1972

This book may be kept

FOURTEEN DAYS

A fine will be charged for each day the book is kept overtime.

OCT 26 '72		
FEB 7 '74		
APR 29 '74		
JUL 3 '75		
EB 26 '76		
MAR 11 '76		
APR 29 '76		
Dec 13 '77		
GAYLORD 142		PRINTED IN U.S.A.

Radical Sophistication

Radical Sophistication

Studies in Contemporary Jewish-American Novelists

Max F. Schulz

OHIO UNIVERSITY PRESS, Athens, Ohio

For Alison, Gavin, and Evan

Preface

INNOCENCE—or the literary expression of it—has been a continuing characteristic of the American experience. R. W. B. Lewis and Leslie Fiedler (to mention two very different kinds of critics) have chronicled its morphology in prior centuries, and Ihab Hassan in our own time. Every force, however, has its counter motion, and it is the philosophy and grammar of one such reaction to innocence that I am primarily concerned with in this book.

Two fictional movements have appeared in the 1950's and 1960's, whose response to mid-century America represents, it appears to me, a departure from the tradition. Both are expressions of a philosophical orientation antithetical to either the illusory optimism or the reactive pessimism that has characterized the faith in a progressive, grass-roots America, which has obstinately become instead a mobile society, fluid culture, and expansive economy. There is the entropic world view of the Black Humorists, of Thomas Pynchon, Bruce Jay Friedman, Vladimir Nabokov, Kurt Vonnegut, Joseph Heller, and John Barth, who in the words of Barth believe that "Nothing has intrinsic value." That is subject for another study. Then there is the humanistic exploration of man's place in society of the Jewish-American writers. Heirs both of an ancient social and religious ethic and of the modern existentialist temperament, they refuse for the most part to assert the pre-eminency of either the group will or the individual desire. They balance between polarities, too honest to human experience as they have witnessed it either to drop out or to falsify, either to opt for the absolutism of a personal decision or to claim the ultimate harmony of contraries. This new Pyrrhonism I have called—with a nod of admiration to Ihab Hassan—radical sophistication.

The number of Jewish-American writers who have emerged in the past two decades almost defies count. Obviously, the select group of authors studied here is expressive, then, as much of my taste as of my thesis. Some criteria have guided me, however, in addition to preference, in the selection of writers. Had my concern been the so-called "Jewish novel," with its description of Jewish manners and its narration of the Jewish experience in America, I would have dealt with a different group: with Daniel Fuchs, Henry Roth, Norman Fruchter, Charles Angoff, Chaim Potok, Wallace Markfield, some of Philip Roth, and much of Ludwig Lewisohn and Meyer Levin. I may appear inconsistent in this regard by introducing the Yiddish story-teller Isaac Bashevis Singer into my discussion; yet he, as well as Bernard Malamud and Saul Bellow, transcend the specific Jewish context of their tales. Ultimately, their response is to man rather than to Jew, to the human dilemma rather than to the Jewish paradox. They confront the contemporary American *Zeitgeist* with sensibilities formed by a technological society and a nuclear age as much as by a special Jewish provenance.

Secondly, I have ruled out as not pertinent to my discussion those novelists, who bulk large in the Jewish fiction of the thirties, treating directly of the socialist movement and the clash between proletarian and owner. I have also placed such fine contemporary writers as Alfred Kazin,

Lionel Trilling, and Harvey Swados with their strong social orientation under the same interdict.

Finally, an explanation should be given for my not considering such admired writers as Herbert Gold and Philip Roth. Frankly, while I recognize their solid achievement, I do not share the enthusiasm of some of my colleagues for them. Radical sophistication occasionally underlies Gold's perception of human aspirations. *The Fathers* is a deft study of the conflicting sensibilities of two generations, without urge to declare in favor of one or the other. In Gold's earlier novels, however, the narrative too often is an inadequate vehicle for the clamoring assertiveness of the language. Stylistically, Gold seeks to resolve what conceptually his aesthetic sense leaves in equipoise. Philip Roth's stringent realism likewise militates against the suspension of judgment that characterizes radical sophistication. Marvelous in its rendering of the appearance of things, his realism seeks to know all, to reduce the infrangible to a surface of details.

While I may appear to be capricious and arbitrary in my exclusion of so many fine Jewish writers, I was not bent on giving a history of Jewish-American fiction in this century; and I have compensatingly kept my guidelines loosely defined and flexible in my discussion of the authors actually treated, for I wished to analyze what strikes me as one of the central contributions of recent Jewish-American fiction, without letting my design harden into dogma. When the consideration of a novel or a writer led away from my thesis, I did not stand on critical scruple, but followed the lure of this new trace. Hence, the chapters that follow may be read both as separate essays and as cumulative contributions to the general statement of the book.

Many people have aided me in its writing. I have profited from the insights of critics who have preceded me, in particular, from Ihab Hassan's _Radical Innocence_ (1961), Marcus Klein's _After Alienation_ (1964), and Jonathan Baumbach's _The Landscape of Nightmare_ (1965). Even though they are not always germane to my study, my pleasure and benefit from reading them has been extensive and intrinsic. In addition, more than one person has generously offered detailed and helpful criticism. For reading sections of the book, I am particularly grateful to L. S. Dembo, Richard Korges, and Fallon Evans. For extended and stimulating discussions about contemporary fiction, I am indebted to my colleagues James Mellard, Glenn Meeter, Dean Flower, and Bruce R. McElderry, Jr. I wish especially to thank my English 532 seminar in the Jewish-American novel for sending me back to my manuscript after every class to revise, to clarify, and to extend what I had already written. Sidney Adler, Michael Cook, Robert H. Deutsch, John Hoag, Moon-Chan Lee, Tony Quagliano, Gary Robertson, Weldon Rogers, Laura Ruby, Barbara Simons, and Dede Wolcott have my gratitude for not letting the teacher-student relationship remain a one-way information center. To Robert Deutsch I owe the original suggestion for the phrase, radical sophistication, although he is blameless of the ways I have used it. Mrs. Marie Buboltz, Mrs. Ruth Decker, and Miss Alexis Rhodes, the departmental secretaries at the University of Southern California, have cheerfully typed and retyped portions of this book, even when my demands for ever new copies appeared (in my eyes at least) to be excessive. Finally, I owe a large debt to Mrs. Susan Schulman and Mrs. Bernice Balfour, who pursued their difficult tasks as copy-editors (not made easier by my going off to Mexico in the middle of the job) with much tact and perspicuity.

Parts of Chapters 1, 4, 6, 7, and 8 have appeared elsewhere. Permission to reprint this material, with changes and additions, has kindly been given by the editors and

Auburn University for "Isaac Bashevis Singer, Radical Sophistication, and the Jewish-American Novel," *Southern Humanities Review*, II (1968); by the copyright owners, the regents of the University of Wisconsin, and the University of Wisconsin Press, for "Mailer's Divine Comedy," *Contemporary Literature*, IX (1968), 36–57; by the editor and Immaculate Heart College, for "Leslie A. Fiedler and the Hieroglyphs of Life," *Twentieth Century Literature*, XIV (1968) 24–34; by the editor, for "Edward Lewis Wallant and Bruce Jay Friedman: The Glory and The Agony of Life," *Critique*, X (1968), 33–47; and by the editor and Newberry College, Newberry, South Carolina, for "Epilogue to *Seymour: An Introduction:* Salinger and the Crisis of Consciousness," *Studies in Short Fiction*, V (1968), 128–138.

I am also obliged to the following writers and publishers for permission to quote from their works: Richard Chase, *The American Novel and Its Tradition* (Garden City, N.J.: Doubleday and Co., 1957); Victor Comerchero, *Nathanael West: The Ironic Prophet* (Syracuse, N.Y.: University of Syracuse Press, 1964); Alan Friedman, *The Turn of the Novel* (New York: Oxford University Press, 1966); David D. Galloway, *The Absurd Hero in American Fiction* (Austin, Tex.: University of Texas Press, 1966); Frederick J. Hoffman, *The Mortal No: Death and the Modern Imagination* (Princeton: Princeton University Press, 1964); Frederick J. Hoffman, "The Fool of Experience: Saul Bellow's Fiction," *Contemporary American Novelists*, edited by Harry T. Moore (Carbondale, Ill.: Southern Illinois University Press, 1964); Stanley Edgar Hyman, *Nathanael West* (Minneapolis, Minn.: University of Minnesota Press, 1962); Stanley Edgar Hyman, *Standards* (New York: Horizon Press, 1966); Frank Kermode, *The Sense of an Ending: Studies in the Theory of Fiction* (New York: Oxford University Press, 1967); Marcus Klein, *After Alienation:*

American Novels in Mid-Century (Cleveland: World Publishing Co., 1965); James F. Light, *Nathanael West: An Interpretative Study* (Evanston, Ill.: Northwestern University Press, 1961); Sidney Richman, *Bernard Malamud* (New York: Twayne Publishing Co., 1966); Walter B. Rideout, *The Radical Novel in the United States 1900–1954* (Cambridge, Mass.: Harvard University Press, 1956); Keith Michael Opdahl, *The Novels of Saul Bellow* (University Park, Penna.: Pennsylvania State University Press, 1967).

Acknowledgments

Permission to quote from the works of the writers discussed in this book has been generously granted as follows:

From *The Spinoza of Market Street* by Isaac Bashevis Singer, translated by Elaine Gottlieb and June Ruth Flaum, copyright 1958, 1960, 1961 by Isaac Bashevis Singer. From *Short Friday* by Isaac Bashevis Singer, translated by Elaine Gottlieb and the author, copyright © 1961, 1962, 1963, 1964 by Isaac Bashevis Singer. From *In My Father's Court* by Isaac Bashevis Singer, copyright © 1962, 1963, 1964, 1965, 1966 by Isaac Bashevis Singer. From *The Family Moskat* by Isaac Bashevis Singer, translated by A. H. Gross, copyright 1950 by Isaac Bashevis Singer. From *The Magician of Lublin* by Isaac Bashevis Singer, translated by Elaine Gottlieb and Joseph Singer, copyright © 1960 by Isaac Bashevis Singer. All reprinted by permission of Farrar, Straus, & Giroux, Inc.

From *Miss Lonelyhearts* by Nathanael West, copyright 1933 by Nathanael West, 1960 by Laura Perelman. Reprinted by permission of New Directions Publishing Corporation. From *The Day of the Locust* by Nathanael West, copyright 1939 by Estate of Nathanael West, © 1966 by Laura Perelman. Reprinted by permission of New Directions Publishing Corporation. From *The Sun Also Rises* by Ernest Hemingway, copyright 1926 by Charles Scribner's Sons, 1954 by Ernest Hemingway. Reprinted by permission of Charles Scribner's Sons. From *Yoshe Kalb*

Saul Bellow, copyright © 1962, 1965 by Saul Bellow. All reprinted by permission of The Viking Press, Inc.

From *The Middle of the Journey* by Lionel Trilling, copyright 1947 by Lionel Trilling. Reprinted by permission of The Viking Press, Inc. From *The Second Stone* by Leslie A. Fiedler, copyright © 1963 by Leslie A. Fiedler. From *Waiting for the End* by Leslie A. Fiedler, copyright © 1964 by Leslie A. Fiedler. From *Back to China* by Leslie A. Fiedler, copyright © 1965 by Leslie A. Fiedler. From *The Last Jew in America* by Leslie A. Fiedler, copyright © 1966 by Leslie A. Fiedler. All reprinted by permission of Stein and Day, Incorporated.

From "The Man Who Made a Nice Appearance" by Edward Lewis Wallant, in *New Voices 3: American Writing Today*, edited by Charles I. Glicksberg, copyright 1958. Reprinted by permission of Hendricks House, Inc. From *The Human Season* by Edward Lewis Wallant, copyright © 1960 by Edward Lewis Wallant. From *The Pawnbroker* by Edward Lewis Wallant, copyright © 1961 by Edward Lewis Wallant. From *The Tenants of Moonbloom* by Edward Lewis Wallant, © 1963 by Joyce Wallant, executrix of the estate of Edward Lewis Wallant. From *The Children at the Gate* by Edward Lewis Wallant, © 1964 by Joyce Wallant. From *The Player King* by Earl Rovit, © 1965 by Earl Rovit. All reprinted by permission of Harcourt, Brace & World, Inc.

From *Stern* by Bruce Jay Friedman, copyright © 1962 by Bruce Jay Friedman. Reprinted by permission of Simon & Schuster, Inc. From *A Mother's Kisses* by Bruce Jay Friedman, copyright © 1964 by Bruce Jay Friedman. Reprinted by permission of Simon & Schuster, Inc. From *The Brothers Ashkenazi* by Israel Joshua Singer, translated by Maurice Samuel, copyright © 1936 by Israel Joshua Singer. Reprinted by permission of Alfred A. Knopf, Inc. From *The Beginners* by Dan Jacobson, copyright © 1966 by Dan Jacobson. Reprinted by permission of The Macmillan Company.

Contents

The Group and the Individual
Character and Narrative

America: Ares and Eros
Rome: Metamorphoses of Stone
China: Philoprogenitive in Perpetuity
The Wild West: Jew, Spade, Wasp

The Polarities of Love
Edward Lewis Wallant
Bruce Jay Friedman
The Polarities of Love: *Ut Poesis*

Prolegomena to *Franny, et al.*
Epilogue to *Seymour: An Introduction, et al.*

Radical Sophistication

1/Introduction

The "Jewish-American School" of Novelists

THERE WAS no Lake school of English poets in 1810, although the *Edinburgh Review* crowd liked to maintain such a fiction. Similarly there is no Jewish school of novelists now. There are only Jewish-American writers practicing their craft. The number currently active is legion. To name them all would be to outdistance in length and in dullness the Homeric roll call of the captains of Agamemnon's army. In ambition they range from the noble infirmity of those bidding for the future to the pragmatism of those dazzled by the glittering present. Their styles encompass the historical romance and black humor; their subjects, the Jewish experience and the human ordeal. What they have in common are a place and a time (America of the 1950's and 1960's) and a set of manners (urban Jewish-American).

How does one explain the emergence in American letters of so many Jewish writers? Irving Howe, in commenting on I. J. Singer's *Yoshe Kalb*, reminds us of the mimetic uses to which the novel puts a set of manners or code of beliefs. The novelist, he remarks, has to be "tightly locked within the premises of his culture" for his work to have validity.[1] The imaginative re-creation of nine-teenth-century East European Jewry by the Singer brothers certainly would support this claim—as would the imaginative achievement of the southern writers of several decades ago. In America no ethnic or regional group presently enjoys more coherent and conscious identification with an older cultural tradition than the American Jew. Yet the literary milieu of the current Jewish-American writers is American rather than Jewish. Few write, as does Isaac Bashevis Singer even after living more than thirty years in this country, about the unique Jewish experience. Furthermore, a Jewish literary tradition has been around for a long time. Why then did the Jewish writers of the thirties fail to produce a viable literature that reached a large American reading public, while the Jewish writers of the sixties succeed beyond belief? A culture which the writer accepts as part of the pulse of his being and which he uses as a point of view for broaching experience may be a requisite, but it is obviously not a necessary catalyst for producing great literature.

Special historical forces must account, if only in part, for the periodicity of art. In 1948 in a symposium on the state of American writing, John Crowe Ransom opined that the condition of great artistic creation is a "kind of exuberance of animal spirits."[2] In saying this he merely alluded to what is itself an effect, not an ultimate cause. Why does the condition for great writing wax and wane in the history of a nation? More than simple exuberance calls writers into being. And why exuberance at one time and not at another? Behind such massive affirmation of life as the Elizabethan's or the Romantic's usually can be found a tension reflecting the merger of social and intellectual forces, which simultaneously brings an old order to an end and a new one into being. For the artist at such moments, life becomes both nostalgically retrospective (or defiantly reactive) and optimistically affirmative. Caught between past and future, he inevitably experiences the conflict of contrary loyalties, of antithetical responses. Out of the resultant tension and the desire to resolve it into meaningful order comes occasionally great art. One thinks of the outburst of poetry and drama in the England of Elizabeth's reign when medieval thought and organization of society were breaking up before the new humanism; and of the poetry in the England of George III's rule when the Augustan world picture of a fixed benevolent nature was giving way to the modern concept of an organic world in perpetual flux. In our time, surely the southern writers of the 1930's and 1940's came in response to the disintegration of the southern agrarian myth under the onslaught of industrialization, with the consequent need to define their minority position as a subculture in relation to the dominant urban Yankee society. In like fashion, historical forces seem to have been at work since the end of World War II to account for the concerted appearance of so many first-rate Jewish-American writers. First, the viability of Israel after the holocaust of Europe in the 1940's has renewed the Jew's pride in his Jewishness, so that he no longer hides it apart in exclusively Jewish enclaves but lives openly, if still self-consciously, with it in Gentile neighborhoods. Secondly, Leslie Fiedler cannot be entirely wrong when he claims even that the urban American Jew "is in the process of being mythicized into the representative American." [3] *Commentary* and *Midstream* as well as Jewish Centers from the East River to the Los Angeles River are lamenting the assimilation of the American Jew—his sense not only of his racial but also of his cultural apartness—into the gray sameness of middle-class America. The tension between the old and new generation, between ghetto and suburb, bar mitzvah and little league baseball, synagogue and college, gabardine and Ivy-League suit, has spurred the

Jewish writer to an evaluation of his heritage as Jew, American, and modern man.

Less concerned than the Jewish writer of the thirties
specifically with the experience of the Jew in America, the
best of the contemporary Jewish-American novelists explore the larger theme of the man of heart in a mass-produced civilization. The characters and manners of his stories are usually Jewish simply because they are what he
knows best; hence only inferentially as part of the larger
issue of the existential posture of modern man does he
touch upon the plight of the marginal Jew. The themes of a
lost past (as much a part of the curdled American dream as
of the Jewish Diaspora) and of the human capacity to feel
and through that feeling to triumph over the computerized
blankness of twentieth-century existence recur in the
works of these men.

The amnesia of Michael Lovett, the narrator of Norman
Mailer's *Barbary Shore*, becomes a precise symbol of the
terrified sense of homelessness of the Jew and of displacement of the modern consciousness. An orphan, raised in an
institution for children (a background shared by Sergius
O'Shaugnessy in Mailer's *The Deer Park*, by Sy Levin and
Frank Alpine in Bernard Malamud's *A New Life* and *The
Assistant*, and in part by Augie March in Saul Bellow's *The
Adventures of Augie March*), Lovett conjectures about
every detail of his past. He cannot even be sure that the
face he sees in the mirror is his, since he is a product of the
plastic surgeon, having been severely burned sometime in
the past. Was it from "the crash of an airplane" or a
"burning house" or a "shell, bombardment"? he forever
queries himself.

> When I stare into the mirror I am returned a face doubt-
> less more handsome than the original, but the straight nose,
> the modelled chin, and the smooth cheeks are only evidence
> of a stranger's art. It does not matter how often I decide the

brown hair and the grey eyes must have always been my own; there is nothing I can recognize, not even my age. I am certain I cannot be less than twenty-five and it is possible I am older, but thanks to whoever tended me, a young man without a wrinkle in his skin stands for a portrait in the mirror.

Nor can he "discern the most casual fact from the most patent fancy, nor the past from the future"; and the details of his own history are "lost in the other, common to us all." Thus, he laments, "I could never judge whether something had happened to me or I imagined it so. It made little difference whether I had met a man or he existed only in a book; there was never a way to determine if I knew a country or merely remembered another's description [ch. 1]."

Here is a disinheritance more radical than the one characterizing Faulkner's idiots, so intense that it includes a separation of Lovett not only from others but even from the image of himself, as the *Dopplegänger* image in the mirror indicates. Paradoxically, the absence of a thought or of a past he can recognize as his own also indistinguishably merges him with the history of his culture. Thus Lovett's amnesia is a hieroglyphic of modern existence, symbolic at once of a submergence of self in the time stream and cultural continuity of a society and of a disenchantment so profound that neither self nor anti-self has recognizable objective existence. Under such circumstances relationships become difficult. Life is a void, events and people disparate and incommunicado. The impersonal rooming house in which Lovett lives supports this situation as does the action of the novel. Lovett has no satisfactory meeting of mind or heart with another person, only momentary impacts (like that of richocheting billiard balls) with similar nullities. His view of human relationships—ironically useless and comfortless for a would-be writer—is summed up by his opening and closing commentary on life: "So the blind lead the blind and the deaf shout warnings to one another until their voices are lost [chs. 1, 33]."

A corollary situation, reflective less of a metaphysical than of a social alienation, is the mixed marriage of Jew and Gentile. Here is no updating of *Abie's Irish Rose*. The sentimentality of a previous generation with its view of the human heart of gold is gone. In Philip Roth's *Letting Go,* Jewish Paul and Protestant Libby Herz are disowned by their parents and left to struggle and starve their way through college. In both of Leslie Fiedler's novels mixed marriages fare badly. In *The Second Stone*, Mark Stone (Jew) is betrayed by his wife Hilda (white Anglo-Saxon Protestant), and Clem Stone (Gentile) is deserted by his wife Selma (Jew). In *Back to China*, Baro Finkelstone's marriage to Nordic Susannah is partly responsible for his transformation into a middle-aged satyr and hers into a frigid dipsomaniac. In Richard G. Stern's *Stitch*, Edward Gunther does not find happiness with his Protestant love Cressida. In Saul Bellow's *Herzog*, Moses leaves a good Jewish wife in his hankering after, first, a Japanese mistress and then a Jewish girl turned Roman Catholic only to be deceived in turn by the latter. In Mailer's *An American Dream*, Stephen Rojack ("half Jewish," half "Protestant. Nothing really.") discovers that his wife Deborah Coughlin Mangaravidi Kelly (descendant of Irish and Italian Catholics) detests "Jewish Protestants and Gentile Jews" because "They know nothing about grace [ch. 2]." So, these writers seem to imply, such is the plight of the Jew who would embrace another cultural heritage and of contemporary man who would trade religious certainty for cosmic flux. Like T. S. Eliot's Magi, in denying old beliefs, while not yet having assimilated new values, they find themselves with nothing, pursuing an empty routine. Such is the fate of Tommy Wilhelm in Bellow's *Seize the Day*. In his youth he had changed his name from Wilky Adler in the false hope of a Hollywood movie career; now at forty-five he is jobless, estranged from wife and children, father, and lover, marking time in an upper Broadway hotel for old people. The failure of these marriages frequently to produce children also emphasizes the division still in effect beneath the surface appearance of union. Paul and Libby Herz commit abortion, and then stop making love to each other out of fear of pregnancy. Augie March finds himself an expatriate in Europe where his wife Stella makes movies—even though he "would have preferred to stay in the States and have children [ch. 26]."

A direct corollary of their isolation is the trial of consciousness through which they flounder. In such an ordeal these characters are searching for an identity, and their creators for a definition of man meaningful for our century. The definition so far (with the possible assertive exception of Mailer) is tentative, hesitant, and humble before the mystery of the human mind and heart. The soul-searching of their protagonists is more reluctant and less apt than the eager omniscience with which the minds of Henry James's heroes and heroines embrace this ordeal. And it is no less tentative than Faulkner's. In contrast to the penchant for self-knowledge of an Isabel Archer or a Lambert Strether, Messieurs Levin, Lovett, Herzog, Tommy Wilhelm, and Buddy Glass flinch at every jolt received by the nerve ends of their sensibilities. Along with Edward Lewis Wallant's Sol Nazerman (*The Pawnbroker*) and Yussel Berman (*The Human Season*) they are prize specimens of the modern urban scene. For sheer intensity of mental and emotional anguish, they outdistance most of the other fictional creations of this century: for example, the Fitzgerald protagonist (more often than not a sophomoric Swinburne), or the Hemingway hero (who really has little aptitude for suffering), or the Faulkner character (who easily translates his pain into the purgative of action, or, if a Negro, stoically endures it).

In one sense this suffering becomes a commentary on the American experience and more specifically a ploy against the mechanization, dehumanization, and conformity of the contemporary scene. It becomes a cry wrung from the heart of one man against the impersonality of existence. Thus, *Seize the Day* ends with Tommy Wilhelm herded by a policeman into a surging line of mourners on Broadway. The pressure of the crowd moves him from the sidewalk into a chapel. There, he stands in front of a coffin and sobs his heart out for the death of a stranger. His appeal for love selfishly rebuffed by his father, his last money bilked from him by an acquaintance, his attempt to reconstruct his life and find happiness in the love of another woman balked by his estranged wife, a "great knot of ill and grief in his throat swell[s] upward" and Wilhelm cries for himself as "the consummation of his heart's ultimate need." With such tears he accepts the bent of his Jewish forebears who have figuratively sat by the waters of Babylon and wailed for themselves for thousands of years. But Wilhelm is also mourning for man. His tears flow before the coffin of a stranger; and the file of mourners and idle onlookers shuffling by react with awe: " 'Oh my, oh my! To be mourned like that,' said one man and looked at Wilhelm's heavy shaken shoulders, his clutched face and whitened fair hair, with wide, glinting, jealous eyes [ch. 7]." And with ironic understatement, Bellow has left the reader looking at Wilhelm through the eyes of this man and the other dry-eyed mourners and the merely curious, envious of his capacity for feeling the ache of life that is the common glory and bitter fruit of humankind, which we have lost the knack for in an age in which emotion is suspect, or simply lacking. Similarly Baro Finkelstone in Fiedler's

Back to China weeps for those loved ones whom he has, despite the best of intentions, hurt and for all the victims of Hiroshima whom he never even knew; and Sol Nazerman in Wallant's *The Pawnbroker* mourns for the man who has taken a bullet fired at him, for his family who died in the gas chambers of a Nazi concentration camp, and for all humankind who bear the stigmata of the cross.

One cannot deny that the American Jew seems to have found the sourness of American Calvinism congenial to the similar strain in his own religious thought. The critics clutch at this propensity for suffering as if it holds for us some profound truth. I wonder, however, if its sacramental importance in the contemporary Jewish-American novel has not been inflated. Suffering looms large in this fiction; yet rarely is it explicitly praised as a virtue. Even those with an apparent genius for sustaining pain—like Tommy Wilhelm, Seymour Levin, Gabe Wallach, or Moses Herzog —are divided against themselves as to its value. In the novels of Edward Lewis Wallant, one might claim that suffering is presented without equivocation as a route to transcendent illumination of one's humanity; even here, however, Norman Moonbloom consciously elects the joyous to the painful route. And in Malamud's novels the ambivalent success of the protagonists by the end of the story must surely compromise whatever affirmation of suffering the mythic structure insists upon. Nor can one gainsay that in *The Assistant* Morris Bober dies cursing the senseless pain of his life and Helen Bober bitterly rejects the funeral sermon in which it is argued that her father's life, because of its fidelity to family and Judaism, has nevertheless had value. It is as if the close call the Jew has had with survival in this century has shaken him to the very roots of his psyche, prompting him to dwell on his—and all men's—capacity for suffering. With his ageless practicality (another word for wisdom) and talent for existence, he knows all the while that pain is essentially destructive and that to prize such masochism is hideous folly. "Don't marry suffering," Tamkin advises Tommy Wilhelm in *Seize the Day.* "Some people do. They get married to it, and sleep and eat together, just as husband and wife. If they go with joy they think it's adultery [ch. 6]." With equal conviction Herzog at the end of his crisis categorically denounces "modern forms of Orphism," [4] with their doctrines or theologies of suffering calculated to intellectualize and spiritualize man. And Yossarian in Joseph Heller's *Catch-22* finally gets so fed up with the negations of war, with its bombing and shooting and its pain caused by the deaths of friends, that he deserts to perform a positive action just once, running off to Rome to save Nately's whore's kid sister. Although Malamud, Bellow, Wallant, and Heller acknowledge suffering to be the *modus vivendi* of twentieth-century existence, they refuse to believe that it is a necessary cautery for society's ills.

These novels remind us in an age excessively rationalized and increasingly computerized of the value of human emotion. Yet the situation is not seen as so desperate that man must opt for a modern vision of religious violence, such as one finds in the stories of Flannery O'Connor. Joy, not unlike Chasidic ecstasy, is still possible, and preferable, to sorrow; affirmation, not rejection, of society is still the goal sought. In spite of the existential preoccupation of our times, these writers in effect question the dogma that the world is totally absurd. They react to man's loneliness in this century, castigating the separation of individual from society as a moral defect. Wallant strikes the characteristic note when, in *The Tenants of Moonbloom*, he questions man's tendency toward solipsism: "One forgets that things exist outside of yourself," Basellecci lectures Norman Moonbloom. "You live alone and you become susceptible to obsessions. . . . There is a selfishness involved, thinking only of yourself [ch. 9]." Man finds his essential humanity when he moves into the terrain of another. So much has been made of the dangling man and the victim of Bellow's two earliest novels that we look for underground men everywhere. The Jewish-American writer is admittedly bitten with the twentieth-century neurosis which regards the mass of people as blind to the real problems of life; hence, in a general way he accepts the idea that the growth of the individual must be achieved, not socially as the Declaration of Independence heralds, but existentially. Yet as a Jew and as an American he never forgets the effect that the private act has on the community. Thus, in his novels the pressure is always toward affiliation of man-alone once again traditionally with the group. The ambivalence of this view is characterized by the ambiguity of the endings of these novels. Their special ambience, which derives from the unresolved tension of such conflicting modes of thought, is strikingly revealed in the writings of Isaac Bashevis Singer, who grew to maturity as the son of a rabbi in the ghettos of Eastern Europe but who has lived the past thirty years in America.

Isaac Bashevis Singer

Singer's is a twentieth-century sensibility attempting an imaginative re-creation of the social and religious milieu of Polish Jewry of the previous three centuries. The unique— and now vanished—circumstances of this society confront Singer's historical consciouness with special irrefrangibility. Tolstoy could revert in *War and Peace* to the time of the Napoleonic invasions without risking intellectual dislocation, for his society still assented essentially to the assumptions of his grandfather. Tension of a profound philosophical order, however, affects the moral pattern of Singer's stories as a result of the radically different *Zeitgeists* of the author and of his dramatis personae. One of the central paradoxes of Singer's fictional world is that even as he pays loving tribute to the value system of a back-country Jewry—dirty, ignorant, but firm in a simplistic faith in what Dr. Yaretsky in "The Shadow of a Crib" calls "a seeing universe, rather than a blind one," [5]—Singer questions such a world picture with the narrative structures he composes for them. His rabbis and pious matrons may think and act in unquestioning accord with a Jewish cosmic vision, but their lives present the absurd pattern familiar to the modern sensibility. It is not without significance that in three of Singer's five novels now translated into English the historical setting is that of a catastrophe wrought upon the Jews by external circumstances, and that his protagonists are caught between rival claims of the Jewish and non-Jewish worlds. As in a Greek tragedy, impersonal fate and individual responsibility merge ambiguously in his stories.

The symbolic overtones implied in the title *The Slave* underscore this ambiguity. Jacob is carried off into slavery in the aftermath of the Chmielnicki pogroms of the second half of the seventeenth century. Yet even as he struggles—in captivity among the Polish peasants to whom he is sold—to retain his Yiddish tongue, to observe his religion, and to recreate in effect the Law, he falls in love with Wanda, the daughter of his master. Rescued after many years by elders of his village, he is driven by his love to return furtively for Wanda and against both the laws of the Jews and the Poles to introduce her into the village, or *shtetl*, as a true daughter of Israel. Thus Jacob is enslaved by man, society, religious law, spiritual fervor, human desires, and earthly passions. Who can discriminate between Jacob the individual who is personally accountable for his actions, and Jacob the victim who is determined by historical, social, and biological forces? Or between the Jacob who observes the historic role of the Jews by bringing Wanda to

God and who fulfills in his life the return to Palestine, and the Jacob who is profoundly alienated from village and synagogue because of these deeds?

Similarly the enlightened and richly human integration of Yasha Mazur, *The Magician of Lublin*, into the free-thinking, mobile, habitat of Warsaw contrasts inexplicably with the escalation of his conscience, the lapse of his skill at lock-picking and gymnastics, and the reversion of his beliefs to the Jewish faith of his forefathers. Three underlying patterns of theme and image provide an ironic commentary on the narrative of Yasha's progress from Pole to Jew. (1) The higher Yasha soars as profane tumbler, the deeper he plunges as sinful man into "the bottomless pit [pt. VI, ch. 9]." Only after his body has fallen from the balcony of the house he has tried to rob, spraining an ankle and arresting subsequent flight, can his soul begin to levitate. The controlling metaphor here is that of Icarus, with Yasha's rise and fall treated dualistically as both grace and damnation. (2) The more freely he roams from mistress to mistress, the more he feels his body to be imprisoned within Poland and his soul within the embraces of women. Only after he quits both roaming and wenching can he hope to be free. The controlling metaphor is that of a prison and of a spider spinning its web to entrap. (3) The more he dissembles, the more he is threatened by disclosure. Only when he renounces deception of his loved ones can he dare to be honest and open with all men. The controlling metaphor is that of a magician or master dissembler.

All three patterns underwrite the change in Yasha as one of religious casuistry. Despite the skill with which they are used, however, Singer is too responsible an artist and too economical a storyteller to indulge in such hackneyed paradigms humorlessly. They reflect rather the skeptical half of his response to his story, supplying us with an ironic measure of Yasha's transformation into a saintly person celebrated (as Emilia's letter is meant to corroborate) all over Catholic Poland. Yasha may have turned his back on his former amoral circus life for the Jewish religious ethos of the *shtetl*, but the mode and consequence of his gesture hardly reassure us of its efficacy. His unJewish antisocial adoption of the monastic ideal, walling himself off from the world as a way of serving both God and society, gives no greater moral illumination or meaningful pattern of his life than had his previous consorting with the thieves of Piask and his roaming of Poland as a performer. The temptations from within and from without—of evil talk, slander, wrath, and false flattery in the form of supplicants who look upon him as a holy man—continue to assail him and to interrupt his meditations. He remains in body and spirit, earthbound, imprisoned, reserved, and secretive; radically alienated from his pious wife and friends, his former associates, and the *shtetl* community; a sainted man holding daily audience to "entertain" the people as the magician in him had done in happier days.

Singer is seriously concerned with the complicated moral and ethical relationships of man to his God and to his society—with the degree to which human conduct describes a moral pattern affecting that of the community and with the extent to which man's actions form pointless arabesques under the indifferent push and pull of historical and psychobiological forces. In *The Family Moskat,* for example, Asa Heshel Bannett and the Warsaw Jews are portrayed as bringing about their own dissolution. Reb Meshulam at the age of eighty lecherously marries for the third time, introducing into the Chasidic community a Galician widow with modernized western habits. With devastating vividness the deterioration of the old pious solidarity of the Warsaw ghetto is depicted in the drunken cynicism, lust, and avarice of the Chanukah Ball, an auspicious place for Asa Heshel, ex-Yeshiva student, to meet his next mistress, the atheistic Communist Barbara. "More sex and fewer children. The bedroom is the key to all social and individual problems [pt. IX, ch. 4]," he tells Barbara. And in its marriage of Spinoza and Malthus, and its aimless, fruitless wanderings, his life passes moral judgment on himself and the Warsaw Jews as a society bent on self-destruction. In the concluding scene of the book he waits resignedly for the Nazi to fulfill his wish to die. He refuses to accompany Barbara, who elects to "keep on fighting for a while," and stands with Hertz Yanovar, religious scholar turned table-tipping occultist, the two quoting to each other in Polish rather than Hebrew the "real truth" of the Bible that "Death is the Messiah [pt. X, ch. 12]." Yet the advent of the Nazi is a jarring note, for in no moral or historical sense can the Warsaw Jews be held responsible for World War II and the Nazi pogrom. The same can be said of the historical phenomenon of the Enlightenment, which claims as victims Asa Heshel, sundry members of the Meshulam family, and Eastern European Jewry in general, diverting them from the paths of righteousness and tradition into the dead end of alienated self-seeking. And there is a sense in which the many chance turns of Asa Heshel's life—for example, his introduction to the libertine Abram Shapiro at the Chasidic synagogue where he had gone fresh from a country *shtetl* for guidance in attending a university—makes him as much a victim of cosmic irony as any of Hardy's characters. This positivist rendering of Asa Heshel's comings and goings on earth denies the contrary structure of meaning in the novel; that is, that there was a moral pattern to his life. With the insistence that there was possibly no coherent relation between him and the world, his life is robbed of moral significance, its events reduced to incoherent moments of sensation.

Clearly, Singer does not find it easy to fix the blame for personal catastrophe, as an older Judaic dispensation

would have—and as Reb Abraham Hirsh in I. J. Singer's
The Brothers Ashkenazi does when he is replaced as general agent of the Huntze factory by his son Simcha Meyer.
Reb Abraham consoles himself with the words of King
Solomon: "there is a time to plant and a time to pluck up
that which is planted, a time to build up and a time to
break down. Nothing happens . . . without the will of God,
not even the breaking of a little finger [ch. 24]." No such
easy comfort is available to Isaac Bashevis Singer, despite
the tender sympathy that he on occasion expresses for
unaffected Jewish ritual and piety, as in the Jewish *Cot-
ter's-Saturday-Night* story, "Short Friday." But even in this
story there is the inexplicable twist of fate, which prompts
the pious couple to copulate after the Sabbath meal, and
then lets them suffocate in their sleep because of a defective stove. I suspect that it is this divorce of his religious
sensibility from precise theological tenets, this drift of his
thought away from the ethical certainties of the Judaic
Law, which allows Americans to read Singer with an understanding and sympathy unavailable to the great Hebrew
writer of this century S. Y. Agnon, and such great Yiddish
writers as Sholem Aleichem and I. L. Peretz. Such stories
as "A Tale of Two Liars," "The Destruction of Kreshev,"
"Skiddah and Kuziba," and "The Shadow of a Crib" drama-
tize the ambiguous hold on Singer's mind of belief and
skepticism. In them believable *shtetl* types jostle with a
wide assortment of supernatural spirits—with the line di-
viding the two very thin at times.[6] The use of an Arch-Devil
narrator simultaneously demonstrates the notion of a
seeing will, purpose, and plan in the everyday affairs of the
shtetl, while underscoring the capriciousness of the forces
manipulating human actions. At other times, in even more
explicit fashion, Singer often parallels, as in "The Black
Wedding" and in some of the stories just mentioned, a
pious account of the protagonist's actions with a psycho-

logical or naturalistic explanation which denies the moral
cohesion of that world. In the story "Cunegunde," for example, he explains the strange nocturnal torments of
abused, demented Cunegunde in her hovel from the viewpoint of her demon-obsessed mind and from that of naturalistic fact: "At night imps came to her bed, mocking her,
wetting her sheet, calling her names, poking and biting her,
braiding her hair. Mice dung and vermin remained after
they had gone." [7]

The danger in this strategy is real, for the coherence of
Singer's fictional world depends on his maintaining a
perilous tension between irreconcilables. If he relaxes an
instant, his story is threatened with fragmentation. The
endings of *The Slave* and *The Magician of Lublin* are painful instances of such falls into disunity. Miraculously, to
transform Wanda the Polish peasant into a Jewish Sarah
and Jacob into a righteous man, or to metamorphose Yasha
Mazur from circus prestidigitator to holy *Zaddik*, is to
sentimentalize their lives under the intolerable pressure to
give some kind of meaningful construct to them.

Singer's mind rejoices in dichotomies. In his autobiographical account of his boyhood he refers to his home as
a "stronghold of Jewish puritanism, where the body was
looked upon as a mere appendage to the soul." One day,
visiting his older brother's atelier, he discovered the artist's healthy respect for the flesh. "This was quite a change
from my father's court," he remarks, "but it seems to me
that this pattern has become inherent to me. Even in my
stories it is just one step from the study house to sexuality
and back again. Both phases of human existence have continued to interest me." [8] The ambivalence of this intellectual position is pervasive in much that Singer writes. Thus
he pays loving tribute to his brother as a "modern man"
with the "high morality . . . of our pious ancestors." [9] Like
the tightrope walker Yasha Mazur, Singer balances be-

tween these contrary modes of thought, his *modus oper-andi* at once archaic and modern, preoccupied with angels and demons and with Freud and Spinoza. He is drawn to the simple piety of his ancestors who never doubted the moral importance of life. He is also a man of the twentieth century, an uprooted European transplanted to America, seized by the contemporary vision of an absurd world—and his artistic integrity will not let the comfortable climate of divine reward and punishment remain intact. In the tension between moral cause and effect which his divided mind creates, his protagonists act out the unwitting drama of their lives. That these stories do not fragment into their unresolved elements attests to the remarkable narrative skill of Singer. That Singer has persisted despite the absence of an answer in posing again and again the question of the moral meaning of human experience attests to the radical sophistication of his vision.[10]

Radical Sophistication and the Jewish-American Novel

It is fashionable these days to see the Jew as the perfect symbol of the Camusian man. Although not as viable a fact in the fifties and sixties as in earlier periods, the Jew's lot of perpetual exile lends itself as a convenient symbol of alienation and hence of what one segment of contemporary thought conceives of as the essential consciousness of being man. Yet only in a highly qualified sense can what I have called the radical sophistication of Singer's vision be considered existential. As a Jew he appeals, however hesitantly, to a construct of beliefs that makes sense of the human experience. Nor does he, like the Christian, reject earth because of the expulsion from paradise. The Jew has historically been God-intoxicated and man-centered. His relationship with the world reveals itself simultaneously as *eros* and as *agapé*. "Mazeltov," Shifrah Tammar greets her daughter the morning after her wedding in Singer's "The

Destruction of Kreshev"; " 'You are now a woman and share with us all the curse of Eve.' And weeping, she threw her arms about Lise's neck and kissed her." [11] Like the holy men of Chasidism bent on the hallowing of each day, she acknowledges the edict that love of man is a prerequisite to adoration of Jehovah. In short, the Jew pursues not the Christian pilgrimage from this world to the next, but performs the miracle of merger of the other world with this one.

During more than two thousand years of Diaspora the Jews have learned to breathe amidst the incertitude that is the daily air of a persecuted minority. A tenuous equipoise of irreconcilables is the best they could hope for; and it pervades their world picture. One could hardly expect otherwise with a people who have persisted for several milleniums in the belief that they are chosen, with a divine mission, when the contrary has been the fact of their daily lives. Out of this knowledge has grown a philosophy—anchored at one end by the teachings of Isaiah and at the other by the realities of this century—which conceives of the Jew as redeemer of the world through his acceptance of God's servitude. [12] But the encumbrance of evil—even when put to the service of God—is an uncertain business, never quite relieving the mind of inquietude. Christianity has stumbled over this legacy of sin since its inception. The Age of Enlightenment could only palely affirm with Alexander Pope that "Whatever is, is right," and "All partial evil, universal good." [13] Among Western men, the Jew has accepted most completely the ambience of this mixed blessing, this gift of the gods to man. The wisdom of the Jew's tragic passiveness is underscored by Singer in stories of what happens to a town when its people covenant with the Arch-Fiend in the interests of God, for example, in "The Destruction of Kreshev" and *Satan in Goray*. Grounded in the harsh realities of this life, the Jew retains unshakable conviction of man's spiritual destiny.

This capacity for belief in the face of "uncertainties, mysteries, doubts" is a radical sophistication that the Jew, with a culture historically of long standing, is currently giving to a century convinced in its existentialist isolation of the incoherence of existence. Today's intellectual, like the Coleridge that Keats characterized as "incapable of remaining content with half-knowledge," clutches at any "fine isolated verisimilitude caught from the Penetralium of mystery." [14] To him the contemporary Jewish novel has much to say. It is a commonplace among Jews that Judaism is not in the habit of disowning its great heretics completely. Rather it accommodates with worldly wisdom what is worthwhile in Spinoza, Maimonides, Freud, and Kafka. This willingness to accept the world on its own terms—disorderly, incoherent, absurd—"without any irritable reaching after fact and reason," and yet without losing faith in the moral significance of human actions, underlies the confrontation of experience in the best of the contemporary Jewish-American novels.

The radical sophistication that I refer to here should not be confused with the open-ended artifact as defined by Robert M. Adams in *Strains of Discord: Studies in Literary Openness* or by Alan Friedman in *The Turn of the Novel.*[15] In one sense, Mailer's, Malamud's, Bellow's, and Salinger's novels conform to the unresolved pattern of assertions that Adams has in mind. That is, their ambiguous endings raise unanswered questions. Do O'Shaugnessy and Rojack make good their rebellious impulse toward existential individuality or do they merely escape the conformity of mass society by fleeing it? Are Hobbs, Alpine, Levin, and Bok triumphant as Grail fertility heroes or badly compromised as human beings? Do Henderson and Herzog achieve loving integration with their fellowman, or do they continue as subtle instances of social and intellectual disinheritance? Is Seymour a modern saint or isn't he? Unlike the open-ended fictional creations discussed by Adams, however, these characters do not have a weak sense of life as pattern. On the contrary, they reflect their authors' convictions about the moral significance of man's actions. Nevertheless, a sense of fractured and divided consciousness paradoxically occurs because these writers are formulating human experience into patterns of conduct at an historical moment when disorder, opposition, and the absurdity of existence have acquired philosophical respectability. It is not then the fictional character who may inhabit an earlier century of faith, as in Singer's stories, but the author who knows with a sophistication radical in its simplism that faith and skepticism comprise less an either-or equation than complementary additions to an indefinite whole. Hence, despite the motive and direction of the protagonist, these novels as structures of meaning are inconclusive.

A difference in openness of a like sort also marks these novels when they are compared to the experiential openness that Friedman explores. Although their conclusions do not conform to the conventional novel's "tapering experience" [16] but instead, like the novels that Friedman examines, end on a new beginning or continuing ethical experience, the openness of this new moral action—unlike the expansive undefined experience which Friedman contemplates—*has been shaped* and, we are led to believe, *will continue to be shaped* by a moral attitude or standard. The paradox here is that whereas the moral inner direction of the protagonist is known, his future experience remains uncertain because he is part of a larger modality of experience, encompassing contradictory concepts with which he is not fully in rapport. The protagonist may have realized a moral stance through his previous confrontation with the existent ethics of society; yet, he continues to resist containment by that society. Thus, in spite of his moral growth having reached thematic climax, his experiential rapport with society remains open-ended. Hence, Friedman is not wholly accurate when he interprets the "flux of experience" in a Bellow novel as being brought to a "balanced irresolution." This may accurately enough describe the sensibility of Bellow but does not do justice to the moral and intellectual resolution with which the Bellow hero comes to terms with his world. Neither Moses Herzog nor Tommy Wilhelm is "poised at the end between two (or three) worlds," [17] as are the irresolute protagonists of John Crowe Ransom's "The Equilibrists." Herzog and Wilhelm each accepts the fundamental prerogative of his heart, even though recognizing its obsolescence in a society managed according to the materialistic and ratiocinative assumptions of mass technology. Hence, the relationship between each of them and society is not static but open to future modification or expansion; and just to that extent are they "poised . . . between . . . worlds" of knowing. As embodiments of a sophistication radical in its illusion, they (and the protagonists of Mailer, Malamud, Wallant, and Salinger) are portrayed as inhabiting (like Tennyson's Ulysses) a limitless world of open-ended happenings devoid of causality, where yet their every action has moral significance.

The Jew seeks to make everything systematic, logical, sensible, and subject to law. So Samuel Talmon rails at his relatives and in-laws in Dan Jacobson's novel *The Beginners*. "When you believed in God, he was a God of laws," he adds. "What is Judaism if not a system of laws, of rules how to live, from one day to the next—even from one meal to the next, if you please? And what do you call Moses, why was he the greatest Jew who ever lived? Because he was Moses the Lawgiver. And you try to carry on in the same spirit now, even though you're modern people and don't believe in God any more. So you try to live by other laws: you still look for reasonable arrangements, orderly developments, clear understandings, settled, sensible ways of living [pt. III, ch. 17]."

The radical sophistication of the Jew, then, like most of the great constructs of western thought is inherently dualistic. The patterns that this attitude takes in the novels of the contemporary Jewish-American writers vary; but most can be reduced to an antinomy which presumes some form of socioreligious determinism, while insisting upon the existential will of the individual. The dilemma—which appears to have become almost a Jewish problem, particularly for the American Jew since the end of World War II—is defined by Lionel Trilling in *The Middle of the Journey*. "How much the idea of personal responsibility had been shaken by modern social science," Laskell muses. "Educated people more and more accounted for human action by the influence of environment and the necessities and habits imposed by society. Yet innocence and guilt were more earnestly spoken of than ever before [ch. 6]." Thus, Malamud may involve his protagonist simultaneously in a mythic and a private quest. Salinger may portray the Glass progeny as hoisted on the petard of their own Zen ideals, by contradictory psychological determinants. Mailer may urge his hero to seek the American dream of illimitable power through sexual release. Wallant may define full spiritual growth of the individual in terms of *caritas*. Fiedler may dance his minority American through a *pas de deux* of cultural betrayal. Bellow may torture his protagonist in a lonely war of mind and heart. Still, these ambivalences are all reducible to the conflict between human autonomy and divine purpose, and its corollary conflict between personal desires and communal needs.

That this version of human experience should suddenly dominate the American literary scene is, of course, one of those cultural mysteries, like the creative outbursts of the Elizabethans and the Romantics, which defies ultimate comprehension. Yet there is discernible a convergence of literary and historical forces that makes the contemporary Jewish-American novel a logical heir of the central tradition of the American novel. This tradition, Richard Chase has defined, in part, in *The American Novel and Its Tradition*, as the discovery of "putative unity *in* disunity" or willingness "to rest at last among irreconcilables." [18] The Jewish imagination similarly has been stirred by the aesthetic possibilities of a radical sophistication, which simultaneously entertains contrary intellectual systems: the secular view of man alienated in an absurd universe and the religious view of man enthroned by divine fiat in God's earthly kingdom.

A corollary factor is the historical parallel between the American frontier and the European *shtetl*. Both environments raised similar questions about individual rights. The American experience continues to grapple with a political and social system, defined by the tension between private freedom and public restriction. Marius Bewley, in *The Eccentric Design*, has brilliantly shown that the conflict over the rights and the powers of the one and the many has been a persistent preoccupation of American thought.[19] The American dream of a freely roving Adamic man was disrupted by the reality of legal restraint almost as soon as the first Puritans put foot ashore on the new land, long before James Fenimore Cooper's backwoodsman Natty Bumppo clashed wills with the townsman Marmaduke Temple, representative of law and order.

Old-World Judaism, in an effort to submerge the individual in the social whole, for internal purposes of psychic and spiritual continuity as much as because of external forces beyond its control, has wrestled with the obverse side of this problem. Seemingly living always as a minority in one pale or another, threatened perpetually by extinction from without and from within, the Jew developed in survival a strong identification of personal observation of the Law with continuation of the community. An individual in the sight of God, he was also a member of an embattled group. His actions affected not only his salvation but also the group's survival. Thus in Singer's stories the *shtetl* defines a moral and ethical principle as much as a physical place and social entity. Both frontier and *shtetl* versions of human aspiration meet in the Jewish-American novel of the past two decades, deepened and universalized by accommodation with the religio-scientific antinomies of Old-World Judaism and of New-World skepticism.

The New Mannerists

In architecture and the visual arts the Italian Mannerists of the sixteenth century pushed against the classical restraints of the Renaissance—the calm of a Raphael, the mathematical ratio and order of a Brunelleschi. Volume and perspective were wrenched and tortured until tension succeeded repose and discordance replaced symmetry. The elongated squeezing of space within the rigid boundaries of the parallel buildings of the Uffizi Palace by Vasari, and the austere interaction of false and true supports in the anteroom of the San Lorenzo Library by Michelangelo, both in Florence, are examples of this Mannerism. The decorative becomes functional in a new grammar of symbolism meant to unite the exaggerated intellectualism of the high Renaissance with the universality of religious affirmation. However, unlike the superhuman struggle between mind and matter that characterizes the late Baroque, Mannerism, according to Nicholas Pevsner, expresses more often than not the frustration of forces frozen in counterpoint.[20] The radical sophistication of some of the current Jewish-American novelists obeys a comparable logic. Like Michelangelo's muscular, earthbound figures soaring in space, straining the bonds of mortality and gravity to realize sublimity, these new Mannerists risk spiritual and moral anxiety to define the secularity of individual experience in the twentieth century in ethical and universal terms, without denying either end of the continuum.

The Malamud story, for example, is characterized, as Sidney Richman has demonstrated, by a violent yoking of colloquial realism to mythopoeic symbolism.[21] Thus, in *The Natural*, rookie pitcher Roy Hobbs's striking out with three pitched balls of Walter (the Whammer) Wambold, the leading hitter in the American League, is defined by the mythic perspective of "David jawboning the Goliath-Whammer, or was it Sir Percy lancing Sir Maldemer, or the first son (with a rock in his paw) ranged against the primitive papa."[22] Note the sudden foliation of alliteration and assonance, which confines the burlesque conclusion in a formal symmetry. Nor is this combination of slang and symbolism a gratuitous display of verbal virtuosity. The two styles lock the narrative into a perilous stasis with the present and the past, the real and the ideal. The Malamud protagonist is a baseball player, a grocery clerk, a college teacher, a handyman compelled to act out the archaic role of folk hero. Here is more than lip service to the fables that baseball is the great American pastime, that the small businessman embodies the American dream, that an ideal can move multitudes. In this era of corporate entities, impersonal computers, and megapolises, Malamud's literal translation of the commonplace into myth stretches the tensile strength of our sensibility. We are always reluctant to let go of the appearance that passes for reality; yet Malamud's prose insists that a baseball player may be a Fisher King, that a grocery store may be a Chapel Perilous, that an ex-stumblebum or a ne'er-do-well fixer may be a Messiah. And in the torsion set up by these extremes our imagination is wrenched, as in the *Last Judgment* of the Sistine Chapel, toward an embrace of earth and heaven, of body and spirit.

Both Wallant and Mailer share somewhat, minus the mythopoeic impulse, Malamud's vision of the interlocked worlds of earth and paradise. They naturally occupy the realm of the emotions—of love-hate, fecundity-sterility, creation-destruction—a much defined territory of the human psyche which they energetically explore as if sleepwalkers had previously crossed its terrain. They extend and redefine its dimensions as if man's nervous system were so much space. Like the entrance to the Biblioteca Laurenziana, where the conventions of pilaster and wall, support and decoration, blur into new relationships that disturb us into fresh awareness of volume and space and of the falsities of harmony and proportion, their mapping of human feeling wrenches us out of our complacency about the directives of our senses.

Wallant's central insight is that to love is to live, and to live is to feel, and to feel is both to cry and to laugh. With passionate single-mindedness, not without occasional crudities, he structures his novels out of the spatial and temporal movements of his protagonists outward from the unbroken membranes of their existences to contact with others and backward from the numbness of their present lives to the vital roots of the past. Life and death are presented as a continuum, underscored by the pervasive imagery of crucifixion and rebirth. Similarly on the level of the language the polarities of emotion form into baroque convolutions of joy and suffering. Thus Norman Moonbloom consistently feels "an exquisite pain" from the bleeding "wounds of his laughter"; yet steadily and with increasing intensity, parallel to his awakening sensibility, "laughter trembled inside him, causing an increase in the pain, which in turn boiled the laughter more rapidly, which increased the pain, and so on [ch. 17]."

With Mailer the satanic reversal of polarity—the expression of love completed as an act of hatred, the creation of life enacted as a maneuver of war—becomes a nightmarish underside of man's straining to realize a whole existence. Thus, in *An American Dream*, Kelly describes the conception of Deborah as a Napoleonic land grab, a forced march of troops to occupy the womb [ch. 8]. And Rojack before his killing of Deborah rarely approached sex as if he were "making life, but rather as if [he] were a pirate sharpening up a raid on life [ch. 4]." Compared to such an austere view of the equilibrium of life, which form and language are marshalled to express, the jeweled elegance of an Updike's humanism appears decadent and puerile. Like Michelangelo's implosion of the monumental in the insignificant and small, Mailer's hipster infusion of danger into love charges the inert with energy. And the increase in consciousness foliates in baroque configurations of olfactory sensations. "The essence of biology," Mailer writes in *The Eighth Presidential Paper—Red Dread*, "seems to be challenge and response, risk and survival, war and the lessons of war." [23] This dialectic of violence as "an indispensable element of life [*Pres*, p. 246]" is extravagantly dramatized in *An American Dream*. Unlike Eitel in *The Deer Park*, who succumbs to the Horatio Alger dream of mass man, returns to Hollywood to make commercial movies and reopen a stale love affair with his ex-wife, Stephen Rojack opts for the Edenic dream of man's birthright "to be free, to wander, to have adventure and to grow on the waves of the violent, the perfumed, and the unexpected [*Pres*, p. 39]." "God owns the creation, but the Devil has power over all we waste," Mailer writes in a fragment of a novel published in *The Twelfth Presidential Paper* [*Pres*, p. 275]; and this anal-genital struggle underlies the narrative strategies of *An American Dream*. Rojack wages titanic battle against the anal demonism of Deborah-Ruta-Kelly (with their taste for sexual acrobatics, pederasty, masturbation, and incest) and the sterile conformism of the Mafia, CIA, TV, and academia to win in the regenerative "quiver of jeweled

arrows" that is the love of Cherry a glimpse of the "heavenly city [ch. 5]." Thus, as with Milton in his portraits of
Samson and Delilah, Mailer explores the ambivalent attrac-
tion-repulsion residual in the relationship of the sexes; and
with the frustrate energy of sixteenth-century Italian Mannerism portrays for us the courage—because of the threat
to us of extinction—which necessarily underlies a vital
sexual life and a healthy growth of the soul.

If Mailer breaks free of the claustrophobic limitations
of what Herzog calls the "potato love [p. 41]" of mass
civilization, Salinger aspires to the profound silence of
Zen-Christian blessedness by way paradoxically of the rational confessions of psychological realism. The psychic
tension of his characters attests to the precarious nodes of
such an effort—as does the ever loosening first person
narrative of his stories. In the self-conscious vocabulary of
the man on a psychoanalyst's couch, the Glass children
clinically evaluate their satoris and epiphanies in terms of
nervous breakdown and emotional crisis. The structure of
Seymour: An Introduction derives from the duality of Buddy's indulging in self-analysis as he struggles to define Seymour's saintliness. Midway in his indication of what Seymour meant to his brothers and sisters, Buddy is invalided
by the sanctified afflatus of his thoughts, suffering for nine
weeks from acute hepatitis. Will the reader, he asks,
"choose to think, on the basis of this Sick Report, that my
personal happiness—so carefully touted at the very beginning of this composition—perhaps wasn't happiness at all
but just liverishness?" This possibility, he confesses, "is of
extremely grave concern to me. For certain, I was genu-
inely happy to be working on this Introduction. In my own
supine way, I was miraculously happy all through my hepatitis (and the alliteration alone should have finished me
off). And I'm ecstatically happy at this moment, I'm happy
to say. Which is not to deny (and I've come now, I'm

afraid, to the real reason I've constructed this showcase for my poor old liver)—which is not to deny, I repeat, that my ailment left me with a single, terrible deficiency." [24] That is, he has developed—only momentarily—writer's block about Seymour! Eventually (naturally) he is able to write again and ends finally with two stories about Seymour's superiority to him in marble shooting and in foot racing. Which leads Buddy to the psychoepiphanic insights: (1) that, in his description of Seymour, his own ego, his "perpetual lust to share top billing" with his sibling rival, "is all over the place" and (2) that, as his saintly brother's keeper, he is also the keeper of all his students whom he must face in two and one-half hours.

> I know—not always, but I *know*—there is no single thing I do that is more important than going into that awful Room 307. There isn't one girl in there, including the Terrible Miss Zabel, who is not as much my sister as Boo Boo or Franny. They may shine with the misinformation of the ages, but they shine. This thought manages to stun me: There's no place I'd really rather go right now than into Room 307. Seymour once said that all we do our whole lives is go from one little piece of Holy Ground to the next. Is he *never* wrong?
> Just go to bed, now. Quickly. Quickly and slowly. [p. 248]

And on the crest of such waves of introspection, Buddy, and Seymour (in "For Esmé—With Love and Squalor"), and Franny (in *Zooey*) balance self-knowledge against illumination, deep sleep against satori.

Fiedler also plays equilibrist, balanced between the frontier dream of beauty, equality, and wholeness of spirit, and the American supermarket culture which hideously parodies the frontier dream. He portrays American political and social reality as a saturnine negative of the positive ideal that purports to direct the underground spiritual flow of American life. Bellow also affirms the human worth of the individual, but with less sardonicism than Fiedler. His heroes stubbornly persist as men of viscera in a world of impersonal collective planning. They recognize sadly, however, that they are quixotic holdouts against the bureaucratization of modern civilization, forlorn survivors of an archaic faith in the primitive order of the emotions.

The mannerism of these writers derives from their effort to incorporate contraries into a comprehensive vision of life, to link the universal with individual experience, to exhibit faith in God and at the same time to express healthy skepticism for the assumed coherence of human events. Their predecessors in this century—Joyce, Proust, Eliot, Pound—sought a solution to the disharmony of modern experience in the divisive forces of time and space. Through the spatiality of form—the fusion of past and present in myth, the use of stream of consciousness, the disruption of narrative sequence—they asserted the aesthetic oneness, at least, of existence. To some extent Malamud, Bellow, and Fiedler also reflect these older means of making sense out of sensory data. Malamud seeks to transmute the time-world of history into the timeless world of myth. Bellow renders the passage of time spatially in *Herzog*, not only through his Joycean reduction of coherent sequence (as in *Ulysses*) but also through his superimposing of the action of the past onto that of the present when he narrates the events of the previous four or five years as a stream of consciousness in Herzog's mind during the five days at Ludeyville which dramatically contain and conclude the novel. The effect is of action occurring simultaneously at different places. And Fiedler in *Back to China* juxtaposes scenes and events from the life of Baro Finkelstone during two widely separate periods of his life—China in 1945 with America in 1965—as the twin halves of one continuing psychic fact.

For the most part in these novels, however, the categories of place and time continue to operate, the worlds of God and man to pursue their divergent courses. Like the Baroque artist who never quite succeeds in making stone suggest the insubstantiality of clouds, so these Jewish-American novelists never entirely manage to adjust an antique dispensation to this century's sense of futility, the old meaning to the new despondency. Yet in the equipoise of form, they try not to let go of either. They resist the luxuriant despair of the Absurd, the smug sentimentalism of Orthodoxy, and the cynical whimsy of Pop. Their mannerism is expressive of a world of tragic frustration. Its achievement is a sophisticated willingness to live consciously with the spiritual and moral anxiety that is the tense inheritance of accepting two contrary explanations of human conduct without insisting on a resolution.

NOTES—CHAPTER 1

1. Irving Howe, "The Other Singer," *Commentary*, XLI (1966), 81.

2. John Crowe Ransom, "The State of American Writing, 1948: A Symposium," *Partisan Review*, XV (1948), 879.

3. Leslie Fiedler, "Saul Bellow," *Prairie Schooner*, XXXI (1957), 105. Fiedler characteristically, however, overstates the case in subsequent essays; cf. "Jewish-Americans, Go Home!" and "Zion as Main Street," *Waiting for the End* (New York: Stein and Day, 1964), pp. 65–103.

4. Saul Bellow, *Herzog* (New York: Viking Press, 1964), p. 317.

5. Isaac Bashevis Singer, *The Spinoza of Market Street* (New York: Farrar, Straus and Giroux, 1958), p. 80.

6. J. A. Eisenberg, "Isaac Bashevis Singer—Passionate Primitive or Pious Puritan," *Judaism*, II (1962), 346.

7. Isaac Bashevis Singer, *Short Friday* (New York: Farrar, Straus and Giroux, 1964), p. 220.

8. Isaac Bashevis Singer, *In My Father's Court* (New York: Farrar, Straus and Giroux, 1966), "The Purim Gift," p. 68; and "The Studio," p. 240.

9. In the dedication of the English translation of Isaac Bashevis Singer, *The Family Moskat* (New York: Noonday Press, 1950).

10. In many unseen and subconscious ways my point of view in this section has been influenced by Irving Howe's suggestive article, "Demonic Fiction of a Yiddish 'Modernist,'" *Commentary*, XXX (1960), 350–353.

11. Isaac Bashevis Singer, *The Spinoza of Market Street* (New York: Farrar, Straus and Giroux, 1958), p. 182.

12. Cf. Michael Fixler, "The Redeemers: Themes in the Fiction of Isaac Bashevis Singer," *Kenyon Review*, XXVI (1964), 380.

13. Alexander Pope, *Essay on Man*, I, 292 and 294.

14. Letter to George and Thomas Keats, 21 December 1817.

15. Robert M. Adams, *Strains of Discord: Studies in Literary Openness* (Ithaca, N.Y.: Cornell University Press, 1958); and Alan Friedman, *The Turn of the Novel* (New York: Oxford University Press, 1966).

16. Alan Friedman, *The Turn of the Novel* (New York: Oxford University Press, 1966), p. 36.

17. *Ibid.*, p. 183.

18. Richard Chase, *The American Novel and Its Tradition* (Garden City, N.Y.: Doubleday and Company, 1957), pp. 7–8.

19. Marius Bewley, *The Eccentric Design: Form in the Classic American Novel* (New York: Columbia University Press, 1959).

20. Nicholas Pevsner, *An Outline of European Architecture* (Middlesex, England: Penguin Books Ltd., 1943, 1963), p. 223.

21. Sidney Richman, *Bernard Malamud* (New York: Twayne Publishers, Inc., 1966), pp. 44–48.

22. Bernard Malamud, *The Natural* (New York: Farrar, Straus and Giroux, 1952), pp. 31–32.

23. Norman Mailer, *The Presidential Papers* (New York: G. P. Putnam's Sons, 1963), p. 167; henceforth referred to as *Pres.*

24. J. D. Salinger, *Raise High the Roof Beam, Carpenters* and *Seymour: An Introduction* (Boston: Little, Brown and Company, 1963), pp. 175–176.

2/ Nathanael West's "Desperate Detachment"

NATHANAEL WEST is reputed to have remained detached from the grotesqueries of Hollywood during the many years he worked there and from the follies of the human world for the thirty-seven years he lived in it.[1] Yet West's novels make it clear that in the deeper reaches of his mind he was obsessed with man's nightmarish dual nature: his neurotic isolation and his social impulse, his self-deception and his self-mockery. Unlike Singer, and so many of the current Jewish-American writers, West was unable to rest content in the human suspension between heavenly aspirations and earthly limitations, belief and skepticism, order and disorder. He portrays life in his novels as a conflict of inadequate imperatives offered to man by society and culture as guides to live by. Conflict supposes not equipoise between codeterminants but supremacy of one over another. In that sense each novel, despite its basic satirical intention, represents a search for absolutes. "Reality! Reality! If I could only discover the Real," John Gilson calls for in his "journal." "A Real that I could know with my senses."[2] In the astringent disillusionment of West's hope of finding something real to believe in—"A Real that would wait for me to

inspect it as a dog inspects a dead rabbit [p. 14]"—each
novel ends as a mocking denunciation of a false dream: the
bardic dream (*The Dream Life of Balso Snell*), the Christ
dream (*Miss Lonelyhearts*), the Horatio Alger dream (*A
Cool Dream*), and the Hollywood dream (*The Day of the
Locust*). West's bitter cognizance of betrayal is pervasive.
The thoroughgoing nature of his sense of the fraudulence
and destructiveness of life is brilliantly, almost excessively,
portrayed by the Trojan Horse correlative in *The Dream
Life of Balso Snell*. Synonymous in Western thought with
falsity and the end of a civilization, the wooden horse—specifically its alimentary canal—becomes the hallucinatory
terrain over which Balso Snell wanders. Thus West clearly
identifies man's dream world with sham and *fin de siècle*.
He uneasily describes its death rattle, while trying desperately to dissociate himself with a comic ploy from emotional involvement in its agony. Unfortunately for the complete success of his stories, he was unable to control his
own sense of outrage and despair. His shriek of laughter, as
Victor Comerchero notes, "keeps breaking into a sob." [3]

The first work of a writer is more likely to rely on
literary analogues than later works which draw directly on
experience for their substance. Such is the case with the
four novels of West. *The Dream Life of Balso Snell* sati-
rizes the ineffectuality of the imagination by way of an
inexhaustible stream of allusions to and parodies of English writers from Dryden to Joyce, and from Dostoevsky to
the French Symbolists and Dadaists, as well as much mis-
cellaneous Western thought. The novel is a book perversely
bent on proclaiming the illusoriness of books. West is reported to have told Liebling "that he had written Balso as a
protest against writing books." [4] That is ostensibly its general satirical aim. In fact, the novel strikes out thematically in a variety of directions, foreshadowing most of the
preoccupations of West in his subsequent novels.[5] Of these

I wish to look at one to demonstrate West's ambivalent involvement in the despairing world that he depicts.

An essential thematic antithesis in the story pits romantic love against the procreative instinct. Like the nympholeptic shepherd-king in Keats's *Endymion* (and like Samuel Perkins, the subject of a biography by Mary McGeeney), Balso Snell swoons in and out of a dream within his dream as he mentally pursues Miss McGeeney, his thoughts struggling "to make the circle of his sensory experience approach the infinite [p. 36]." The prevailing situation is one of incompatibility. Lust encounters conditions of courtly love, and sacred love the wiles of the seducer. "Oh, I loved a girl once," Balso Snell laments:

> All day she did nothing but place bits of meat on the petals of flowers. She choked the rose with butter and cake crumbs, soiling the crispness of its dainty petals with gravy and cheese. She wanted to attract flies, not butterflies or bees. [p. 57]

This perverse merger of the fleshly and the ethereal becomes inextricably ambiguous in the witty biography of Saint Puce, the flea "who was born, lived, and died, beneath the arm of our Lord [p. 11]." In his daily sensations of supping on Christ, whose body provided him with both meat and drink, Saint Puce enacted perpetual Holy Communion.

As the ironic tone of these two examples indicates, West will not allow the mystery of the "Two-become-One" to remain intact. For him the contraries reconciled are always coming undone. Like Fra Lippo Lippi he forever sees "the garden and God there / A-making man's wife"; and this lesson of "The value and significance of flesh" he "can't unlearn ten minutes afterward." [6]

If the spiritual cannot exist without the incarnate, through substance then must we confirm our substancelessness. Thus West fashions his own infernal mystery. The ideal vanishes into solid flesh. "Who among us can boast that he was born three times, as was Dionysius?" B. Hamlet Darwin asks caustically.

> Or who can say, like Christ, that he was born of a virgin? . . . Alas! none of us. . . . You who were born from the womb, covered with slime and foul blood, 'midst cries of anguish and suffering.
> At your birth, instead of the Three Kings, the Dove, the Star of Bethlehem, there was only old Doctor Haasenschweitz who wore rubber gloves and carried a towel over his arm like a waiter.
> And how did the lover, your father, come to his beloved? . . . Did he come in the shape of a swan, a bull, or a shower of gold? No! But with his pants unsupported by braces, came he from the bathroom. [p. 55]

Unfortunately for West's peace of mind, as the savage despair of the passage suggests, he found no satisfaction in this reduction of the infinite into the corporeal either. In an acrid satire of fleshly desire the story (and dream) concludes with Balso having a nocturnal emission. (The entire story represents the strenuously intellectual efforts of Balso's body to have a wet dream.) Even sex, the urge to procreate, ends as a pointless solo exercise in release of tension, likened to "the mechanics of decay [p. 61]." At the instant of emission, West exultantly informs us that Balso's "body broke free of the bard" and "took on a life of its own" "that knew nothing of the poet Balso [p. 61]." Despite this freedom from the false constraints of the categorizing imagination, not life, not the organic, but death and the mechanical describe the evolutions of the body. The basic metaphor used is that of an army performing "the manual of disintegration," maneuvering automatically "with the confidence and training of chemicals acting under the stimulus of a catalytic agent [p. 6]." Release is described in terms of a mortally wounded soldier: "His body screamed and shouted as it marched . . . then with one heaving shout of triumph, it fell back quiet . . . victorious." Thus the "miracle was made manifest" in the One, West says sardonically.

> The One that is all things and yet no one of them: the priest and the god, the immolation, the sacrificial rite, the libation offered to ancestors, the incantation, the sacrificial egg, the altar, the ego and the alter ego, as well as the father, the child, and the grandfather of the universe, the mystic doctrine, the purification, the syllable "Om," the path, the master, the witness, the receptacle, the Spirit of Public School 186, the last ferry that leaves for Weehawken at seven. [pp. 61–62]

In the diminishing manner of the burlesque stanzas of Byron's *Don Juan*, this catalogue of the body's regality ("the Spirit of Public School 186"!) underscores the skepticism with which West assents to the enthronement of matter.

Worse, yet, mind returns in the form of false literary sentiment to adulterate further the autonomous reality of the body. In a brilliant analysis of its style, Victor Comerchero [pp. 57–61] shows how Balso's imagined copulation with Mary McGeeney is a parody of the melting, swooning seduction of eighteenth-century sentimental literature, of the stereotype passion of pulp fiction, of the hard-boiled back-seat wrestle of the realistic school, of the decadent *fin de siècle* dreams of encounters with an oriental *femme fatale*, and of the Molly Bloom monologue at the conclusion of Joyce's *Ulysses*. Saturninely, if comically, West reveals that even Balso's "dreams have been corrupted by literature. When he dreams, even a wet dream, it is a literary one." [7] Driven by sexual desire, Balso Snell in his dream exploration of the nature of mind and matter may have discovered complacently that the body reigns supreme; but West's interpretation of the same event is less optimistic. In acrid disillusionment he concludes (corroborated by the dream context of the narrative) that Balso's solution to the hopeless bifurcation of life is as chimerical as the empty constructs of the mind, which man fools himself into believing are a pledge of meaningful order in the world.

"If there is a vision of love" in West's fiction, Josephine Herbst has remarked, "it is etched in the acid of what love is not." [8] *The Dream Life of Balso Snell* presents a satyr's conception of love, *Miss Lonelyhearts* that of the whorehouse madam turned church-choir mistress. From cynical exploiter of his correspondents' cries for help, Miss Lonelyhearts metamorphoses into a Christlike savior of these lost and lonely souls of modern civilization.

West's point of view, however, is more subtle and complex in *Miss Lonelyhearts* than in his other three novels. His virulent skepticism is forever testing the validity of a thought and seeking the motive behind an action. Thus, he constantly and ambivalently undercuts his effort to find a pattern in existence. The horrifying lives of Miss Lonelyhearts' readers unquestionably moves the columnist to sincere desire to succor them. But his conversion from hardboiled columnist to soft-souled evangelist is compromised at every turn. The psychology of sex—the twentieth-century substitute for previous centuries' religious faith—is the instrument of his betrayal of others as well as of himself. More often than not he is depicted as selfishly demanding rather than selflessly giving of his love. His impulse toward the Divine Love of man and "all God's creation [p. 75]" advocated by Father Zossima in *The Brothers Karamazov*, which he has been reading, manifests itself in sexual cruelty, self-loathing seduction, latent homosexuality, and religious hysteria. Like infernal stations of the cross in his outrageous progress toward saintly love of humanity, he bloodily bungles (in a dream) the sacrifice of a lamb, viciously tugs at the nipples of his fiancée's breasts, brutally twists the arm of an old homosexual, calculatingly attempts to seduce his boss's wife, distastefully submits to the sexual advances of a correspondent, ardently holds hands with her crippled husband, eventually strikes the housewife seductress in the face again and again, and finally achieves union with Christ while in a fever.

Throughout this inverse way of the pilgrim, religious ardor is confused with sexual desire, love with lust, and lust with violence and destruction. Miss Lonelyhearts' addresses of love to Betty, Mary Shrike, and Mrs. Doyle are associated with a Mexican War obelisk that like a giant phallus "lengthening in rapid jerks," and "red and swollen in the dying sun," seems "about to spout a load of granite seed" of death [p. 89]. The arm of the "clean old man [p. 85]," who was pulled from the stall of a public restroom and accused by Miss Lonelyhearts of being a pervert, becomes "the arm of all the sick and miserable, broken and betrayed, inarticulate and impotent . . . of Desperate, Broken-hearted, Sick-of-it-all, Disillusioned-with-tubercular-husband [p. 88]." In its effort to create order out of the entropy about him, Miss Lonelyhearts' sensibility, ill from its encounter with Fay Doyle, nightmarishly grapples with the contents of a pawnshop window, "the paraphernalia of suffering." Out of this jumble of articles it attempts to construct a phallus. Failing in this, it works to form the paraphernalia into a gigantic cross on the shore of an ocean, but

> . . . every wave added to his stock faster than he could lengthen its arms. His labors were enormous. He staggered from the last wave line to his work, loaded down with marine refuse—bottles, shells, chunks of cork, fish heads, pieces of net. [pp. 104–105]

The linkage of Christ with the sea has strong libidinous overtones (cf. pp. 75–76, 138–139, where Christ and a phallic snake and Christ and a fish are also joined). The prior encounter with Fay Doyle is described in marine terms. Her undressing in the dark is heard by Miss Lonelyhearts as "sea sounds":

> Something flapped like a sail; there was the creak of ropes; then he heard the wave-against-a-wharf smack of rubber on flesh. Her call to him to hurry was a sea-moan, and when he lay beside her, she heaved, tidal, moon-driven.

And in language that foreshadows his subsequent building of the cross, he staggers out of bed fifteen minutes later "like an exhausted swimmer leaving the surf [p. 101]." In short, moved by the inadequacy of sex to steady his nerves and allay his self-hatred, he sublimates his eroticism in Christian humility, as a complementary form of therapy.

West could not formulate the ambivalence of his hope for a religious solution to life more clearly. As if the condemnation of *agapé* is not vehement enough, Miss Lonelyhearts' religious conversion, as Victor Comerchero demonstrates conclusively, has a homosexual origin, further underlining West's "mythic, mocking, agonizing" suspicion that "true compassion" is unendurable in this decaying world.[9] In the plight of Miss Lonelyhearts West portrays a devastating debasement of the Ulysses and Sirens motif. And the blasphemously blind universe that he envisions, in which "the Miss Lonelyhearts are the priests of twentieth-century America [p. 122]," receives full confirmation when Miss Lonelyhearts interprets his fever as a religious experience and climbs out of bed to embrace the crippled Doyle, whom he believes "God had sent him so that Miss Lonelyhearts could perform a miracle and be certain of his conversion [p. 139]." But West in his heart of hearts knew that God was dead. Miss Lonelyhearts never quite qualifies for membership in Graham Greene's pantheon of tainted saints. West's faith is at once too strong of desire and too weak of belief. Miss Lonelyhearts' need for a confirmatory miracle italicizes this profound skepticism. And the consequences of his desire for certainty are ironically devastating on both the sacramental and psychological levels of the narrative. He rushes to embrace the cripple and heal his leg. Doyle, however, is terrified by Miss Lonelyhearts' mad charge and by Betty's sudden appearance at the bottom of the stairs. As they grapple, a pistol Doyle is carrying accidentally fires, killing Miss Lonelyhearts. Locked in each other's arms they roll down the stairs. The symbolic union of the two men at the end is no doubt on one level expressive of Miss Lonelyhearts' spiritual yearnings; but their embrace, as Stanley Edgar Hyman observes, is also homosexual, the one ironically penetrating "the body of the other with a bullet," "while the woman stands helplessly by." [10] The disparity in the novel between the simple narrative affirmation of religious faith and the underlying metaphoric insinuation of Oedipal obscenities adumbrates the tortured ambiguity of West's imagination—its attraction to a Christ dream that it could not believe in.

In *A Cool Million* and *The Day of the Locust,* West explores the *Zeitgeist* of the cheaters and the cheated on native grounds. The dreams are now distinctly the homegrown variety found sprouting in the land of opportunity. "America takes care of the honest and industrious and never fails them as long as they are both," Nathan "Shagpoke" Whipple expounds from his perch on a cracker barrel. "The story of Rockefeller and of Ford is the story of every great American," he tells Lemuel Pitkin, "and you should strive to make it your story. Like them, you were born poor and on a farm. Like them, by honesty and industry, you cannot fail to succeed [p. 150]." The rest of *A Cool*

Million is West's saturnine retort. Not from rags to riches but to the same old shirtsleeves, not from log cabin to White House but to the same old mortgaged farm house—this is the just reward of the barefoot, but honest and industrious, American boy. With acrid irony West equates business enterprise with the imagination, foresight, and aggressiveness of Wu Fong's white slavery emporium; and economic success with unapprehended chicanery and thievery. The American capitalistic system is posited on the productive ideal that the building of a better mousetrap is always good for the community. West's answer is to demonstrate that the folklore of Horatio Alger is more likely to be destructive of the individual than to be beneficial to society. And so he gives us the allegory of Lemuel's inexorable dismemberment on the barricades of capitalism: *sans* teeth, eye, thumb, scalp, and leg. To the memory of this derelict of the American way of life, the fascistic "Leather Shirt" followers of Shagpoke Whipple shout at the conclusion in a national holiday celebration of Lemuel's birthday, "All hail, the American Boy! [ch. 31]."

Victor Comerchero contends that because of the broadly comic tone of *A Cool Million*, a reversion to the tone of *The Dream Life of Balso Snell*, it fails to engage the reader. Consequently one tends to miss the serious point of the novel; "one is so amused by America as West presents it that one is neither frightened nor angered by it [p. 118]." In his effort to set up a critical issue, a straw man, so to speak, Comerchero exaggerates the difficulty posed by the blurred focus of the book's tone. The plain fact is that few readers (critical commentators, that is) have missed the central warning of the novel. Comerchero's observation, however, about the strange refusal of the story to take itself seriously is penetrating. The "personal involvement" that he suggests as an explanation has more than a grain of truth in it, as this essay, I hope, makes clear. But Comerchero does not, unfortunately, make anything more of this insight.

With what in the story is West involved? One cannot see the temperament and agony of West in either Lemuel Pitkin or Shagpoke Whipple, as one can in Balso Snell, Miss Lonelyhearts, and Tod Hackett. Hence the disturbing reserve of the story, by way of its excessiveness, does not derive from West's effort to dissociate himself from the central characters. Closer to the simple truth, probably, is that West, like his great predecessor Swift, is engaged in a lover's quarrel with a world that does not live up to his expectations. The broadly vulgar style in which he tells the story is, of course, on one level a parody of the crass, didactic prose of the Horatio Alger tale. Not so much the economic system, however, as the noisome aura of sanctity which enshrouds it is the object of his attack. After all, in writing his books, West himself hoped to turn an honest dollar. That hope was appropriately enough strongest with *A Cool Million*.[11] The pious cant of a Shagpoke Whipple celebrates the manufacturing process and the pursuit of gain as the golden ends of human activity. The result is that the manufactured article deteriorates into a by-product and man is lost sight of altogether, transformed into a helpless ministrant to his own inexorable dehumanization. In the "Chamber of American Horrors, Animate and Inanimate Hideosities," West brilliantly pictures the debasement of taste and of sensibility produced by this carnival atmosphere. Here the flotsam of an industrial civilization buttressed by a false ethic is accorded the revered permanence of museum exhibits. Man's Hippocratic ideal is enshrined in the patent medicine offerings of the drugstore: in a "Hercules wearing a small, compact truss" and in "a copy of Power's 'Greek Slave' with elastic bandages on all her joints." Technical know-how is displayed in the cheap imitative tricks of paper "made to look like wood, wood like rubber, rubber like steel, steel like cheese, cheese like glass, and, finally, glass like paper [ch. 28]." So the inconstant and the deceptive are memorialized with sneaking admiration as a tribute to American technological genius.

In Greenfield Village, Henry Ford's monument to Americana, there is an ash heap meticulously encased and labeled as having come from behind Thomas Edison's Menlo Park laboratory. Gazing at this dump pile, one can never be quite sure of the degree of fetish worship and, contrariwise, of sly humor that it represents. Nor can one categorically isolate West's attitude in *A Cool Million*. Shagpoke Whipple, the homespun American philosopher, wins our sufferance; but Shagpoke the politician, the Americafirster, terrifies us. Lemuel, the innocent pawn, evokes our pity; but Lemuel the fool, the classic rube, equally arouses our derision. The names that West chooses for his characters are invariably witty wordplays, adding an extra dimension to our understanding of that person. Lemuel Pitkin's last name is close in sound to pipkin. Whether we are right to associate pipkin with Lemuel, we cannot avoid the scathing sense of the diminutive in his name; hence in comparison to his namesake Lemuel Gulliver, his misfortunes are seen as a diminuendo echo of the Brobdingnag gulling suffered by Gulliver on *his* Whittingtonian travels in search of fame and fortune.

The big lie is certain. Less evident is the source of the lie: the ideals of the American Way of Life? the naïveté of such simpletons as Lemuel? the "sophisticated aliens [ch. 31]" decried by Whipple? or the ingrained evil of an economic system? The tone of *A Cool Million* reflects West's own uncertainty of what to finger. For all his pessimism he was not a little bitten with the American dream of a new Eden in the wilderness, as Betty's and Miss Lonelyhearts' nostalgic interlude on the farm in Connecticut hints—a surprising performance for seemingly so confirmed an urban novelist. There is also his love of the Bucks County countryside and of hunting and fishing. And there is the prophet's fervent need to believe in something, which in West is strung taut by the contrary pull of the cynical side of his nature. It is no wonder in his daily life that he strove to divorce himself from the furious indignation which drove his artistic vision.

With *The Day of the Locust*, West's view of life approaches Swift's in the fourth book of *Gulliver's Travels*. Spectators and performers alike feel the lash of his derision. Attracted by its semblance of life, Midwesterners come to Hollywood only to be tricked into death by a diet of sophisticate sex. They gyrate from movie premiere to movie premiere, as much automatons as the celluloid celebrities they push and shove to glimpse. The cinematic promise of ripe love and of a richer, fuller life never materializes. Faye Greener is a pathetic imitation of the Hollywood sex goddess, her thoughts and mannerisms a pastiche of Grade B movies. Both Homer Simpson and Tod Hackett (note the puns on death and havoc in the latter's name) discover in her ever fresh lure of sexuality a fey, receding will-o-the-wisp. Her appearance promises love, but it proves no more rewarding than the suggestive accents and movements of a screenland heroine. Each one's desire for renewal of person is eventually betrayed by her beauty, "whose invitation wasn't to pleasure, but to struggle, hard and sharp, closer to murder than to love [p. 271]." The mechanically destructive recoil of the mob at the end of the novel reflects West's view of what happens to man when his hopes end as tattered scarecrows of reality. The adulatory pursuit of celebrities blurs sinisterly into the sexual violence that underlies emotional hunger. Spasms surge periodically through the crowd. Smutty remarks pass freely from stranger to stranger. Men hug passing complacent women. With such senseless eroticism, the mob apes the dark underside of the lives of its screen heroes and heroines. Death is inextricably linked to love. Human energy is easily diverted from a life instinct to a death impulse. Thus the adoration of the premiere mob is manifested as the blight of locusts, just as the alteration of the primordial hills of southern California into travesties of exotic architecture is another manifestation of the locust's presence.

The Westian novel is concerned at its center with the instability of existence, which derives basically from a metaphysical reaction to the modern world picture of everything being in flux. What more frighteningly askew world of metamorphosis can one imagine than the one of architecture, aesthetics, music, and mathematics Miss McGeeney tells us that Samuel Perkins discovered "in the odors of a woman's body [p. 36]." In these terms the Hollywood setting of *The Day of the Locust* provides West with the most perfect of the correlatives he has used to set forth his vision of life. As is proper in the city dedicated to the making of movies—to the creation of shapes that alter before one's eyes—the guises and gestures of the celluloid world of shadowy change, of make-believe, become the status quo. A fat lady in yachting cap converts into a housewife going shopping; a man in Norfolk jacket and Tyrolean hat, an insurance agent returning from his office; and a girl in slacks and sneakers with a bandanna around her head, a receptionist leaving a switchboard. The painted canvas, plaster, and lath sets on the back lots of the film studios reappear as the Mexican ranch houses, Samoan huts, Mediterranean villas, Egyptian and Japanese temples, Swiss chalets, and Tudor cottages that line Pinyon Canyon at the end of Vine Street. Repeatedly the Westian man transmutes into a woman. John Gilson as Raskolnikov, after murdering a dishwasher, caresses his breasts "like a young girl who has suddenly become conscious of her body on a hot afternoon." He imitates "the mannered walk of a girl showing off before a group of boys," flirts with some sailors, going "through all the postures of a desperate prostitute," and "camping" for all it is worth [p. 22]. Lemuel is transformed momently into a male prostitute in Wu Fong's establishment. And Miss Lonelyhearts exhibits more than one symptom of the homosexual. The many periods in history endlessly shift their outlines. Searching for Faye, who has a bit part in the movie "Waterloo," Tod Hackett wanders through a kaleidoscope of time and place and of the artifices of civilization:

> The only bit of shade he could find was under an ocean liner made of painted canvas with real lifeboats hanging from its davits. He stood in its narrow shadow for a while, then went on toward a great forty-foot papier mâché sphinx that loomed up in the distance. He had to cross a desert to reach it, a desert that was continually being made larger by a fleet of trucks dumping white sand. . . .
>
> He skirted the desert, making a wide turn to the right, and came to a western street with a plank sidewalk. On the porch of the "Last Chance Saloon" was a rocking chair. He sat down on it and lit a cigarette.
>
> From there he could see a jungle compound with a water buffalo tethered to the side of a conical grass hut. Every few seconds the animal groaned musically. Suddenly an Arab charged by on a white stallion. He shouted at the man, but got no answer. A little while later he saw a truck with a load of snow and several malamute dogs. He shouted again. The driver shouted something back, but didn't stop.
>
> Throwing away his cigarette, he went through the swinging doors of the saloon. There was no back to the building and he found himself in a Paris street. He followed it to its end, coming out in a Romanesque courtyard. He heard voices a short distance away and went toward them. On a lawn of fiber, a group of men and women in riding costume were picnicking. They were eating cardboard food in front of a cellophane waterfall. [p. 351]

Faye Greener and her father, Harry, have maintained their theatrical poses of movie siren and vaudeville clown so long that, in the words of Comerchero, each "has been dispossessed of his personality—of his identity—through disuse [p. 138]."

West's obsession with flux is a central controlling force in *The Dream Life of Balso Snell*. In keeping with the protean nature of a dream, shapes are forever altering before Balso's eyes. His first sight of Miss McGeeney is of a slim young girl "standing naked before him . . . washing her hidden charms in a public fountain." She calls to him in the erotically charged language of the Romance.

> Throwing his arms around her, Balso interrupted her recitation sticking his tongue into her mouth. But when he closed his eyes to heighten the fun, he felt that he was embracing tweed. He opened them and saw that what he held in his arms was a middle aged woman dressed in a mannish suit and wearing hornrimmed glasses. [pp. 31–32]

Balso's orgasm at the end of the book, while dreaming of having sexual intercourse with Miss McGeeney (changed again, "alas! but with much of the old Mary left, particularly about the eyes," p. 57), enacts not only the completion of his own desire but also the wish fulfillment of John Gilson's schoolboy dream of sleeping with her. Dreams figure in all the novels except *A Cool Million*—where the dream is conceived of as a nationwide and patriotic preoccupation with the getting and keeping of money. Critics have made much of the Freudian and Surrealistic impulse in West's frequent resort to dreams, and rightly so; but their significance for West is not restricted to the psychological and aesthetic. In their reflection of a volatile universe, they also have a strong metaphysical import.

Another instance of West's preoccupation with the metamorphosis of things is the recurrence in his novels of

performers and of the blurring of distinction between performer and spectator. In one way or another almost all his
characters pursue an occupation, usually as writer or
actor or painter, which transforms one kind of reality into
another kind. The poet Balso discovers to his dismay that
the wooden horse "was inhabited solely by writers in
search of an audience [p. 37]." Instead of writing he finds
himself involuntarily reading the work of others. *Miss
Lonelyhearts* is a story about a nameless man writing the
daily "agony column" for a newspaper, answering letters,
written under pseudonyms by the afflicted, for the enter-
tainment of the majority of its readers. Here columnist and
correspondent blur together in their dual categories of
writer and reader. Even Lemuel Pitkin ends as a human
prop at the Bijou Theater, dismantled nightly of his toupee,
false teeth, glass eye, and wooden leg by the comedy team
of Riley and Robbins. The complete symbiosis of performer and spectator occurs in *The Day of the Locust*,
when the surrealistic actions of the mob become confused
in Tod's mind with his painting of "The Burning of Los
Angeles," which depicts such a mob savagely chasing the
objects of their adulation. Here participant and observer
(not to mention the actual and the fanciful) fuse indistinguishably into a macabre dance of death, celebrating the
impermanence of all things.

The despair implicit in this obsession with change cannot be exaggerated. West's Jeremiahlike search for permanent values was forever overturning proof of the tran-
siency of things. "West's brilliance" as a novelist, Comerchero observes, "proceeds from his ability to generalize
frustration [p. 163]." West's vision of frustration stems
from his metaphysical sense of the helplessness of man
trapped in an unstable universe.

"If I could be Hamlet, or even a clown with a breaking
heart 'neath this jester's motley," the writer of The Pam-

phlet exclaims, "the role [of being man] would be tolerable. But I must always find it necessary to burlesque the mystery of feeling at its source; I must laugh at myself, and if the laugh is 'bitter,' I must laugh at the laugh [p. 27]." These lines are often quoted as expressive of the strenuous effort of West to dissociate himself from the horrors of his age. In his novels he tried to realize distance by treating his fictional characters with extreme objectivity. But the cold malice with which he analyzes their faults, like the excessive scatology or sexual and bodily nausea found in all his writing, reveals the radical nature of his revulsion, and the extremity of his reaction, to the frustrated aspirations of his protagonists—which were also (with the exception of homosexuality) his own frustrations. The Westian man is an early species on the evolutionary scale of *genus victima*. Like the Neanderthal man, as compared to present-day *Homo sapiens*, he excites our morbid interest and disgust more than our sympathy or love. West's involvement with him is that of the prophet. He has the reformer's instinct. He wishes reality to be different from what it is and people from what they are. He hates what will not heed his jeremiads, unlike a Malamud or a Bellow, who can love their fictional *schlemiels* without feeling a strong urge to reform them. In this fact lies one of the fundamental differences between the idealistic naïveté of West and his generation and the radical sophistication of the Jewish-American writers of the fifties and sixties.

Strong overtones of antifascism and anticapitalism characterize West's novels as sincere expressions of their time. As Josephine Herbst remembers him, "The horror of this age was in West's nerves, in his blood." [12] In his passionate search for something to believe in, West exhibits the desperate commitment of the thirties; but in his bitter sense of betrayal by ideas, he suffers the anguished disillusionment of the liberal of the thirties in the decades that followed. His need for detachment was intense; but the age and his background made that well nigh impossible for him to realize. At a time when most of his Jewish contemporaries were still writing realistically of the Jewish experience in America, West was attempting to define symbolistically the larger American experience. His vocabulary necessarily relied heavily on literary fashion. His vision of American life was inevitably narrow and limited. His insecure control of his material, despite his inventiveness and his expenditure of incredible labor on his stories, foredoomed the results to shakiness of form, uncertainty of tone, inconstancy and occasional vulgarity of language, and finickiness of output. His passionate involvement in ideas led to his quasi-identification with the search for values of his central characters. Unfortunately, such identification with his fictional creations also inhibited his judgment of their quest. His stories are more heated and polemical than is good for them. He too often lost what a later generation would call his cool. Yet in his exploration of the meaning of Hollywood and in his probe of the psychic blows suffered by being American, he courageously homesteaded forty acres on which Mailer, Bellow, Fiedler, and the other contemporary Jewish-American novelists are currently building a Levittown.

NOTES—CHAPTER 2

1. Cf. James F. Light, *Nathanael West: An Interpretative Study* (Evanston, Ill.: Northwestern University Press, 1961), pp. 151–152.

2. *The Dream Life of Balso Snell* (1931) in *The Complete Works of Nathanael West*, edited with an introduction by Alan Ross (New York: Farrar, Straus and Cudahy, 1957), p. 14. All references to this and the other novels—*Miss Lonelyhearts* (1933), *A Cool Million* (1934), and *The Day of the Locust* (1939)—cite this edition.

3. Victor Comerchero, *Nathanael West: The Ironic Prophet* (Syracuse, N.Y.: Syracuse University Press, 1964), p. 71.

4. Quoted by Richard B. Gehman in the introduction to *The Day of the Locust* (New York: New Directions, 1950), p. xv.

5. Cf. James F. Light, *Nathanael West* (Evanston, Ill.: Northwestern University Press, 1961), who considers the basic theme to be "the struggle between the spirit and the flesh [p. 46]"; Victor Comerchero, *Nathanael West* (Syracuse, N.Y.: Syracuse University Press, 1964), who defines its central theme to be "literary falseness versus the truth of reality [p. 52]," and its variants "the sexual origins of human behavior [p. 64]," and "the disparity between men's spiritual aspirations and their physical reality [p. 70]"; and V. L. Lokke, "A Side Glance at Medusa: Hollywood, the Literature Boys, and Nathanael West," *Southwest Review*, XLVI (1961), who reads the book as a denunciation of "the dreams of the creators of *avant-garde* art as well as the fantasy world of the middle-brow intellectuals who consume the product [p. 36]."

6. Robert Browning, *Fra Lippo Lippi*, 11. 266–269.

7. Victor Comerchero, *Nathanael West* (Syracuse, N.Y.: Syracuse University Press, 1964), p. 60.

8. Josephine Herbst, "Nathanael West," *Kenyon Review*, XXIII (1961), 611.

9. Victor Comerchero, *Nathanael West* (Syracuse, N.Y.: Syracuse University Press, 1964), pp. 95–102.

10. Stanley Edgar Hyman, *Nathanael West* (Minneapolis, Minn.: University of Minnesota Press, 1962), pp. 22–23.

11. Cf. James F. Light, *Nathanael West* (Evanston, Ill.: Northwestern University Press, 1961), p. 128.

12. Josephine Herbst, "Nathanael West," *Kenyon Review*, XXIII (1961), 611.

3 / Bernard Malamud's Mythic Proletarians

AT THE END OF *The Assistant,* Frank Alpine converts to Judaism. Thus, in his person as well as in his maintenance of the Bober store and family, Frank insures continuation of the dead Morris Bober's richly human ethics. In his essay "Jewish-Americans, Go Home!" Leslie Fiedler exclaims: "This solution of Malamud's already begins to look a little old-fashioned, appearing as it does in a book which seems a belated novel of the thirties, a last expression of the apocalyptic fears and Messianic hopes of those terrible but relatively simple times."[1] In this offhand remark Fiedler inadvertently identifies one of the two grammars which control the form and content of the Malamud novel. As the Depression milieu of *The Assistant* and the pre-Bolshevik context of *The Fixer* insist, these novels are mutations of the proletarian impulse of the Jewish intellectual of the 1930's. As the baseball rites of *The Natural* and the wasteland motifs of *A New Life*[2] slyly (and at times not so slyly) insinuate, the fictional worlds of these novels also accommodate as a second grammar a mythic pattern of vegetation ritual and Grail quest.[3] The Malamud novel conceptualizes this duality of theme and structure in the appropriately disparate language of realism and symbolism. Sidney Richman comments perceptively in reference to *The Natural* that this "deliberately impure yet perfectly organized style" alternates "Passages of idiomatic, terse, and slangy prose . . . with passages of lyrical intensity." [4] The skill with which Malamud combines the colloquial and mundane with the incantatory and religious is paralleled by his capacity to fuse the assumptions of Marx with the patterns of myth. In the Malamud novel the cosmogonies become one. The historical determinism of socialism merges with the cyclical inevitability of mythos; the proletarian hero winning justice for society, with the mythic hero renewing life for the community. That this identification is in some respects inevitable, Frank Kermode has demonstrated in his exploration of *The Sense of an Ending*; for the tendency of any mental structure or "fiction," once it forgets its fictiveness, especially if it has millennial expectations, is to regress into myth.[5]

The Malamud protagonist is a haunting leftover of the Depression years, his sensibility scarred by economic and social inequities. His past life reads like a "Hobo News" true confession of the down-and-outer of the thirties. Sy Levin is an ex-drunkard—son of a thief and a suicidal madwoman—who had drifted sodden with drink in rotting shoes for more years than he could say from "somebody's filthy cellar" to "small dark rooms" in rooming houses "overrun by roaches and bugs" [pp. 186–187]. Frank Alpine's early life was similarly "made up of lost chances" until "he gave up and let himself be a bum," sleeping in gutters and cellars, eating "what he scrounged out of garbage cans, . . . bearded, smelly, dragging himself through the seasons without a hope to go by [p. 74]." The Depression "mentality" of a Bottom Dog [6]—with his burning sense of the haves conspiring to maintain the servile status of the have-nots—colors the thinking, as well, of Morris

Bober, Roy Hobbs, and Yakov Bok and the tone, particularly, of *The Assistant* and *The Fixer*. Morris bitterly laments the lack of reward for his honesty and industry, while the dishonesty of his ex-partner and the perfidy of his neighbor Karp are allowed to prosper. Roy's request for more salary is sanctimoniously but curtly denied by Judge Goodwill Banner, the penny-pinching majority owner of the New York Knights; while Pop Fisher, the manager of the Knights, is constantly thwarted in his efforts to produce a pennant-winning team by the greed of the front office. And Yakov sees himself as a naked little man, with only his integrity to pit against the impersonal implacability of a monstrous Russian bureaucracy. Malamud's characters have understandably loomed large among the alienated figures of contemporary fiction. Of more significance probably for mastering the vocabulary of his fictional world is to recognize that this alienation assumes the gestures socially of the oppressed victim of an absurd economic system and symbolically of the sick Fisher King.

One of the persistent themes of the radical novels of the thirties and the forties is the conversion of the hero from accommodation with the world of economic power to belief in the worker's cause.[7] This *engagement* is analogous to the commitment of the mythic hero to the redemption of the community.

The Malamud hero is, at first, determined to make his fortune. With Roy Hobbs, it is his Indian Summer career as a rookie home-run king; with Frank Alpine, his aborted effort as a robber Prince; with Sy Levin, his "new life" as a college teacher; and with Yakov Bok, his masquerade as "a sort of Christian overseer [p. 46]." In each instance, however, his selfish search for gain or personal satisfaction metamorphoses into a social and ritualistic quest that ends in at least quasi-revival of spirit in the land. The individual who began as a self-server involuntarily assumes the contrary role of scapegoat and redeemer.

Significantly each Malamud protagonist journeys from his previous abode to a moral and / or economic wasteland, whose regeneration enlists his energies. Roy Hobbs "still in motion [p. 36]" from fifteen years of wandering joins a "last place, dead-to-the-neck ball team" suffering already in early summer from "a blasted dry season [p. 34]." Frank Alpine, newly arrived from the West Coast, assumes the dull routine of assistant grocer in a transitional East Side neighborhood delicatessen. Sy Levin steps off the train from New York City in the Northwest town of Marathon, Cascadia, to join the intellectually moribund English department of Cascadia State College. Yakov Bok leaves his country *shtetl* for Kiev, where he saves the life of an anti-Semite and goes to work as overseer of the man's seedy brickyard.

Inexorably each finds himself championing a struggle against repressive, annihilative forces. Roy's prowess at the bat revives the New York Knights. Their game-winning streaks make them a pennant contender and the idols of the aroused fans. Roy's homers act as a tonic for hospitalized boys and unwed mothers. Against the ravages of age and the obscene manipulations of the front office with gambling interests, he battles to keep the hopes of the team and its fans alive. Frank's back-breaking hours of unremunerated labor prop up both the Bober store and family, and halt their going under from the attrition of the Depression and a marginal neighborhood. Sy's energy and idealism as a teacher make him the leader of a Young Turk's rebellion against the desiccated policies of the Old Guard. Yakov's endurance of brutal imprisonment without trial for a crime he did not commit attracts revolutionary support. He refuses a pardon and insists on a trial to redeem his name and the names of all Jews in the anti-Semitic eyes of Russian officialdom. This social action of the hero as proletarian fuses with the regenerative role of the hero as mythic savior. "A good teacher is a liberator," Sy Levin tells himself [p. 167]. "You suffer for us all," the lawyer Ostrovsky tells Yakov Bok [p. 305]. The political and archetypal nature of the allusions here underscores the dual regenerative role played by the Malamud protagonist. As a baseball hero—an idol of America's national pastime—Roy Hobbs's fate, especially if one listens to the roar of the crowd, seems to affect the nation's fate. His home runs can redeem a people's faith in itself.

One might say with some accuracy that the proletarian sense that gives these novels their deepest life has a mythic sense intruded upon it. Onto the social action of the narrative Malamud superimposes a framework of vegetation ritual, Grail quest, nature cycle, and wounded Fisher King. Enough has already been written of the symbolic presence of these elements—and such others as the Jungian bird, "terrible mother" archetype, wasteland motif, father-son displacement, Christ rebirth, and pastoral *Sehnsucht*—in the Malamud novel so that detailed verification would be gratuitous. Indeed, the mythic trail is so thoroughly marked by Malamud, that once a few signs are identified one can follow the trail backward from the contemporary urban scene to the primordial grove, and forward again, without the need of a guide. If one is looking for ways to fault the novels, one can easily point to the obtrusiveness and non-structural function of this symbolism. Rarely do the symbols seem to emerge naturally out of the exigencies of plot and character; rather plot and character appear to exist primarily as vehicles for the symbolism. Birds arbitrarily sprout wings on Roy's baseballs, determine Frank's hang-up on St. Francis, elude Sy's bird-watching excursion in the woods, and fly past Yakov's cell window or metamorphose into a bomb thrown at him, to remind us of each one's unhealthy mother fixation and hence psychic wound as Fisher King. Harriet Bird, Memo Paris, and Avis Fliss suffer from sick breasts to identify them as "terrible mother" figures and as victims of the wasteland. Marcus Klein and Philip Roth [8] have complained that the Malamud novel lacks realistic specificity. Even in such a resolutely realistic novel as *The Assistant*, with its hallucinated aura of the thirties, place and time remain undefined. This vagueness clearly allows the mythic superstructure to assume great thematic importance. Characters and incidents are easily abstracted into symbols and universals. A Roy Hobbs or a Frank Alpine becomes important not for what in himself as a fictional creation he tells us about the human situation, but for what as a symbol he represents in a mythic frame of reference. Such an apparent limitation in Malamud's presentation of human experience, however, can be defended as a strategy of containment, so to speak, to gain a limited but important aesthetic objective.

The overall thematic ends of Malamud's myth-haunted novels are readily evident. Where one may easily go astray is in evaluating the ambiguity of tone which characterizes the fate of the protagonist and the outcome of the action. Roy Hobbs, Frank Alpine, Sy Levin, and Yakov Bok are all symbolically conceived of as maimed kings; their flaw, self-interest. As a great ball player "What will you hope to accomplish?" Harriet Bird asks Roy. His disappointing answer is that he will gain fame and wealth from being the best in the game. "Isn't there something over and above earthly things—some more glorious meaning to one's life and activities?" she responds [p. 27]. Her subsequent shooting of him is thus a mythic enactment of this psychic wound; for it is his narcissistic longing for the luxury-loving Memo Paris and consequent blindness during much of his career to the health of the community that allows him to make a deal with the club owner to throw the play-off game for the pennant. Frank Alpine equally seeks shortcut methods to "live like a prince [p. 74]." Stealing becomes a habit. He pilfers Morris Bober's cash register and ultimately Helen Bober's virtue and self-respect. Sy Levin indulges himself in an adulterous affair with the wife of his colleague and senior member of the English department. Yakov Bok denies his Jewish blood and breaks the Gentile rule against Jews working outside the ghetto. Each transgresses against the moral and legal code, setting his desires above the law and needs of the land. Yet each eventually wins a moral victory over his old self through his conversion to concern for the larger unit of the group. In mythic terms of the regeneration he brings to society, he proves to be a true folk hero. Roy repudiates the syndicate, rejecting Memo Paris's seductive bribe in favor of Iris Lemon's gift of fruitful love. Frank converts to Judaism, keeps the store open and Helen Bober's love alive. Sy regenerates the intellectual life of the English department and arouses love in barren Pauline Gilley, who quickens with his child. And Yakov awakens in the oppressed Russians the power of resistance to tyranny. Each pursues his role of culture hero seemingly to a successful conclusion. New life after a fashion comes to the afflicted land, for the Malamud hero cannot elude entirely the fated outcome of his ritual servitude, but it comes without grace. His flawed character compromises on the realistic level of the story any clear-cut victory posed by such mythic and tragic archetypes.

There is a marked discrepancy between the affirmative claims of the moral, and the negative implications of the social, levels of the action. In the ancient ritual of the vegetation cult, the king's death was a willed sacrifice to ensure continuation of the annual rebirth of nature. The Malamud hero, contrariwise, does not will his fulfillment of the conditions of the archetype. Despite the moral order gained, he remains a victim of what Jason Compson sardonically calls the "rear guards of Circumstance." [9] Furthermore, his mental hesitations and ethical timidities, when measured against the full affirmation of the archetype, seriously qualify the hope that the mythical level of the ending holds out to us. Only after he has wasted three times at bat and beaned Iris with a foul ball does Roy respond to her cry for love and protection: "Win for us, you were meant to [p. 180]." Determined now not to throw the game, Roy ironically strikes out in the ninth inning anyway to retire his team and lose the play-off for the pennant. Suspected of a sellout, he is finished in organized baseball. His is the first of those Pyhrric victories with which Malamud, the severe moralist, burdens his heroes at the end of each novel. Frank's vision of life cannot see beyond his possession of Helen, which he identifies with maintenance of the store. He and Helen will marry in time and repeat, despite Helen's dream of a better existence, the nightmare death-in-life drudgery of her parents, incarcerated day and night in the tomb of the marginal neighborhood store. Sy leaves Cascadia, terrifyingly saddled with another man's children and wife, whom he is not sure he even loves, and with his promise given never to teach again. Even granted the circumstances, his recurrent impulse to flee and his silent reservation about marrying Pauline after her divorce are comically unheroic. Yakov goes before a hostile court for his trial, whose outcome remains decidedly uncertain; but the exploding bomb and hostile crowds that line the street through which his closed carriage passes imply that he will have little to do with the eventual determination of his fate. As he helplessly watches the bomb thrown, he frantically ducks. "If this is my death I've endured for nothing [p. 329]," he pathetically thinks.

The archetypal inevitability of nature's seasonal cycle is analogous in its optimism to a secular faith in the histori-

cally determined growth of society toward perfection. Both
guarantee the fulfillment of human activity—the triumph
over death and the emergence of utopia—that is, if man
could consistently observe this blueprint for paradise.

Unfortunately, one cannot arbitrarily propel society toward absolute ends. Man lives in time, not in eternity—in
what Frank Kermode defines as *chronos* or passing time, in
opposition to *kairos* or moment of crisis, "the season, a
point in time . . . charged with a meaning derived from its
relation to the end." [10] Both his sense of self and his sense
of his relationship to society, conceived of as instances of
consciousness, can occur only in time. In this existential
situation neither moral nor social perfection is obtainable,
for in time man is an incomplete creature of process. The
Malamud hero, typically, is bent on finding a new identity,
and with it a new rapport with society. Eternity furnishes
man with the absolute yardstick of his growth and actions.
Myth in the Malamud novel functions similarly. It links
man in an "ennobling interchange" [11] with the permanent,
while starkly reminding him of his mortality which alien-
ates him from wholeness of being. The rebirth of the Malamud hero as a new person is formulated in the life-death
terms of resurrection. As with the womb-tomb-pit symbolism that figures in D. H. Lawrence's concept of what is
called "a reconstitution of the human personality" by Frederick J. Hoffman, "Death is in this sense the cessation of a
false, a blind, way, succeeded by the assumption of the skin
and soul of a new personality." [12] Accession to a new being
is thus analogous to the story of Christ's resurrection.
Mythically, then, the Malamud hero is identified with the
Christ-Dionysius-Fisher King polarity in the story. Separated from the archetype, however, like Christ separated
from his divinity, the Malamud hero becomes merely a
scapegoat. Socially and psychically, not release to a new
life but imprisonment by the old Adam marks his efforts to

transform himself. One thinks of the pitch black office of the Judge (not to mention the dark pools of water) through which the new Roy gropes to face and recognize himself with hatred, the tomblike store that claims the new Frank Alpine, the dreams of death by water that torment Sy Levin, and the prison cell that possibly still awaits Yakov Bok.

The mythic and social levels of the Malamud novel face each other in a perfect stand-off. The incompleteness of human nature, Malamud seems to say, precludes any final design. So he gives us Roy Hobbs, a Paul Bunyan of the baseball diamond with a flawed bat; Frank Alpine, a drifter and thief, who inhabits obstinately the airless confinement of a Jewish delicatessen in a Gentile neighborhood, out of mixed motives of guilt, lust, and *caritas;* Sy Levin, a New Yorker, who quixotically seeks fresh air in the sterile vacuum of a cow-college in the Northwest, out of a naive faith in Horace Greeley's slogan about the West; and Yakov Bok, scapegoat of society as the pun on the German meaning of his name suggests, who trades the claustrophobia of the *shtetl* for the spiritual expansion of a Russian prison cell. Each aspires (as the puns on Alpine's and Levin's names suggest) to renewed kinship with man; but each is hobbled (implicit as morpheme in Hobbs's name) by the limitations of a past and by the shortsightedness of self. The feeling of being trapped haunts all Malamud's protagonists.

The most difficult problem for the proletarian novelist in the first half of this century, according to Walter B. Rideout, has been the conclusion to his book. Revolutionary optimism and Marxist reasoning dictate that his story end in a vision of the classless society. In this sense Marxism is as relentlessly apocalyptic as myth. The conventions of realism which govern the form require that the internal logic of the story prefigure the affirmative note at the end. Since capitalism and a class-structured society stubbornly persist in America, and most of the radical novelists of the thirties especially "were not really novelists at all but Tractarians," they were forced to "sloganize" their endings, "flatly asserting a doctrinal message in their own persons or through inadequately concealed mouthpieces." A few of the best—James T. Farrell, Henry Roth, Robert Cantwell, and Nelson Algren—refused either to "consider the possibility of overt moralizing" or of "forced optimism." They persisted in letting the "logic of their design" come honestly to its bitter, negative end. Surprisingly, Rideout remarks, almost none of these novels "turned fully to symbolism as a solution to the problem of the ending; for the symbolic conclusion can be either a thrusting toward intensified vision or an easy retreat from it into verbal wish-fulfillment." [13]

Malamud in a bravura extension of form has utilized the solution of symbolism, while maintaining the integral thematic development of his story. In the symbolism of the Grail and vegetation myths, he has a human drama as inexorable in its insistence on the renewal of life as that of socialist dialectics. In the quest hero he has as committed a national redeemer as the proletarian revolutionary. And in the moral victory of this protagonist over material corruption and fleshly temptation, which ironically limits the full achievement of his earthly dreams, Malamud retains the psychological and structural consistency of the story.

It should be clear by now that the mythic superstructure of the Malamud story satisfies the affirmative demands of the proletarian novel; and that the antithetical requirements of the symbolic and realistic strata of the story dictate the ambiguity of the Malamud conclusion.

One additional point as regards this dichotomy may be worth mentioning. Systems of dialectical contraries such as Hegel's, Blake's, and the NeoPlatonists's presuppose an ultimate synthesis, or in the case of Blake at least a persistent balance, of contraries. The Marxist viewpoint, working ostensibly within the same framework of thought, similarly anticipates a final solution. Yet underlying the Marxist formula, and intrinsic to most nineteenth-century designs of progress toward perfection, is the Darwinian notion of conflict and never completed process. The Marxist belief in the inevitability of class warfare betrays its Darwinian genes. This contradictory note of continual becoming, which precludes of course any final form of being, is ironically inimical to an archetypal vision of human nature. Hence, a mythic affirmation necessarily defines perfection in a frame of reference distinct from that characterizing a social *promise* of completeness. The special ambience of the Malamud novel derives essentially from this tension between the ideal and the actual.

The Malamud protagonist functions simultaneously as mythic savior and as social scapegoat. His growth in conscience represents symbolically a victory for society and the forces of life. His personal transgressions (bribery, theft, adultery, rape, perjury), which eventually cause him to fall short of his human goals, provide society with a vicarious castigation of its recurrent failure to realize utopia. In the refusal of the novels to resolve these rhetorical equivocations, Malamud opts firmly and unambiguously for a radically sophisticated comprehension of the human predicament.

NOTES—CHAPTER 3

1. Leslie Fiedler, *Waiting for the End* (New York: Stein and Day, 1964), p. 92.
2. Bernard Malamud, *The Natural* (New York: Farrar, Straus and Cudahy, 1952), *The Assistant* (New York: Farrar, Straus and Giroux, 1957), *A New Life* (New York: Farrar, Straus and Giroux, 1961), and *The Fixer* (New York: Farrar, Straus and Giroux, 1966). All references are to these editions.
3. Passing critical allusion to the mythic elements in Malamud's

novels has become *de rigueur*. Only a few critics, however, have addressed themselves directly to this problem. They include Norman Podhoretz, "Achilles in Left Field," *Commentary*, XV (1953), 321–326; Earl R. Wasserman, *"The Natural:* Malamud's World Ceres," *Centennial Review*, IX (1965), 438–460; James M. Mellard, "Malamud's Novels: Four Versions of Pastoral," *Critique*, IX (1967), 5–19; Sidney Richman, *Bernard Malamud* (New York: Twayne Publishers, Inc., 1966); and Jonathan Baumbach, "The Economy of Love: The Novels of Bernard Malamud," *Kenyon Review*, XXV (1963), 438–457; and also his *The Landscape of Nightmare* (New York: New York University Press, 1965).

4. Sidney Richman, *Bernard Malamud* (New York: Twayne Publishers, Inc., 1966), p. 46.

5. Frank Kermode, *The Sense of an Ending: Studies in the Theory of Fiction* (New York: Oxford University Press, 1967), pp. 35–43.

6. From the title of Edward Dahlberg's novel *Bottom Dogs* (New York: Simon and Schuster, 1930).

7. Walter B. Rideout, *The Radical Novel in the United States 1900–1954* (Cambridge, Mass.: Harvard University Press, 1956), p. 73 and *passim.*

8. Marcus Klein, "Bernard Malamud: The Sadness of Goodness," *After Alienation: American Novels in Mid-Century* (Cleveland: World Publishing Company, 1964), pp. 247–293; Philip Roth, "Writing American Fiction," *Commentary*, XXIII (1961), 228–229.

9. In the Dilsey section of William Faulkner's *The Sound and the Fury.*

10. Frank Kermode, *The Sense of an Ending* (New York: Oxford University Press, 1967), p. 47.

11. William Wordsworth, *The Prelude*, XII, 376 (1805); XIII, 375 (1850).

12. Leslie Fiedler, *The Mortal No: Death and the Modern Imagination* (Princeton, N.J.: Princeton University Press, 1964), p. 411.

13. Walter B. Rideout, *The Radical Novel in the United States* (Cambridge, Mass.: Harvard University Press, 1956), pp. 222–224 and 228.

4/ Norman Mailer's Divine Comedy

ADVERTISEMENTS FOR MYSELF *and* THE PRESIDENTIAL PAPERS:
Testaments I

IN HIS idealistic desire to reform society Norman Mailer
has moved steadily away from his early agitation for a political solution toward the call for an erotic, quasi-religious
redefinition of the modern consciousness. In the process
the unorthodox methods he advocates have obscured the
traditional character of the values espoused in his fiction.
Only George A. Schrader,[1] to my knowledge, has hinted his
recognition, in passing, that Mailer's ideas fit into a tradition; but Schrader is narrowly concerned with Mailer's divergence from European existentialism and does little
with his insight. Essentially Mailer is in the tradition of
eighteenth- and early nineteenth-century English and American primitivism. He believes man to be essentially good, or
as he puts it, "man is . . . roughly more good than evil, that
beneath his violence there is finally love and the nuances of
justice."[2] Visions of human goodness inevitably acquire
either rational or theological overtones. In Mailer's writing
the latter appears to dominate. With a diction weighted as
heavily with religious as with erotic terms, he speaks out
like a moralist, thundering anathemas not at the licentious

of heart but at the insensible of spirit. Nor, as Diana Trilling notes in her excellent analysis of Mailer's intellectual position,[3] is his invitation-to-sin-so-that-we-may-find-grace an unfamiliar heresy.

Where Mailer departs most from his early political activist position is in the configurations he makes of personal being and economic theory. Man's puny or *bad* orgasm, as contrasted with his apocalyptic or *good* orgasm (to use Mailer's Hemingway manner with the hipster's *graffiti*), Mailer defines in "Reflections on Hip" and in "Hip, Hell, and the Navigator" as manifestation of a dying which is evil. For, "as one dies a little more, one enters a most dangerous moral condition for oneself because one starts making other people die a little more in order to stay alive oneself [*Adv*, p. 385]." The Mephistopheles in this drama of human diminuendo is vaguely our capitalistic economy. "Built on property and such inhuman abstractions of human energy as money, credit, and surplus value," Western society has congealed the texture of being, the "productive, purposive, creative, and sexual energies," into an ice age of "cancerous ambivalences and frustrations [*Adv*, pp. 362–363]." Clearly the case is no longer the simple nineteenth-century one of mercantilistic haves and proletarian have-nots. Hence, in part, Mailer's loss of enthusiasm for the cause of Marxism is explained. The emergent affluent society, however, as he sees it, poses new dangers to the human spirit. At "the center of the problem," which he defines in "Heroes and Leaders," is the paradox that "life in America becomes more economically prosperous and more psychically impoverished each year."[4] To combat these doldrums of the flesh and the spirit, Mailer prescribes strong existential medicine. Man, he advocates in "The White Negro," is to "find his courage [his sense of life, of being,] at the moment of violence, or realize it in the act of love [*Adv*, p. 351]."

If Mailer seems to occupy the incongruous philosophical position of advocating change of the politico-economic structure of society by a revolution in its habits of coition and achievement of utopia through the apotheosis of murder, his worship of the power that devolves from sex and murder would seem to be even more perverse. Power is a key concept for him. In this respect he is a legitimate heir of the reformers of the last century. Yet careful distinctions must be made here, or one errs like Diana Trilling and others in mistaking Mailer's ambivalent fascination for a Croft or a Faye as an admiration for the courage and willed power drive of the fascist. It is true that Mailer is interested in the uses and abuses of power, and that he sees clearly that sex and killing are the ultimate forms of human power. Yet power per se is peripheral, not central (as Edmond L. Volpe [5] contends), to most of the novels. The use of sex and killing to gain control over another appears to be an evil to Mailer as it does to others. Whereas *The Naked and the Dead* is conceived in terms of political and military authority, the subsequent novels increasingly define power in terms of religious and psychological growth. A conventional release of spirit, a going out of self with its resultant joy—an existential control over self, not a totalitarian authority over others—is what ultimately fascinates Mailer in the mystique of sex and death. Is not this the belief that informs his remarkable Carlylean analysis in "Heroes and Leaders" of John Fitzgerald Kennedy's failure as a leader and a man? In this respect Mailer is not unlike the eighteenth-century antinomian Blake, who started out a political revolutionary, became disillusioned by the excesses of the French Revolution, and turned increasingly to advocacy of a Gestalt revolution in the concept of self as a means of man's gaining psychic and spiritual health. Like Blake, Mailer calls repeatedly for man to restore his vitality "by an exceptional demonstration of love" [6]—to work a second revolution in this century that moves "not forward to the collectivity which was totalitarian in the proof but backward to the nihilism of creative adventures . . . backward towards being and the secrets of human energy [*Adv*, p. 363]."

As for his offensive pitch in "The White Negro" for the hipster's "incandescent consciousness" based on a knowledge of the "possibilities within death [*Adv*, p. 342]," Mailer's essay on "The Existential Hero" makes clear that his faith in the frontier myth of Edenic America and primal purity has supplied his rationale as much as has the raffish camaraderie of his Greenwich Village escapades. Echoing the corollary disillusionment of the Adamic fall, which accommodates to this myth the contrary reality of industrial America, Mailer acknowledges a fall "from individual man to mass man [*Pres*, p. 39]." Yet the old myth "that each of us was born to be free, to wander, to have adventure and to grow on the waves of the violent, the perfumed, and the unexpected" survives, leading a subconscious existence in our psychic lives. Hence a split personality afflicts the American character, which Mailer formulates thus:

> Since the First World War Americans have been leading a double life, and our history has moved on two rivers, one visible, the other underground; there has been the history of politics which is concrete, factual, practical, and unbelievably dull if not for the consequences of the actions of some of these men; and there is a subterranean river of untapped, ferocious, lonely and romantic desires, that concentration of ecstasy and violence which is the dream life of the nation. [*Pres*, pp. 38–39].

Schrader has observed that Mailer is a romantic who "would undo the Fall of mankind" and "carry the human race back to the Garden of Eden on his own shoulders." [7] The novels since *The Naked and the Dead*—*Barbary Shore*, *The Deer Park*, and *An American Dream* [8]—are attempts to construct fictional worlds that tell how the lost American can gather together the scattered parts of his being and find his way back to a Gestalt existence, a unified emotional life. A reminder of Mailer's intentions with *The Deer Park* is instructive in grasping their overall design. Mailer told Richard Stern in 1958 in reference to the play version that he thought of the characters as existing in Hell and not knowing it. Thinking of the Prologue in Hell, which Mailer had written to introduce the play, Stern asked ironically, "How about a Prologue in Heaven?" Mailer answered, "Oh, it would be more interesting. . . . But it would be more difficult. That was beyond my grasp." [9] By 1964 his ambition and skill were sufficient to turn the trick with *An American Dream*. Whether he is fully aware of his frame of conceptual reference is problematic, but in these three novels Mailer has written a divine comedy of modern love. *Barbary Shore* depicts the purgatory of disordered love in contemporary life. *The Deer Park* describes the hellish "depths of the dead" into which commercial onanistic man descends when he turns inward and in the dark terror of his soul worships what Mailer (in "The Existential Heroine") has called "the voice of . . . pinup magazines, dreamy, narcissistic, visions of sex on the moon." [10] *An American Dream* presents the heavenly city of ecstasy glimpsed phoenix-like by those who dare to leave the "antechamber of Hell," mounting "fire stairs . . . through locks and ambushes" (as Rojack conceives fantastically of the route of his ascent to Kelly in the Waldorf Towers) "up through vales of anathema . . . fear and fever [*AD*, ch. 7]," until they emerge, scalded clean of middle-class moral funk, in the expanding continuum of life and death.

BARBARY SHORE: *Purgatory*

Barbary Shore comes closest of Mailer's novels to having an allegorical surface. Ostensibly, it is a political polemic in the Huxley tradition of the novel of ideas. Actually, it is a modern morality play in which is acted out the agonizing drama of contemporary man's effort to find through the dynamics of love some kind of human restoration in contemporary society.

Here politico-economic allegory coincides with existentialist ethics more firmly than in the two novels that follow it. Hell, as well as purgatory and heaven, are states of mind in Mailer's cosmology in addition to being places of abode. Mailer identifies the commercial mind (typed "Moneybags, the haunted [ch. 24]" by Lovett) with hell, the world of self-interest. In the economic sphere this selfishness reveals itself as acquisitiveness and in the psychological and social sphere as narcissism. The goal of Dante's journey in *Purgatorio* was earthly paradise, won by purging the self of the sin essentially of disordered love. "Set love in order, thou that lovest me," is the dictum on which, according to Edmund G. Gardner,[11] *Purgatorio* rests. Most twentieth-century men, Mailer contends, subsist in purgatory. With dormant hearts they long for the sweet emotion that will change for bad or good their future. The contemporary scene, as Mailer conceives of it, offers us a halfway house of penance, a wild border, a Barbary shore, between the hell of flaccid feelings and a heaven of dynamic being—a purgatory where, morally and emotionally bent by circumstances, we either retreat into solipsistic sensuality (whose hell is pictured in *The Deer Park*) or advance toward existential renewal (whose heaven is depicted in *An American Dream*). Hence, unlike Dante, Mailer begins his triptych of society with purgatory.

Purgatory in the world of *Barbary Shore* is presented as a penitentiary of cubicles in anonymous brownstone rooming houses. Here dwell the transitory and the faceless for whom time has run out. Lovett is an amnesia victim who has "no past [ch. 24]." Lannie is a mental patient who has lost the "record of [her] self [ch. 17]" during a series of shock treatments. McLeod, in fleeing both the Communist Party and the FBI, had destroyed his identity ten years earlier and has been "obliged to take up a wholly new existence [ch. 24]." Hollingsworth is an equally anonymous government agent. Their surrealistic isolation extends even to an absence of commercial ties with life. Lovett as a would-be writer has no steady job. Lannie has lost hers. McLeod has quit his. And Hollingsworth is "on vacation" from his dummy cover-up job in a broker's office.

In purgatory one's past is initially judged, one's sins contritely acknowledged, and one's progress toward moral regeneration begun. Although almost all the characters in *Barbary Shore* are engaged in such a pilgrimage, the man whose soul is most concentrated on this struggle with itself is McLeod. Pursued by the inexorable "guards" of the two rival economic powers, capitalism and communism [cf. ch. 23], his effort to save his life is presented as an allegory of a twentieth-century soul's penitential progress toward salvation. Ten years ago he had gone underground, severing his connections with both political apparatuses. Since quitting the world, so to speak, he has devoted his energies to the selfish task of saving merely his skin. To create a new identity he has married and had a child. But the marriage has been contracted out of selfish reasons. His wife, Guinevere, accurately has tagged her marriage when she accuses McLeod, "I'm your bloody salvation, that's all [ch. 26]."

Mailer's language, here, and throughout the novel, performs on two levels, the political-economic and the psychological-moral—one literal and the other usually ironic. Guinevere has been McLeod's savior for an unspecified number of years in that his pursuers, the agents of America and Russia, have mistakenly sought an unmarried man.

This mask, however, does not protect McLeod indefinitely. After ten years of running he has been tracked to his attic hideaway in his wife's rooming house by Hollingsworth, an American agent. If ultimately she does not save his life (body), she does in the end prove ironically to be the savior of his soul, in a sacramental sense instrumental to his salvation.

To document the means of this salvation—*agapé*—is to define a central tenet of Mailer's ethics. McLeod's marriage had been one of expedience. Out of selfish concern for his own safety he had taken a woman with rich resources of love, who was in his own words "ready to share" herself "with somebody." It was "the only period of your life," he admits to her, "when you could have been in love. And I betrayed that potentiality. You needed a man who would give you a great deal, and I gave you very little [ch. 26]." He is guilty of warping a second being into the inward bent of the purely private life that tortures his own heart. His living apart from his wife and daughter in a barren room separated by three floors from their apartment, with none of the other roomers aware of his identity, skillfully dramatizes his isolation and emotional sterility. Similarly, Guinevere's promiscuity and responsiveness to Lannie's homosexual advances presents in vivid allegory the extent to which McLeod's selfishness has pushed her into narcissism. Thus, Guinevere is a witness to the "wrongful love" that is denounced by Dante in the tenth canto of *Purgatorio*. She is witness to the involuted excesses into which another's refusal of love can mislead the heart.

Mailer underscores this role of Guinevere in the comic charade of her first meeting with Lovett. "I'm a Witness [meaning Jehovah's Witness]," she lies to him outrageously. But she speaks with poignant truthfulness in terms of the sacramental level of the story. "We're going to Gethsemane, that's the truth. We're going to be destroyed [ch. 4]," she harangues Lovett. Again the words refer both to the political theme that the two capitalistic systems are driving the world to the brink of barbarism and to the ethical theme that commercial emotionalism—acquisitiveness of the heart—is damning mankind to narcissism and sterility. "The world is so full of sin. Nobody loves his neighbor any more [ch. 4]," she laments in pointed allusion to the latter theme.

Denial of love has been McLeod's sin (and political crime, since an additional irony is that he has dedicated himself to the socially ameliorative task of guiding man "from hell to Arcady [ch. 29]," paradoxically by performing the professional revolutionary role of the notorious "Hangman of the Left Opposition [ch. 20])." Conversely, an avowal of love marks his moral reintegration. For ten years McLeod concentrated with single-minded devotion on saving his skin. His bitter summary of those misspent years is, "I devoted myself to nothing [ch. 24]." He has in mind his cessation of political activity; but he also recognizes that his life has been empty. "Petrified in my bones," he confesses to Lovett, "I was already dead so I must call on [Guinevere] to thaw me out, and I've never given her the time of day [ch. 25]." To "force a revolution into [his] life," he seeks out his daughter in play. "I'd give an arm to have the child love me," he avows to Lovett [ch. 19]. He also confesses to Lovett his discovery that he could now "feel the most intense love" for his wife [ch. 25].

The first step in moral regeneration is to admit one's guilt with a contrite heart. McLeod's confession of his frozen heart prefigures its thaw. And the narrative underpinnings support this renewed flow of his feeling for Guinevere. There is his obsession with cleanliness—especially his regular scrubbing of the bathroom—which symbolizes a state of mind desirous of purification. A similar longing for the grace of illumination is indicated when he turns the

lamp bulb, in sardonic parody of the third degree Hollingsworth is about to resume, "so the light glared into his eyes
[ch. 20]." Following his long audience with Hollingsworth,
McLeod admits to being the mysterious "Balkan gentle-
man" high up in the Bolshevist apparatus and to having
stolen a "little object" from the American organization
[ch. 24]. He then exposes to his own eyes and to Lovett's
through one night and most of another "the last festering
cocci of the sore" of his life, in a lacerating search "deeper
and deeper into the mesh of motive," in an effort to bring
the "moralist and the criminal . . . to dock" together [ch.
25].

The ultimate disposition of McLeod's fate depends on the
outcome of his duel of nerves with Hollingsworth. Hence
Hollingsworth could be mistaken for the angel of divine
judgment, particularly since the informal hearings he holds
in effect trigger McLeod's final reformation. A sardonic
irony, however—key to the *Weltanschauung* of *Barbary
Shore*—is involved in the actual details of Hollingsworth's
background. On the surface he passes as quite orthodox.
Hailing from a small town in the Midwest, he is presenta-
ble, polite, a freckled, blue-eyed boy with a corn-colored
cowlick. Lovett   imagines   "the   places   in   which
[Hollingsworth] had slept through his boyhood: a bed, a
Bible, and in the corner a baseball bat perhaps [ch. 5]."
God's emissary as the boy next door! Disturbing contradictions, however, qualify our response to these marks of
respectability. He is brutal toward women, lecherous,
hard-drinking, a lowbrow, with a mind (according to
McLeod) "like a garbage pail." His mirth is indistinguishable from "the mechanical laughter in a canned radio
program, the fans whirring." His eyes are "Two circles of
blue, identical daubs of pigment . . . opaque and lifeless
[ch. 5]." Like Faulkner's detestable emblems of twentieth-century civilization, Popeye and Flem Snopes, Hol-

lingsworth has something mass-produced, stamped, and labeled about him.

Hollingsworth's intention is to double-cross his superiors by making a private deal with McLeod in a power drive to gain the unidentified object he has been sent to get back. As recompense Hollingsworth promises to "save" McLeod. The situation has strong overtones of the classic contest of bartering for one's soul with the Devil. But McLeod's developing conscience prevents his succumbing to the temptation of "playing upon [Hollingsworth's and his own] cupidity." He recognizes that he would leave the house "alive and better off dead." In a cryptic formula, reminiscent of the ancient mariner's encounter with Nightmare-Death-in-Life in Coleridge's *The Rime of the Ancient Mariner*, McLeod reduces his choice to "alive it's dead, and dead I'm alive [ch. 25]." The phrasing is charged with Christian overtones. To save his soul ("the little object") McLeod must risk losing his life.

The purgatorial investigation of McLeod which Hollingsworth has been unofficially conducting is then a black parody of Saint Peter's justice. Hollingsworth represents not Christ's mandate but Antichrist's. His organization is the identical twin of the enemy organization. The Gods of both are "collective [ch. 21]," dedicated to "standardization," and "abdication of the best in human potentiality." Both preach "exploitative systems [ch. 29]"; and, appropriately, Hollingsworth in his cover-up job is associated with a Wall Street firm. To deal with him then is to sell one's soul to the Devil. Neither capitalistic power, McLeod comes to see, is interested in him personally; both want only "the little object" he possesses, his integrity, his soul. "If possession of the little object by neither power is a disadvantage to both," McLeod postulates, then "to deprive them is a moral act [ch. 24]."

To act upon this insight, however, he must progress

beyond his narrow claim of love for Guinevere to the Socialist ideal of love he has proselytized for so many years. This selfless love of mankind McLeod rises to when he relinquishes Guinevere and his daughter to Hollingsworth as the price of salvaging "the little object" (that is, the human soul) for all men. As he prepares to face Hollingsworth for the last time with his final answer of "no," McLeod bequeaths the "object" to Lovett (surely a pun is intended), who despairingly had "lived like the hermit in the desert who sweats his penance and waits for a sign [ch. 1]," and who had been "at the crossroads [ch. 2]" of his life when he met and accepted McLeod's legacy of "the rudiments of selfless friendship [ch. 33]." McLeod's "exceptional demonstration of love [*Pres*, p. 51]" not only restores Lovett's faith in man but also Lannie's. As Dante climbs upward to the sixth terrace of Purgatory [Canto 22], he is instructed by Virgil that "Love, / Kindled by virtue, always has inflamed / Another, if its flame were but displayed." When McLeod takes leave of the emotionally exhausted Lannie, he asks Lovett to treat her with "a little mercy." His overflowing heart touches Lannie's and inflames her love for man and rekindles her hope for the coming of a new Jerusalem [ch. 30]. Here the political-economic and existential-ethical levels of the narrative unite in one vision of brotherly love. As an ex-Trotskyite Lannie alludes, of course, to the true (as opposed to Bolshevist) inauguration of Socialist justice on earth. Also, under the pressure of the story of the regeneration and salvation of McLeod's soul, she alludes to the institution of that earthly paradise (which Dante portrays all penitent souls toiling upward toward) atop the mountain of purgatory.

One hesitates to call Mailer a Christian apologist; yet in *Barbary Shore* he has written a modern morality play that seems to advocate traditional Christian values. Everyman McLeod (the politico-economic creature in this century of passionate ideologies) saves his soul through apparently orthodox means. Surely his death at the end is a sacrificial slaying, not the suicide that all the critics claim. Unless he is lying, he indicates to Lovett every intention of joining up with him after the final unpleasant interview with Hollingsworth. At the moment of McLeod's death, Lovett overhears Hollingsworth say, "You've hurt a fellow's feelings . . . and that is why I am forced to punish you"; then Lovett imagines "the slow rapt movement of each man about the other" and finally hears "some sound of attack [ch. 31]." This hardly sounds like suicide! In an existential act of will McLeod elects to withdraw his allegiance from the two great commercial systems of the world in favor of an utopian faith in the human heart. In that decision he confronts "the possibilities within death" which Mailer claims in "The White Negro" provide "the curious community of feeling in the world of the hipster [*Adv*, p. 342]." The result is McLeod's death but also, in the legacy of "the little object" consecrated with his life that he passes on to Lovett, a confirmation is made of the inexhaustible power of the heart's "love for every man our brother." Here, Mailer seems to say, is the choice open to contemporary man: to be a prosperous cannibalistic digit in the calculating machine of bureaucracy or to be an enriched psyche at the "limits of [its] growth [*Pres*, p. 21]" in a full emotional life.

THE DEER PARK: *Hell*

The Deer Park extends Mailer's exploration of political-economic and psychological-moral patterns of conduct, centering on the American tendency to identify man's acquisitive and erotic instincts and on the debilitating effect of this confusion of values for a whole society. Eros is the totem of Hollywood; its directors, producers, actors, and hangers-on buy and sell love as readily as they contract to make a movie. Under the tyranny of such contempt for life, the buried nature of man—"the noble savage" Eitel calls it —is "changed and whipped and trained by everything in life until it [is] almost dead [ch. 11]." The chief eunuch of this "deer park" is the film mogul Herman Teppis, who connives, for example, to marry his top sex goddess Lulu Meyers to his leading matinee idol—but notorious homosexual —Teddy Pope, because the marriage would give Supreme Pictures "a royal couple, the Number One married lovers of America [ch. 20]," and hence be good for business. A widower, he derives sexual satisfaction from demeaning young girls, Hollywood hopefuls supplied regularly from the stock room by his son-in-law and producer Collie Munshin. Motherhood, sex, compound interest, religion, and patriotism are hypocritically jumbled in his thought and speech until they lose all identifiable value.

In the contrapuntal structure of the novel, the apparent opposite of Teppis's sentiment is Marion Faye's hard-boiled existential idealism that has only scorn for the "self-swindles" of Hollywood. A "religious man turned inside out [ch. 13]" by his distaste for the human race, he sees himself as a Baudelairean "saint in Hell," bent on purifying his soul through "some black heroic safari" of complete submission to sin [ch. 25]. His motto is that "There is no pleasure greater than that obtained from a conquered repugnance [ch. 13]." Since he most detests people, he systematically occupies himself with love—of all varieties and degrees of perversion—until, guided by his misanthropy, he drifts into the role of professional procurer. Thus, in his pursuit of nobility, he succumbs to the same vice of commercialized love that Teppis does, and in his private life becomes an ironic confirmation of his belief that nobility and vice are "the same thing" viewed from different directions [ch. 13].

Between sentimental submission to commercial con-

formism and perverse assertion of individual integrity,
Charles Eitel and Sergius O'Shaugnessy act out the compromises of their lives. In the story of Eitel, Mailer most
fully develops the political-economic and psychological-
moral structures of meaning of his novel. An idealistic film
director, Eitel had refused to testify before a congressional
investigating committee and had been blacklisted by the
movie industry. To that extent he had striven to dissociate
himself from Hollywood commercialism; but he moves
only as far as Desert D'Or, a satellite of the film capital two
hundred miles away, where his sentimental faith in love
and his reputation as a proficient man in bed become his
major occupation. Inevitably, sex stales. To sweeten his
soured life, he eventually cooperates with the investigating
committee so that he can return to Hollywood—and the
confusion of economic, sexual, and ethical motive is significant—to make profitable movies whose dishonest excel-
lence his professionalism "lusted for [ch. 15]." He is
last seen manipulating a press release for Lulu Meyers, an
ex-wife, with whom he is conducting a postmarital affair.

The Deer Park, then, depicts the failure in human spirit
of the Horatio Alger dream. In one way or another the
transients of Desert D'Or find themselves permanent occu-
pants of the treadmill of a self-indulgence—whether economic power as with Teppis or erotic power as with Eitel
—that is infernally sanctioned as the goal of their society.
Only O'Shaugnessy resists the twin temptations of love and
money, rejecting an offer to star in the filming of his life
story and losing Lulu Meyers as a result. In the aftermath
of this decision, he inhabits the literal hell of a restaurant
kitchen where he attends a steam-heated dishwasher, burning himself week after week on the hot dishes, "mortifying
my energy," as he puts it, "whipping my spirit, preparing
myself for that other work I looked on with religious awe
[ch. 21]." Bent on making himself into a writer he escapes

Desert D'Or; but whether he escapes the hell of the spirit, which is the real meaning of Desert D'Or, is problematic, since in the second half of the story he is a shadowy undeveloped figure. With the possible exception of O'Shaugnessy, the moral experience of the novel is directed toward the dismal round of life that has submitted to mass commercial values. Love is treated in this context as an expedient way of cashing in on people, of using them for one's own ends. The movie industry exploits love as a commodity, idealizing it, ironically, into the ultimate expression of individual sincerity and morality. The circularity of the cash-sex nexus portrayed here is only too apparent.

In the symbolism of place and time as well as in the narrative of events, this tautology of existence is emphasized. Unlike the transient world of *Barbary Shore*, the ethos of *The Deer Park* is without hope, fixed in the windless lee of stopped time. Parched for nine months of the year, Desert D'Or burns without surcease from a sulfurous sky that blasts every living thing and from the lusts of the flesh that enthrall every inhabitant. It is an analogue of "that second circle of sad Hell," where, Keats tells us,

> . . . in the gust, the whirlwind, and the flow
> Of rain and hailstones, lovers need not tell
> Their sorrows.[12]

Like those living in the Valley of Ashes in *The Great Gatsby*, the sojourners of this desert community are indistinguishable in appearance and spirit from the landscape. They are exiles, renegades, ex-movie stars, has-beens, temporary and permanent refugees from the film capital, drifters—the damned and the defeated—all reminiscent of the lost souls of Sartre's *The Flies* and of the Paris expatriates of Hemingway's *The Sun Also Rises*. Self-loathing is only second to hatred of others as the principal emotion. Eitel sums up the response to life in words that sardonically reverse those of Brett Ashley at the end of *The Sun Also Rises*: "In the end that's the only kind of self-respect you have. To be able to say to yourself that you're disgusting [ch. 22]."

In such a context of hatred, ironically, the preoccupation of the denizens of Desert D'Or is love. But their pursuit of adulation and orgasmic gyrations as panaceas merely confirms their self-disgust and moribund sensibilities. They begin each affair "with the notion that life [has finally] found its flavor, and end with the familiar distaste of no adventure and no novelty [ch. 16]." What could conceivably be more hopeless than this new version of the myth of Sisyphus? Each is interred within his loathed self, doomed to a tautological titillation of his own sensations, unable to communicate with another even through love-making. Instead of being productive of life, sex has become a death-trap. Thus, Eitel makes love to a prostitute, all the while having "never felt so lonely in his life." An hour later, crying "I love you, I love you," in the monotone of an acolyte chanting the dead form of a once meaningful rite, he makes love to his stale mistress, whose body has become "a cove where he could bury himself." Then he takes a sleeping pill in order to drift into unconsciousness. Despairingly, he considers himself "locked in Elena's love [ch. 16]."

In an essay in the February 1963 issue of *Commentary*, Mailer defines hell as "a pantomime of small empty activities." [13] So it is with these lost souls, for whom love remains an enervating round of solipsistic movements across the bleak terrain of oneself.

"And who do you love now?" Eitel asks Elena in the first rank bloom of their love.

"You," she said, and then looked away. "No, I don't. I don't love anybody at all."

"You feel on your own?"
"Yes."
"It's a good way to feel." [ch. 10]

Such solo love, advocated here by Elena and Eitel in dialogue that makes them a parody of the Hemingway hero and heroine, is a charade, a "closed rehearsal of the comic and the entertaining [ch. 10]," condemning each actor to the treadmill of inventing endless new games of sex to make it palatable. Hence Lulu and Sergius play at being model and photographer, movie star and bellhop, queen and slave. "She was never so happy," Sergius recalls, as when she played "the bobby-soxer who sat with a date in the living room and was finally convinced, always for the first time naturally enough [ch. 12]." Understandably, these profane souls, condemned to such mummery, fail even through ordinary discourse to communicate with each other.

In handling this theme of incommunicability, Mailer makes the most of a defect in the structural pattern of the novel. In both *Barbary Shore* and *The Deer Park* he appears to have conceived of his narrative as a dialogue between two men, an experienced mentor and a neophyte writer who puts himself to school under the older man's somewhat tarnished but still idealistic tutelage. Neither story, however, is as successful as its prototype *The Great Gatsby* [cf. *Adv*, pp. 235, 242–243] in coping with its dual assignment of two centers of consciousness, particularly since in each instance the first-person narrator (Lovett, O'Shaugnessy) never seems certain which story, his or the older man's (McLeod, Eitel), should occupy center stage. The problem is brought into the open when O'Shaugnessy recalls the night that Eitel related his theory about human nature. "Although I do not want to go into theory,"

O'Shaugnessy hastens to say, "maybe it is a part of character. I could write it today as he said it, and I think in all
modesty I could even add a complexity or two, but this is
partly a novel of how I felt at the time, and so I paraphrase
as I heard it then, for it would take too long the other way
[ch. 11]."

Although the characterization of Eitel suffers, as in this
instance, from the indirection of the first-person narrative
and from the divided emphasis on two heroes, the characterization of O'Shaugnessy suffers even more from this
general lack of dramatic development. For *The Deer Park*
is essentially the story of Eitel (as the pun on his name, "I
tell," would suggest), not of O'Shaugnessy who was, as
Mailer admits in *Advertisements for Myself*, "the frozen
germ of some new theme [p. 236; cf. pp. 237, 242–243]."
Mailer also implies as much in his subsequent attempt to
write the story of Sergius O'Shaugnessy in an as yet unpub-
lished novel [cf. *Adv*, pp. 248, 478–503, 512–532]. Still,
sketchiness in *The Deer Park* regarding O'Shaugnessy
serves a thematic function. Since it leaves his connection
with Eitel shadowy and lacking in dramatic development,
it underscores the irresolvable gap of time and space that
separates the cynical commercialism of the older man
from the existential *Angst* of the younger. And at the end of
the novel O'Shaugnessy imagines Eitel, years later and a
continent away, remembering with a pang "the knowledge
he wanted to give me, suffering the sad frustration of his
new middle age, since experience when it is not told to
another must wither within and be worse than lost [ch.
28]."

Considering the cul-de-sac into which the denizens of
Desert D'Or have relegated love and life, the novel ends on
an additional irony when Sergius asks in a fancied dialogue
with God,

"Would You agree that sex is where philosophy begins?"
But God, who is the oldest of philosophers, answers in
His weary, cryptic way, "Rather think of Sex as Time,
and Time as the connection of new circuits." [ch. 28]

The infernal reference to life in Desert D'Or is only too
self-evident. For like hell, the desert metropolis exists in a
state of suspended time. The horror of unending sameness
of existence has been vividly evoked by poets from Greek
myth onward. The Struldbrugs of *Gulliver's Travels* and
the Tithonus of Tennyson convey with considerable pathos
this dilemma of man's experience with time. Blake renders
the paradox eloquently in *Milton* when he writes:

Time is the mercy of Eternity: without Time's swiftness
Which is the swiftest of all things: all were eternal
    torment. [I, xxiv, 72–73]

Life in Desert D'Or consists of moribund activities performed without hope of surcease by way of what Blake
elsewhere calls the "production of time." Its inhabitants—
the "middle-aged desperadoes of the corporation and the
suburb"—have lost their past, living in an "airless no-
man's-land of the perpetual present." [14] Its inferno-like environs merge day and night into a sequence of endless
sameness. In his opening description of the place, Mailer is
at considerable pains to make this clear. "Everything,"
Sergius tells us, "is in the present tense." "Built since the
Second World War," he adds, "it is the only place I know
which is all new." Drinking in the "air-cooled midnight of
the bar," he remarks,

I never knew whether it was night or day . . . afternoon was
always passing into night, and drunken nights into the dawn
of a desert morning. One seemed to leave the theatrical darkness of afternoon for the illumination of night, and the sun
of Desert D'Or became like the stranger who the drunk imagines to be following him. [ch. 1]

Thus, Mailer works brilliantly to efface the boundaries of time, consigning Desert D'Or to an Alice-in-Wonderland where seconds and minutes, days and nights, consume each other into faceless limbo. And this horror of arrested time carries over as a leitmotif in the published fragments of an unfinished novel that presumes to continue the life and times of O'Shaugnessy. The title of one section, "The Time of Her Times," oracularly calls attention to this self-conscious obsession with duration. In the other fragment, a Joycean "Advertisement for Myself on the Way Out," time —or more accurately not-time—figures as a narrative strategy for limning the paradox of modern consciousness.

Writers are fond of imagining love as an experience capsuling time (and space) into momentary experiences of eternity (and infinity). Contrariwise, love is naturally associated with the temporal rhythms of life: with the sequences of fertility and the periods of gestation. Through its generative connection with life, love links man to past and future. In this sense God's fancied answer to Sergius that sex is time, and time the connection of new circuits, is meaningful. But when the Delphic assertion is used as a lens through which to see and measure Desert D'Or and the "life" of its people, it becomes an acrid summary of what has transpired in the story. Trapped by the stifling commerce of their egos, their lives endlessly the same, Eitel, Elena, Lulu, Dorothea O'Faye, Marion Faye, and the others seek to escape into the outer world of sentience. Sex offers them the semblance of life, but even with it they know only the dry salvages of lust.

The receptacle for all the human refuse of Hollywood, that gaudy symbol of American civilization, Desert D'Or represents rather precisely (given Mailer's special Messianic views) the deadened nerve ends of a commercial society which has lost the secret of feeling and thinking morally but continues to sleepwalk through the dead forms of an old dispensation. Thus, in *The Deer Park* Mailer explores the nightmare world of emotional totalitarianism, when bereft of all but "the scurry beneath the stone [ch. 10]." In the third of this trilogy, *An American Dream*, he attempts through the fictional parable of "Raw-Jock" Rojack to teach modern man, a twentieth-century Pilgrim afflicted with "anxiety of the anxieties [ch. 7]," how to renew his "exhausted spasm of the heart [ch. 8]."

AN AMERICAN DREAM: *Paradise*

At the conclusion of *The Deer Park* Eitel in imagined dialogue with O'Shaugnessy declaims dejectedly, "One cannot look for a good time . . . for pleasure must end as love or cruelty . . . or obligation." Sergius objects to this sermon of the commercially respectable and the ideologically cynical with the inspired fervor of an incipient hipster:

> I would have told him that one must invariably look for a good time since a good time is what gives us the strength to try again. For do we not gamble our way to the heart of the mystery against all the power of good manners, good morals, the fear of germs, and the sense of sin? Not to mention the prisons of pain, the wading pools of pleasure, and the public and professional voices of our sentimental land. If there is a God, and sometimes I believe there is one, I'm sure He says, "Go on, my boy. I don't know that I can help you, but we wouldn't want all *those* people to tell you what to do."
> . . . Then for a moment in that cold Irish soul of mine, a glimmer of the joy of the flesh came toward me, rare as the eye of the rarest tear of compassion, and we laughed together after all, because to have heard that sex was time and time the connection of new circuits was a part of the poor odd dialogues which give hope to us noble humans for more than one night. [ch. 28]

Before selling out to Hollywood and big business Eitel had tried to serve this "joy of the flesh," theorizing that love fed the happy blossoming of one's blood. The core of his faith was that people had a buried nature—"the noble savage" he called it—which was changed and whipped and trained by everything in life until it was almost dead. Yet if people were lucky and if they were brave, sometimes they would find a mate with the same buried nature and that could make them happy and strong. At least relatively so. There were so many things in the way, and if everybody had a buried nature, well everybody also had a snob, and the snob was usually stronger. The snob could be a tyrant to buried nature. [ch. 11]

The Deer Park is about Eitel's defeat by the "public and professional voices" of emotional totalitarianism. *An American Dream* is an audacious romantic assertion that the embattled "noble savage" in man, given the courage and strength and luck, can prevail against the establishment of the tyrannical snob.

Put simply, *An American Dream* narrates Stephen Richards Rojack's recovery from "a private kaleidoscope of death [ch. 1]," engendered by his killing of four German soldiers during World War II and by his barren love for his wife Deborah Kelly. His recovery with its "new grace [ch. 1]" of life is triggered by equally strong medicine: the purgative murder of his carnivorous wife and the avowal (with the consequent underworld threat to his personal safety) of love for the nightclub singer, Cherry. Stated thus blatantly in terms of its bare story line, the novel becomes a travesty of human action and religious values. As polemic it advocates something just short of running amok, replete with the metallic distaste of lust and murder. To deal with the book on its own terms, however, one needs also to consider its dialectical conception and rich texture of language.

A few years ago, in a brilliant article on Faulkner, Jean-Paul Sartre argued that to know an artist's metaphysics is to know his form.[15] This is true no less for Mailer than for

Faulkner. A Manichaeism with its "lights and darks, and all the other mysterious dualities of our mysterious universe" [16] provides a substratum to much of Mailer's analysis of man and society. His social revolutionist's faith in a dialectic that reduces the world to stark blacks and whites is at odds, however, with his artist's sensibility, which finds complex patterns of parallels and contrasts in otherwise simple designs. Such fracturing of a neat dualism into a dynamic continuum of human reactions appears in his definition in "The White Negro" of the "curious community of feeling" to be found in the world of the hipster. It is, he says,

> a muted cool religious revival to be sure, but the element which is exciting, disturbing, nightmarish perhaps, is that incompatibles have come to bed, the inner life and the violent life, the orgy and the dream of love, the desire to murder and the desire to create, a dialectical conception of existence with a lust for power, a dark, romantic, and yet undeniably dynamic view of existence for it sees every man and woman as moving individually through each moment of life forward into growth or backward into death. [*Adv.* pp. 342–343]

In Mailer the American faith in the efficacious event is united uneasily with an older European allegiance to the conceptual and the ideological. This unstable syndrome of contraries can serve as a gloss to *An American Dream*.

The near alliance of the "desire to murder and the desire to create"—"eternal Eros" and "his equally immortal adversary," as Freud called the two "heavenly forces" in *Civilization and its Discontents* [17]—particularly fascinates Mailer. The narrative design of the novel takes its shape from the yoking of these incompatibles: Rojack's love for Deborah that contains in it also a yen to kill her; his rapid movement in less than twenty-four hours from the murder of Deborah to the love of Cherry, as if the two disparate

acts were links in a chain of cause and effect; his eagerness
to test his new love by challenging death in the persons of
Shago and Kelly, and by walking the parapet of Kelly's
penthouse balcony. But equally significant is the way these
incompatibles mold the texture of the language, giving the
surface statement some of the metaphysical substance that
Donne's puns on death have. Thus, Deborah's love "always
offered its intimation of the grave." Rare was the instance
of making love to her that Rojack did not feel "a high
pinch of pain as if fangs had sunk into" him, his "mouth on
hers, not sobbing but groping for air [ch. 2]." After their
separation, his telephone talks with her were moments
when he felt he was committing hara-kiri, with the remains
of his love for her "drawing from the wound [ch. 1]."

One could cite many more examples of this marriage of
love and hate, of life and death; but it is the corollary
heaven-hell antithesis which more narrowly defines the
symbolic action of the novel—that is, the central struggle
of Rojack, somewhat intuitively, to find his way between
the opposing claims of what one might call old-fashioned
good and evil. As he quipped on his TV program, "God's
engaged in a war with the Devil and God may lose [ch.
8]."

Arrayed on the side of Satan are Barney Oswald Kelly
and his daughter Deborah, who is the Devil's own child.
Kelly describes her conception as occurring under Luci-
fer's aegis. "I took a dive deep down into a vow," he discloses to Rojack, and "said in my mind; 'Satan, if it takes
your pitchfork up my gut, let me blast a child into this
bitch!' [Deborah's mother] And something happened, no
sulphur, no brimstone, but Leonora and I met way down
there in some bog, some place awful, and I felt something
take hold in her. Some sick breath came right back out of
her pious little mouth. 'What the *hell* have you done?' she
screamed at me, which was the only time Leonora ever

swore. That was it. Deborah was conceived [ch. 8]." Married to her, Rojack finds himself to his bewilderment and eventual horror in the constant presence of the Devil. The "afterbreath" of making love to her leaves him in hell: "floated on a current of low heavy fire, a sullen poisonous fire, an oil on flame which went out of her and took me in [ch. 2]." Hers is a subtle Satanism. She "did not wish to tear the body, she was out to spoil the light." She appears to him ironically and dualistically as "ministering angel (ministering devil) [ch. 1]," whose "grace always offered its intimation of the grave [ch. 2]."

Through his murder of Deborah, then, Rojack rids himself of the haunting presence of Satan and begins his return to paradise. At the moment of her death, his "flesh seemed new," he "had not felt so nice since [he] was twelve [puberty?]." He felt that he had acquired a "new grace [ch. 1]," but he still has a far road of soul rebuilding to travel. And the distance is measured by the love he makes to two women, Ruta (root, of the earth, dark) and Cherry Melanie (virginal in the sense that none of her lovers until Rojack has succeeded in bringing her to an orgasm), both former mistresses of Barney Kelly.

With these two women Rojack enacts the existentialist's progress from mass conformity to individual choice. Thus, their narrative function further defines the Manichaean frame of conceptual reference of the novel. Ruta continues in the service of Kelly, ostensibly as a maid to his daughter but actually as a spy for him. Cherry has courageously cut free of him and the Mafia at the risk of her life. Rojack encounters Ruta twice: minutes after killing his wife in her apartment and twenty-four hours later in Kelly's Waldorf Towers suite. In his first encounter with Ruta, the life-death antithesis predominates. To him paradoxically her flesh seems alive, her skin dead. "Cold gases" exhale from her womb; her vagina is a "storehouse of disappointments." He breaks into her bedroom immediately after killing Deborah to find her masturbating. In subsequently making love to her he alternates between sodomy and fornication—between what, through a perverse reversion in her, is identified as her "bank of pleasures" and her "deserted warehouse, that empty tomb." This quickly becomes a contest in Rojack's mind between "a raid on the Devil and a trip back to the Lord." At the moment of orgasm he has a choice. At first he selects the "deserted warehouse . . . a chapel now, a modest decent place"; but he can still "feel the Devil's meal beneath, its fires . . . lifting through the floors." At the last minute he switches to the Devil and "felt low sullen waters wash about a dead tree on a midnight pond." He is not yet ready to pay his "respects to God," he concludes [ch. 2]. Evil, lust, and sterility are the keynotes of this love-making.

The contrast between Ruta and Cherry is nowhere better illustrated than in this sterility-fertility motif. At first (as with Rojack and Ruta), Rojack and Cherry meet each other with locked wills. There is a "casing of iron about [his] heart, and . . . her will [is] anchored like a girdle of steel about her womb. . . . Nothing was loving in her; no love in me; we paid our devotions in some church no larger than ourselves." When he removes her diaphragm, however ("that corporate rubbery obstruction" to the realization of life), their wills "begin at last in the force of equality to water and to loose tears, to soften into some light which is shut away again by the will to force tears back, steel to steel, until steel shimmers in a mist of dew," and Rojack hears "a voice like a child's whisper on the breeze" and glimpses "that heavenly city which had appeared as Deborah was expiring in the lock of my arm." They both happily believe that they have conceived. Symbolic of a new dawn and renewed life, this hoped-for conception occurs the morning after Deborah's murder [ch. 5]. Later that night

Rojack and Cherry meet a second time and find that the iron in their wills has fully dissolved, replaced with "one cornucopia of flesh." "God," Rojack in effect prays, "let me love that girl and become a father, and try to be a good man [ch. 5]."

The antitheses are self-evident. In the course of twenty-four hours Rojack progresses from lust to love, from sodomy to fruitful coition, from selfish willfulness to willed selflessness, from the stench of stale gases to the aroma of honeysuckle [ch. 5], from the neighborhood of hell to the environs of heaven.

Not without Hemingway aplomb and manner, Mailer develops Rojack's intuitions of the flesh into a code of bravery that Jake Barnes and Brett Ashley would happily assent to. As he unites with Cherry, Rojack senses in the room a "sweet presence" of wings, which "spoke of the meaning of love": " 'I think we have to be good,' " he says to Cherry, "by which I meant we would have to be brave [ch. 5]." Rojack is no antinomian of the flesh. The penance of courage must precede the sacrament of love. He "believed God was not love but courage. Love came only as a reward [ch. 8]." The reason is that evil can also masquerade as love. This is the lesson he learns from his love bouts with Deborah, Ruta, and Cherry. When love is a sensation which belongs to one alone (as Mailer shows in *The Deer Park*), it is the "art of the Devil [ch. 6]." Only when it includes transcendence of self in willing "journey of knowledge . . . from the depth of one being to the heart of another [ch. 1]," does it become the gift of God. The latter demands courage. And Rojack, who has lived for years in cowardly capitulation to the Daddy Warbucks milieu of the Kellys, has to practice bravery if he is to deny power and to affirm love. This is the significance of the opening references to a wartime experience that has continued to haunt him. As a "stiff, overburdened, nervous young Second Lieutenant," he had found himself trapped in World War II by four German machine gunners, with "the full moon giving a fine stain to the salient of our mood (which was fear and funk and a sniff of the grave) [ch. 1]." His marriage to Deborah and submission to her world of the New York *Times* only confirmed the "sickness and dung" that filled "the sack of [his] torso [ch. 1]." He discovered that swimming in the well of her evil intuitions brought him nearer to his memory of the four Germans than anything encountered before or since. Not until the barren and hence occultly sinister ninth year of their marriage is he finally goaded by Deborah into a fury sufficient to push him to strangle her. An outgrowth of this act is the will to face the tests of courage, which the love of Cherry demands. Hence the vomiting by his "burned-up lungs" of all "the rot and gas of compromise, the stink of old fears, mildew of discipline, all the biles of habit and the horrors of pretense," when he goes to the nightclub where Cherry sings [ch. 4]; and hence his set-tos after this prelude of ritual cleansing, involving repeated threats to his life, with Ike "Romeo" Romalozzo, Shago Martin, and Barney Kelly—all contenders for her love.

This is Hemingway brought up to date—the not unnatural ethic of Rojack, a man who is a university "professor of existential psychology with the not inconsiderable thesis that magic, dread, and the perception of death were the roots of motivation," who "had one popular book published, *The Psychology of the Hangman* [ch. 1]," and who taught as a corrective an anti-Freudian metaphysic that "the root of neurosis is cowardice rather than brave old Oedipus [ch. 8]." Although a distortion of reality, when viewed according to traditional morality, this philosophy of eros / agapé is not Priapus run riot, but an honest effort to wrench experience into a shape answerable to the needs of the times. Following its exercises, Rojack realizes the power and the glory of the golden age of sexuality. This is not the power which so many of the characters in *An American Dream* (Deborah, Ruta, Kelly) exercise. This is not Satanic power with its totalitarian drive to gain ascendancy over another, which "is only power for the sake of power, and . . . is cowardly power for it masquerades in coy and winsome forms." [18] This is rather the Godly power of the uninhibited innocent sexuality that controls human actions from womb to tomb. It is regained by commercially and culturally brutalized man's purging from himself "the lead and concrete and kapok and leather of . . . ego [ch. 1]" and thereby winning mastery over the circumstances of his life.

Mailer can assert this Godwinian-Rousseauistic faith in human goodness, because he holds an essentially monistic view of being. That is, he believes man to be intrinsically good but affected physiologically, and hence psychically, by external substances and stimuli. In the dialogue on "The Metaphysics of the Belly," written in July 1962, he defines *being* as a wedding of matter and soul: "*Being* is first the body we see before us. That body we see before us is that moment of the present for a soul, a soul which must inevitably be altered for better, for worse, or for better and worse by its presence in a body [*Pres*, p. 295]." And the body he argues, using the conceit of eating, is engaged in a constant digestion of the external world of experience, with "the possibility of illness every time opposites do not meet or meet poorly, just as there is the air to gain life every time opposites meet each other nicely [*Pres*, p. 290]." In this respect Mailer would appear to look upon love as not unlike the impulse that leads primitive man to eat his enemy's heart to gain its courage. Significantly, after he kills Deborah, Rojack imagines himself and her maid supping on Deborah's flesh for days while "the deepest poisons in us would be released from our cells [ch. 2]." Mailer then sees the choices of evil or good as physiological gratifications from which man realizes either adulterated fragmentation or healthy unity of self.

Brom Weber has rightly called our attention to the ambiguous meaning of the title.[19] It is an ironic comment on the tenuousness of the official American dream, "that hyperconglomerate of success, salesmanship, health, and wealth," [20] so perfectly epitomized in the life story of Barney Kelly. At the same time it is a straightforward assertion of the frontier dream that still obsesses the American below the surface of his respectability. That is, the dream of "ferocious, lonely and romantic desires, that concentration of ecstasy and violence which is the dream life of the nation [*Pres*, p. 38]." *An American Dream* is, ultimately, an audacious effort to show Americans how to shuck off old habits and return to the primal innocence that "the fresh, green breast" of this continent has for hundreds of years beguiled man into believing was possible in the New World (so Nick Carroway epitomizes it at the end of *The Great Gatsby*). The novel thus simultaneously restates one of the most persistent of American illusions and attempts to blaze another Northwest Passage to its elusive Cathay.

CANNIBALS AND CHRISTIANS: *Testaments II*

Barbary Shore, *The Deer Park*, and *An American Dream* are honest statements of an original, independent mind. They argue stubbornly that the Northwest Passage of violence will lead not only the deadened soul of Rojack but the "electronic nihilism" of all men to similar renewed joy at the "core of life [*Adv*, p. 385]." In this respect the three novels accurately reflect Mailer's nonfictional polemics against "modern man's ability to swallow nausea." [21] Mailer's Socratic dialogue, "The Political Economy of Time," stands at the end of *Cannibals and Christians* as a summation to date of his fears and hopes. Here he reiterates his insistence that the only "true and passionate lovers are those who love each other because they give life to one another," and that "There are souls which can be expressed —that is, *un*deadened—only by violence [*CC,* p. 342]."

Despite the coherence of a unified view that the novels and testaments alike present, there is reason to suspect that Mailer is ambiguous in feeling, if not outright doubtful, of the rightness and certainty of this faith that the individual can prevail against the pressures toward conformity of mass culture. Hence, doubtless, his gradual shift from advocacy of social action to enthusiasm for spiritual nodes becomes clear. The ending of each novel doggedly hints as much. With collapsed hopes, McLeod goes not unwillingly to his death. Lovett becomes a fugitive, fleeing "down the alley which led from that rooming house . . . only to enter another, and then another . . . obliged to live waiting for the signs which tell me I must move again [ch. 32]." Eitel succumbs to the blandishments of a congressional investigating committee, testifies in open hearing, is reinstated in the good graces of Hollywood, and deteriorates into making commercial movies and carrying on an affair with his ex-wife Lulu Meyers. O'Shaugnessy flees to a university in Mexico where he subsists on the G. I. Bill of Rights. Shago and Cherry meet violent deaths. And while Rojack wins out over the police and the Mafia in his revolt against society, with the resultant reassertion of his individuality, he does not in the end seem to have succeeded wholly in realizing his desires. With Cherry dead, he drifts off to Yucatan, a finesse that ends his confrontation with society.

The uncertainty and even masochism of such gestures is self-evident. Despite his noisy claims for the hipster as existentialist man, Mailer still remains essentially a disgruntled intellectual in search of something to believe in. Both McLeod and Eitel, who most nearly represent the

idealists Mailer has created, exist in a state of existential
doubt. Bereft of ideational belief and stuffed with frustrated fervor, each is left with only his frantic assertion of
self, which ironically seems to win for him only physical
death or spiritual torpor. Hence, Mailer desperately re-
sorts, in F. J. Hoffman's words, to "passion without a context." Analyzing Mailer's opening statement in *Advertisements for Myself*, Hoffman concludes,

> It is all here: the rage at the state of "The Republic," the
> retreat from the shock of annihilation, the recourse to
> "nihilism," the dependence upon minimal physical verities,
> which are not attached to a cause or a principle since these
> seem to have become inoperative. Courage, sex, conscious-
> ness, the beauty of the body, the search for love: these are
> minimal necessities of a passionate life, but they are not
> identified with any specific form of justification or objective.
> They are simply, nakedly there, to be rescued from annihila-
> tion, to be revalued without recourse to ideological strategy.
> . . . Mailer is reduced to the task of describing passion with-
> out a context, or at best within a context that is entirely
> misunderstood.
>   When Mailer becomes "philosophical," as he must, it is in
> terms of an unphilosophical situation: nondidactic, self-
> defensive, expansively hopeful, and frustratingly, repeti-
> tiously sentimental, or passionate. The dynamics of "courage,
> sex, consciousness, the beauty of the body" are all a part of
> a self-consuming passion; vigor seems to contain its own
> philosophical reward. The self is preserved through its re-
> location at "the center of the Universe." [22]

Consequently, Mailer in all honesty finds great difficulty in
imagining either Lovett or O'Shaugnessy as very successful
in "the reconstitution of the self" [23] through sex and violence; nor is his selection of their mentors, for whom both
ideas and passion have staled, guaranteed to lead them out
of the wilderness. O'Shaugnessy breaks free of the false
world of Hollywood; but ends up playacting at violence and

love by operating a matador's school for frustrated girls in a Greenwich School warehouse loft. Rojack fares more successfully; but he too at the end lights out for Yucatan.

So far Mailer has been standing on dead center ideationally. Expressive of this fact is that the fictional worlds he has created exhibit unresolved tension that eventually goes slack and is allowed to leak away. Whether Mailer will ultimately resolve his own doubts is, of course, problematic. Should he bring it off, he may yet realize his ambition, audaciously confessed in *Advertisements for Myself* [p. 477], to "hit the longest ball ever to go up into the accelerated hurricane air of our American letters."

There is no doubt of Mailer's ambitions for the novel in general—and for his own in particular. He admires the work of realism done for the nineteenth century by Balzac and Zola and chides his contemporaries that someone has not yet done it for the mid-twentieth century. In an address to the American Studies Association of the Modern Language Association in 1965, he defined the two dominant impulses in the American novel as realism and manners. Both, he believes, have deteriorated from the range of achievement of Dreiser and Henry James to the restricted localism of a Steinbeck and the camp of a Terry Southern.[24] At other times, with more clear-cut antithesis, he has characterized American fiction as devoted to either a social or psychological point of view. The serious novel, he says, begins today from "a fixed philosophical point—the desire to discover reality—and it goes to search for that reality in society, or else must embark on a trip up the upper Amazon of the inner eye [*CC*, p. 128]."

Some of Mailer's problems as a novelist stem from his effort to write both kinds of novel at once. The schizophrenia of *Barbary Shore* and *The Deer Park* derives in part from his dualistic conception of Eitel and O'Shaugnessy, McLeod and Lovett, as twin routes into the unexplored world and into the unknown self. Undoubtedly, disjunction between the social and the psychological accounts for some of the surrealistic focus of these two novels. In *An American Dream* Mailer most successfully combines the two aims in one of the few courageous attempts in this century at a novel of manners embracing a comprehensive picture of American society, which is also a psychological novel traveling "unguided into the mysteries of the Self [*CC*, p. 129]." Unlike the eight heroines of Mary McCarthy's *The Group*, whom Mailer flagellates in *Cannibals and Christians* for remaining classbound, Rojack comes "from one class" and makes "heroic journeys to other classes [*CC*, p. 136]." And the novel's violent style, while underscoring the unreality of the "postwar" era, aims at breaking through the routine of fixed and minimal standards. Not since Scott Fitzgerald has a writer come directly and so close to the reality of the modern American experience.

To date, however, one cannot say in all honesty that Mailer has succeeded in rendering fictionally the plan I have described at great length in this essay. The language and narrative of his novels outline his views, but the characterization is flawed. Eitel, O'Shaugnessy, and Rojack never convince us of the larger spiritual reference of their sexual lives. Not love but lust with its rancid smell haunts their sexual acts in spite of the nervous pitch of the language claiming otherwise. Perhaps this reaction derives in part from our ingrained moral resistance to sexual license and lawless violence. We dissent to the possibility (as Mailer claims for all besieged souls in his essay "The Metaphysics of the Belly") that Rojack is sweetened and softened to love by way of the violent murder of his wife. We dissent to his capability of leaving "the bitter sores" of his soul behind and ascending by way of his fetid flesh into the jeweled light of spiritual bliss, even as the rhetoric convinces us of his emotional regeneration. This failure would suggest that Mailer's style has risen to the demands he has increasingly placed on it, but his novelistic skills have not matured comparably.

Indeed, Mailer's language is clearly an achievement. A prose style is difficult at any time to realize—and hence rare in the history of English literature. Mailer bids fair to pull off this feat. Furthermore his style rarely bores. It does not, like Salinger's with increasing frequency, impose on the reader; nor, like Philip Roth's, sap one's interest and strength with arid wastes to traverse; nor, like Bellow's, move unevenly between precision tooling and mass production; nor, like Wouk's, blunder past the target. At its best, it is feisty, yet virile, at once personal and universal.

Even more praiseworthy, Mailer's style at its best is expressive of his ideas. Most commentators agree about the controlled rhetoric of *The Presidential Papers*, but boggle at the baroque excesses of *An American Dream*. Stanley Edgar Hyman in a review of that novel has considerable fun at Mailer's expense decrying what he calls "Mailer's immortal longing, to be a *big* fancy writer like Thomas Wolfe." [25] He deplores Mailer's poetic inversions, unidiomatic tenses, syntaxless sentences, tritely romantic and deranged similes, and mystique-of-spirit odors, quoting at great length instances of these faults—a practice reminiscent of the early nineteenth-century critiques of such offenders against the aesthetic decorum of that day as Wordsworth and Keats. Hyman seems to have set himself up as an unofficial watchdog over the purity of the language. Witness his title *Standards* for the selected edition of his reviews in *The New Leader*, and his quotation on the title page of the definition of the word from Webster's Second (not Third!) International Dictionary. As with Croker and Lockhart in their day, so with Hyman in ours, long quoted lists of blemishes torn from their context fail to grapple with the aesthetic problem of the work of art as a conceptual unity of theme and form. Surely Brom Weber is more to the point when he suggests that *An American Dream* depicts Rojack's psychic growth, hence the importance of the style, with its intense psychological and sensory perception, which shows the extent to which Rojack has "escaped the banal and become aware of himself." [26] In a review of Victor Lasky's *John Fitzgerald Kennedy: The Man and the Myth*, Mailer asserted that Kennedy "was without principles or political passions except for one. He knew the only way he could re-create the impoverished circuits which lay between himself and the depths of his emotions was to become President [*CC*, p. 170]." With a few changes these words equally describe the efforts of Rojack to revive his deadened nerve ends on a nourishment of murder and sex, with the violent imagery of the book nervously underscoring this trauma of growth. The mystique-of-spirit odors, which so offends Hyman, is in fact then a superbly functioning vehicle for the dramatization of character and development of the central thesis of the novel.

Similarly the extensive cave and dungeon imagery in *The Deer Park*, descriptive of the solipsistic hell in which its protagonists exist, conveys, as in Blake's poems, a metaphysical undercurrent of meaning heavily charged with emotional connotations. One example of the rich resources of language at Mailer's disposal will suffice. After she leaves Eitel, Elena goes to live with Marion Faye. Bent upon an existential resistance to his fear of death and to his revulsion from nauseating sensory experiences, he welcomes Elena as a further mortification of his flesh. But his defenses are insufficient to withstand the seductive temptation of answering Elena's human cry for help to stave off loneliness. To his chagrin he finds himself "Jailed in the keep of his bed with Elena beside him, enduring the venial mortification of having his skin itch near her presence, his nostrils repelled by the odor of her body which Eitel had savored so much [ch. 25]." The ironic union of contrary situations in the metaphor of the fortress-become-jail reverberates to the multiple strands of the tale. It echoes in its primary sense the embattled isolated existence of the denizens of Desert D'Or. It defines Faye's retreat from love, illustrated also by his engaging "in the trade" of prostitution. It characterizes his (as well as the other Desert D'Orites') belief that sex is a divisive strategy for gaining power over another instead of a unitive expression of procreative love for another. Furthermore, it comments on his failure to keep himself emotionally uninvolved and condemns him as the criminal in his sacrifice of humankind to his existential needs. He fails in his repellent effort to drive Elena to commit suicide, hence also in his desire to confront death vicariously. He is compromised by a feeling of pity for her. In desperation, while taking her to the airplane which will return her to Los Angeles, he steers his car into the path of an oncoming truck. Thus he is forced irrationally as a result of his failure with Elena to court the suicide himself.

Not since the nineteenth century and the heyday of the Darwinian hypothesis has a writer used images of war, march and countermarch, as compulsively as Mailer. Given his view of twentieth-century man as locked in a struggle for the survival of his integral self, a combatant against the forces of a world which believes in the New York *Times*, Mailer exhibits in his use of this battle metaphor a cohesive, synthesizing imagination that works with powerful directness to organize experience into meaningful order. If he shows weakness in creation of characters, he reveals on the other hand an attraction to ideas and great inventiveness in finding objective correlatives for these ideas. Most importantly, he has an imagination that deploys language and the larger structural units of the novel with the ruthless deft hand of a sergeant-major. And like a gung-ho marine he will take chances, risk defeat, to win large objectives. The faults of exuberance of such a mind are the faults not of a minor, but of a potentially major, artist.

With the publication of *An American Dream*, Mailer appears to have reached the end of one line of development as a thinker and as an artist. The three novels *Barbary Shore*, *The Deer Park*, and *An American Dream* present a fully articulated view of life. And in *Cannibals and Christians* [p. 248] he indicates that he has grown tired of the word *orgasm*. He can now do one of two things: (1) continue to explore the territory whose boundaries these novels have surveyed, or (2) make a fresh start, as he did after *The Naked and the Dead*. Which route he will pursue remains to be seen.

NOTES—CHAPTER 4

1. George A. Schrader, "Norman Mailer and the Despair of Defiance," *Yale Review*, LI (1961–62), 267–280.

2. Part of Mailer's reply to Jean Malaquais' reflections on "The White Negro" (Part 4, "Reflections on Hip"), included in *Advertisements for Myself* (New York: G. P. Putnam's Sons, 1959), p. 363; henceforth referred to as *Adv.*

3. Diana Trilling, "Norman Mailer," *Encounter*, XIX (1962), 45–56; reprinted as "The Radical Moralism of Norman Mailer," *The Creative Present*, eds. Nona Balakian and Charles Simmons (Garden City, N.Y.: Doubleday and Company, 1963), pp. 145–171.

4. Norman Mailer, *The Presidential Papers* (New York: G. P. Putnam's Sons, 1963), p. 4; henceforth referred to as *Pres.*

5. Edmond L. Volpe, "James Jones-Norman Mailer," *Contemporary American Novelists*, ed. Harry T. Moore (Carbondale, Ill.: Southern Illinois University Press, 1964), pp. 106–119.

6. "Superman Comes to the Supermarket," *The Third Presidential Paper—The Existentialist Hero* [*Pres*, p. 51]. The specific referent of this phrase is the hope that the Democratic party had for John F. Kennedy as President.

7. George A. Schrader, "Norman Mailer and the Despair of Defiance," *Yale Review*, LI (1961–62), 278.

8. All references are to the following editions: *Barbary Shore* (New York: Holt, Rinehart and Winston, Inc., 1951), *The Deer Park* (New York: G. P. Putnam's Sons, 1955), *An American Dream* (New

York: The Dial Press, 1965); henceforth referred to as *BS*, *DP*, and *AD*.

9. "Hip, Hell, and the Navigator, an Interview with Norman Mailer by Richard G. Stern," *Adv*, pp. 383–385.

10. "An Evening with Jackie Kennedy, or, The Wild West of the East," *The Fifth Presidential Paper—The Existential Heroine* [*Pres*, p. 94].

11. Edmund G. Gardner, *Dante* (New York: E. P. Dutton's Sons, 1923), p. 176.

12. John Keats, "On a Dream," 11. 9–12.

13. Reprinted as "Responses and Reactions II," *Pres*, p. 154.

14. So Mailer characterizes America in "She Thought the Russians Was Coming," *The Second Presidential Paper—Juvenile Delinquency* [*Pres*, p. 21]; and in "An Evening with Jackie Kennedy, or, The Wild West of the East," *The Fifth Presidential Paper—The Existential Heroine* [*Pres*, pp. 95–96]. Cf. Mailer's remark in "The Metaphysics of the Belly," *The Twelfth Presidential Paper—On Waste*: "I write often of the enormous present, of psychopathy, of how mass man has no sense of past or future, just now [*Pres*, p. 279]."

15. Jean-Paul Sartre, "Time in Faulkner: *The Sound and the Fury*," *Faulkner: Three Decades of Criticism*, eds. Olga W. Vickery and Frederick J. Hoffman (East Lansing, Mich.: Michigan State University Press, 1960), pp. 225–232.

16. So Mailer wrote in *The Village Voice* in a note on obscenity, reprinted in *Adv*, p. 288.

17. Sigmund Freud, *Civilization and Its Discontents*, trans. Joan Riviere (Garden City, N.Y.: Doubleday and Company, Inc., 1958), p. 105.

18. Norman Mailer, "Power," *Fifth Advertisement for Myself* [*Adv*. p. 287].

19. Brom Weber, "A Fear of Dying: Norman Mailer's *An American Dream*," *The Hollins Critic*, II (1965), 1–6.

20. *Ibid.*, p. 2.

21. Norman Mailer, *Cannibals and Christians* (New York: The Dial Press, 1966), p. 247.

22. Frederick J. Hoffman, *The Mortal No: Death and the Modern Imagination* (Princeton, N.J.: Princeton University Press, 1964), p. 478–479.

23. *Ibid.*, p. 483.

24. Norman Mailer, "Modes and Mutations: Quick Comments on the Modern Novel," *Commentary*, XLI (1966), 37–40.

25. Stanley Edgar Hyman, *Standards* (New York: Horizon Press, 1966), p. 278.

26. Brom Weber, "A Fear of Dying: Norman Mailer's *An American Dream*," *The Hollins Critic*, II (1965), 4.

27. Since I wrote this chapter, Mailer has published two books. *Armies of the Night* (New York: New American Library, 1968) continues the nonfictional ambience of personal confession and social-political journalism of *Advertisements for Myself, The Presidential*

Papers, and *Cannibals and Christians.* Devoted to an odd combination of dispassionate analysis and provoking narration of the Washington peace march and riots of several years ago (in which history and fiction are curiously blurred), it need not concern us here. *Why Are We In Vietnam?* (New York: G. P. Putnam's Sons, 1967) is a novel of considerable power, wit, and ultimately the source of much exasperation. That it promises a new fictional direction, however, is not clearly enough presaged.

Both old and new Mailer leave their imprint on the novel. The preoccupation with the Hemingway cult of physical bravery shows no sign of dimming. Nor has Mailer rid himself as yet of the naughty boy syndrome that delights in shocking the stuffy respectability of one's elders with dirty words. A case can be made for his stress on the scatalogical and the obsessively sexual, given the narrative point of view of a wise-acre Texan adolescent, with a family background of more money than breeding; but the exuberant excesses of Mailer's language inevitably end up pummeling the reader into stunned insensibility. In this respect, a concern for America's psychic and sexual health continues to exercise Mailer and to betray him into extravagances.

Yet *Why Are We In Vietnam?* is by no means the instance of stunted powers, of solipsistic infantilism, that so many of the reviewers would have us believe. Indeed, the novel shows Mailer still ready to take chances, still determinedly striking up the Amazon River of the American psyche. And the indication is that he has grown in literary power and sophistication, in his ability to work within a literary tradition, drawing strength from it without being overpowered by it. His updating of Faulkner's *The Bear,* by placing that Mississippian tale of initiation and Southern guilt into the contemporary frame of national guilt and Texan sanctimony and bumptiousness, contributes startlingly to the continuing discovery of America. His control of narration, point of view, character, and particularly dialogue, is firmer than in the past. There is also heard the saving grace of humor, a new note of willing suspension of judgment that augurs well for the future. Whether this growth adds up to a new departure is a moot point; but it does indicate that Mailer cannot yet be written off as a writer who never realized his initial promise.

5 / Saul Bellow and the Burden of Selfhood

The Head and the Heart

IN A bitter exchange with his father that brings him close to tears, Tommy Wilhelm begs for a show of sympathy, an expression of love, in return for the deep feeling he has for the older man. In the abasement he feels as an aftermath of the quarrel, Tommy dimly perceives "that the business of life, the real business"—as opposed ironically to the crass commercial scruples of his father—is "to carry his peculiar burden" of being human, "to feel shame and impotence, to taste . . . quelled tears." When the heart was responding, "the only important business, the highest business was being done [ch. 4]."

One hesitates to place possibly the most cerebral novelist of the current scene in the anti-intellectual camp of American fiction; but like Melville and Hawthorne and such recent contemporaries as Hemingway and Faulkner, Saul Bellow displays marked distrust of the human mind. Bellow is sufficiently disturbed by the cool intellectual to characterize him usually as an IBM machine of obstinate calculation. Dr. Adler, Simon March, and Madeleine Herzog confront the human world as an I-It relationship. They use

people like things. On the same continuum Lucas Asphalter, the physiologist friend of Herzog, translates his scientific passion into obsessive love of a monkey. It is a measure of Bellow's compassion and skill as a novelist that
neither Dr. Adler nor Simon nor Madeleine nor Lucas becomes inhuman to us by virtue of their contempt for man.
Simon's frozen anguish even engages our pity—as it does
Augie's. Yet Simon does not elicit Bellow's fondness—even
admiration—as does Tommy Wilhelm or Augie or Henderson or Herzog, men of heart and dark solitariness, who
figure in his recent novels as heroes.

J. V. Levenson [1] sees all Bellow's heroes as dangling men,
alienated from society. Augie, Henderson, and Herzog may
share some of the blood of Joseph, Leventhal, and Tommy
Wilhelm (who is transitional in the evolution of the Bellow
protagonist) but their kinship is of the kissing cousin variety, for Bellow has not continued from novel to novel to
draw carbon copies of the "absurd man." Ihab Hassan [2]
defines more precisely the multifacets of the Bellow hero
as he has evolved from communicant with death to cele-
brant of life in *Dangling Man* to *Henderson the Rain King*. [3]
He may still be a victim—suffering contemporary man,
irascibly alien to his machine-tooled culture—but now not
only is he frequently overemotional, and often enthusiastic
to the verge of dyspepsia, but he is also possessed with joy.

Bellow is fond of quoting Blake, as are his fictional
creations, especially Augie and Herzog. When he went to
stay with the Himmelsteins, Herzog included among his
meager necessities "an old pocket edition of Blake's poems
[p. 80]." Like that sublime antinomian of the eighteenth
century, Bellow paradoxically sees the mind and the heart
as antithetical, while conceiving of man ideally as a *Gestalt*
of reason, emotion, instinct, and imagination.

Unfortunately for the tranquility of the human spirit,
man's reason has tyrannically ruled his being since at least

the scientific revolution of the seventeenth century. Blake
analyzes this historical plight of "the Sons of Albion" with
devastating clarity in *Jerusalem*:

> They take the Two Contraries which are call'd Qualities,
>   with which
> Every Substance is clothed: they name them Good & Evil;
> From them they make an Abstract . . . / . . . it is the
>   Reasoning Power,
> An Abstract objecting power that Negatives every thing.
> This is the Spectre of Man, the Holy Reasoning Power,
> And in its Holiness is closed the Abomination of Desolation.
>   [ch. 1, plate 10]

Instead of permitting the mind to usurp the self in this way
(Blake argues fervently in chapter 4, plate 98, of *Jerusalem*), man should rejoice in the Divine Vision of his
"Unity / In the Four Senses." Bellow embraces this insight
with equal fervor. To be divided from within or, which is
identical, to be divided from without, by denying one's
fellow man (for "we are One Family" so Blake contends in
chapter 3, plate 55, of *Jerusalem*) is to enter the hallucinatory world of Leventhal and Allbee in *The Victim*. Bellow's
heroes are accused by the "Reality-Instructors" (as Herzog
terms his friend Sandor Himmelstein, p. 30) of "ignoring
the reality principle and trying to cheer up the dirty scene."
"Accept the data of experience," Augie is counseled by his
friend Clem Tambow [ch. 21]. But as Blake (and Bellow
with disciplelike zeal) never weary of dramatizing, the data
of experience are the product of the mind, of "the rotten
rags of Memory [*Milton*, ch. 2, plate 41]." And like the
bleak, colorless, soundless universe fashioned by New-
tonian physics, which Blake imaginatively refuted, the
mind's experience concentrates narrowly (and perversely)
upon the profane. "Facts *are* nasty," Himmelstein snarls at
Herzog [p. 86]. And to the Himmelsteins of this world,

Herzog muses savagely, "truth is true only as it brings down more disgrace and dreariness upon human beings, so that if it shows anything except evil it is illusion, and not truth [p. 93]." Worse, to restrict one's life to the data of experience is to deliver oneself into bondage to Urizen, the despotic reason.

The seriousness with which Bellow views this danger is indicated by the pervasiveness in his books of prison / bondage images and by his recurrence to it in nonfictional statements about his craft. The immensity of population and elaborate organization of society, he notes in "The Writer and the Audience," have produced a system which directs the individual in how to deal with the majority of situations. The system, however, "loves abstractions" (here Bellow's language becomes strikingly Blakean) "and is not friendly toward the imagination; it prefers preparedness to impulse."[4] Most men, he protests, have accepted the central tenet of Western empiricism that all life can be accounted for in terms of the reason. Fixed in this belief, the modern consciousness turns on itself and destroys human dignity. "It throws shit on all pretensions and fictions," Herzog laments, and then makes new "realities nobody can understand [p. 193]." The extreme instance is Bateshaw, in *The Adventures of Augie March,* who is maniacally determined—ironically at the cost of his human feeling—to create a serum which will eliminate boredom and allow love to fill the world. As an antidote to the modern personality's reliance on system in lieu of immediacy of response, Bellow contends, the writer must find "enduring intuitions of what things are real and what are important."[5]

Thus Augie, Henderson, and Herzog reject modern positivist systems of thought in favor of a more human embrace of experience. "You must cleanse the gates of vision by self-knowledge," Herzog tells himself [p. 86], echoing

without acknowledgment a key dictum of Blake's. One
might say that Bellow's most recent novels pose their heroes increasingly at a critical stage in their struggle to
discover, like Augie as a "Columbus of those near-at-hand"
"in this immediate *terra incognita* that spreads out in every
gaze [ch. 26]," their own natures in the light of the assumptions of their society. The beatific endings of these
novels (not without the ghostly laughter of Bellow's comic
muse echoing in our ears) occur when the hero finally
accepts his nature for what it is—and society for what *it* is.
Augie sees with pity how much Bateshaw is trying to be
barren of "in order to become the man of his ideas." The
incongruity of Bateshaw's person and goal strikes Augie
forcefully: Bateshaw wants "to bring about redemption
and rescue the whole brotherhood of man from suffering,"
by acting "mainly from the head rather than from the
heart [ch. 25]." For a time Henderson, following Dahfu's
theory of life, submits to the indignity of crawling on all
fours and roaring like a lion. But Henderson finally rejects
a theory which perversely argues that the route to humanity is by way of animality. "And so I was the beast," he
concludes, and "This is where I ended up. Oh, Nebuchadnezzar! How well I understand that prophecy of Daniel.
For I had claws, and hair, and some teeth, and I was burst-
ing with hot noise [ch. 18]." This lament of Henderson
recalls Blake's powerful engraving at the end of *The Marriage of Heaven and Hell* of Nebuchadnezzar on hands and
knees like a beast in the field feeding on grass. Here, on all
fours—Blake pictures, and Bellow limns with resounding
echo—is where reason brings man: to the death of what in
him is human. And Augie sums up the response of Bellow's
heroes to this *reductio ad absurdum* when he tells Clem
Tambow that "It can never be right to offer to die, and if
that's what the data of experience tell you, then you must
get along without them [ch. 21]."

Bellow's most recent heroes are yea-sayers and visionaries even in defeat. "I may well be a flop" at my line of endeavor, Augie cheerfully admits at the end of the novel, but "Columbus too thought he was a flop, probably when they sent him back in chains. Which didn't prove there was no America [ch. 26]." Their misfortune—and the world's —as Bellow sees it, is that they run counter to the data worship of our age, which artists in moments of desperation have reduced to Dada. To the myopia of the *Massenmenschen* (who resist the lesson of life learned by Augie, Henderson, and Herzog, and prefer to grow burning sores instead of coming-to, as Henderson laments [ch. 22]), they are an object of derision and pity. When Augie returns from Mexico, the worse for wear after his caper with Thea Fenchel, he is greeted by Clem Tambow, the student of psychology, with the snickering question: "How is your campaign after a worthwhile fate, Augie?" But Augie wonders,

Alas, why should he kid me so! I was only trying to do right, and I had broken my dome, lost teeth, got burned in my progress, a mighty slipshod campaigner. Lord, what a runner after good things, servant of love, embarker on schemes, recruit of sublime ideas, and good-time Charlie! Why, it was a crying matter, no fooling, to anyone who might know which side was up, that here was I trying to refuse to lead a disappointed life. A hell of a cause of sympathetic tears but also, as Clem saw, of haw-haws, as great jokes often are. [ch. 21]

Henderson in his angry, frustrated, stubborn longing to raise himself into another world [ch. 19] finds himself ostracized, shunned by his peers as if he were a madman or a leper. "We're supposed to think that nobility is unreal," he muses,

But that's just it. The illusion is on the other foot. They make us think we crave more and more illusions. Why, I don't crave illusions at all. They say, Think big. Well, that's baloney of course, another business slogan. But greatness! That's another thing altogether. Oh, greatness! Oh, God! . . . I don't mean inflated, swollen, false greatness. I don't mean pride or throwing your weight around. But the universe itself being put into us, it calls out for its scope. The eternal is bonded onto us. It calls out for its shore. [ch. 21]

And Herzog, "predictably bucking" the distortions of reality "had characteristically, obstinately, defiantly, blindly . . . tried to be a *marvelous* Herzog," an aristocrat, a man of pretensions, a duke, as his name in German means, who, "perhaps clumsily, tried to live out marvelous qualities vaguely comprehended [p. 93]."

If these men speak at all for Bellow, then he is a hybrid genus, practicing the realism of the thirties and forties and the symbolism of our age, while professing a modified Romantic faith in man of the last century. "Truth, love, peace, bounty, usefulness, harmony! [*ecce* Augie, ch. 22]" become seriously treated concepts. More important, they are within the reach of all. Man can refuse time's computerization of human events. As Henderson puts it, this life is "not a sick and hasty ride, helpless, through a dream into oblivion. No, sir! It can be arrested by a thing or two [ch. 12]." And Augie seconds him in his belief that "all noise and grates, distortion, chatter, distraction, effort, superfluity" can pass away

like something unreal. . . . At any time life can come together again and man be regenerated, and doesn't have to be a god or public servant like Osiris who gets torn apart annually for the sake of the common prosperity, but the man himself, finite and taped as he is . . . will be brought into focus. He will live with true joy. Even his pains will be joy if they are true, even his helplessness will not take away his power, even wandering will not take him away from himself, even the big social jokes and hoaxes need not make him ridiculous, even disappointment after disappointment need not take away his love. [ch. 22]

This paean of Augie's is Blakean in its *Gestalt* vision of man, as are the means by which he believes man can revive the moribund fragments of his being in joyous assent to existence. The age of science, however, with its deification of reason, the faith in which man has lived for 250 years, forces both Blake and Bellow (although they call for coordinated use of the whole man) to emphasize the contrary underdeveloped faculties of imagination and emotion. Thus, Henderson accepts the Blakean notion that art checks the senseless speed of life, redividing time. Music and the great cathedrals of France arrest time for him, merging the moment with eternity [ch. 12]. "Humankind has to sway itself more intentionally toward beauty [ch. 19]," he comes to believe; and he is seconded by Dahfu's conviction that "one imagination after another grows literal. . . . All human accomplishment has this same origin, identically. Imagination is a force of nature. . . . Imagination, imagination, imagination! It converts to actual. It sustains, it alters, it redeems [ch. 18]." Blake would have given hearty assent to these words, so hortatorily reminiscent of his own.

There is similar agreement among Augie, Henderson, and Herzog that man may realize resurrection from what Henderson calls burial in oneself [ch. 19] through the corollary way of love. Herzog tells himself that love is a transcendence of one's body of death through "our employment by other human beings and their employment by us [p. 272]." This vision of human relationships is akin to Blake's dialectical concept of love as a marriage of contraries, of individualities which undergo no change while combining into something new. By this avenue, man realizes his humanity and divine brotherhood with man. In his essay on

the "Distractions of a Fiction Writer," Bellow has com-
mented on the excessive systematizing forces of our age.
To counteract their reductive effects, he held up the need to
believe in the importance and existence of human beings.
This belief, he said, quoting Simone Weil, is love and alone
matters.[6] Hence, "Amorous Herzog, seeking love, and
embracing his Wandas, Zinkas and Ramonas, one after another [p. 94]" in an effort to inject emotion into an otherwise rational modern world! And with a touch of Rabelai-
sian humor, the international scope of his love-making
hints at his evangelistic desire to save mankind by transforming the world through sexual passion into the divine
Jerusalem of Blake's vision. Similarly, *The Adventures of
Augie March* in raffish picaresque fashion chronicles Augie's capacity for love, the "involutional, busy, dippy horse-
fly in [him that] made such a mad fuss of love over this
treasure of crystal-sugar esteem [ch. 18]." And the laughing, jeering world involuntarily acknowledges their loving
natures by coming to them for comfort, help, consolation.
It is not her lover Frazer but Augie whom Mimi appeals to
when she finds herself pregnant, and Augie whom Stella
"chose . . . to consult with and to ask for help." And just
as he is forever understanding and forgiving his brother's
lapses of love, he sees Stella's employment of him as "a
kindness she did me and I was under obligation to her
before she spoke even a word [ch. 18]."

One can, of course, overindulge. One cannot help thinking that Herzog comes close to this error in the years
following his estrangement and divorce from Daisy when,
his emotional and rational natures at strife, he measures
time by the days and weeks he spends with a revolving bevy
of international beauties. Bellow, like Blake, advocates
participation in life of the whole man. Excess occurs when
one faculty—it can be the heart as easily as the mind—

dominates our being. In our time, however, as in Blake's, the tyranny of the mind has been most prevalent.

The contrast between the old and the new Henderson vividly illustrates the transforming power of love. For more than fifty years emotionally constipated, unable to communicate his feeling to his wives, he lies buried deep within himself [ch. 19], savagely, caustically, lashing out at the world to give expression to the inarticulate hurt he suffers internally. When this "sleep is burst [ch. 22]," there is a loving transformation in his response to life, dramatized for us in the conclusion of the book. Admittedly, Henderson's new-found-land is the "gray Arctic silence [ch. 22]" and his stay there consists of a romp around an airplane which will quickly wing him elsewhere. These ironies are expressive of Bellow's radically sophisticated resistance to both the despair that grips the existential man as he stares into the void of his self and to the naïve optimism that stirs the institutional man as he peddles his social panaceas and spiritual nostrums. Bellow's mature protagonists realize that the world is no longer an Eden and that the cause of life's glory is also the cause of its ache; but more importantly, the shock of this recognition darkens their joyous assent to existence while enlarging their affective capacity for it. Thus Henderson, the man who had prevented his daughter from mothering a Negro foundling baby, now nurses a lion cub and befriends an orphan boy, "a black-haired boy, like my own. This kid went to my heart. You know how it is when your heart drops. Like a fall-bruised apple in the cold morning of autumn [ch. 22]." The man who had abused his wife and fled from her to Africa now anticipates the happiness of meeting her at Idlewild. The man who had incurred the enmity of his friend's bride by forgetting to kiss her, even as the best man, now rhapsodizes, like Chaucer in the Miller's Tale over the fresh spring of Alison's beauty, about the eternally renewable glimpsed in the person of an airline stewardess. Gratefully he realizes that "Whatever gains I ever made were always due to love and nothing else [ch. 22]."

Blake wrote in *Jerusalem* that an abstract of reason "is a Negation / Not only of the Substance from which it is derived, / A murderer of its own Body, but also a murderer / Of every Divine Member [ch. 1, plate 10]." Embodying all men in the figure of Albion, Blake lamented his enslavement to the hypocritical "Loom of Locke," whose "Reasonings like vast Serpents / Infold around" man's limbs [*Jerusalem*, ch. 1, plate 15]. Bellow too equates the cerebral, rational life with narcissism, imprisonment of the spirit, deceit, death, and finiteness; and the visceral, emotional life with joyful regeneration, creation, liberation, honesty, life, and infinity. Tommy Wilhelm, Augie, Henderson, and Herzog awaken to the knowledge that "all the forms of love, eros, agape, libido, philia, and ecstasy" are the answer, as Augie learns, to *moha*, "meaning opposition of the finite . . . the Bronx cheer of the conditioning forces" of modern technological death-in-life [ch. 22]. They come to this knowledge and acceptance of themselves as loving natures through the state of experience, which is suffering and "death," to use not inappropriate Blakean terminology. The head can know "the facts of life . . . the truth [p. 91]" abstractly and discourse endlessly with "the cant and rant of pipsqueaks about Inauthenticity and Forlornness [p. 75]" without ever experiencing any of it. So Herzog (man of heart as his name *Herz* underscores) reproves Shapiro, the man of theory unquickened by life into warm sympathy for his fellow human.

All Bellow's protagonists feel the pain of existence. All are profound sufferers. But if Bellow appears to place a positive value on suffering in his rendering of Tommy Wilhelm, he has moved, as the comic mode of *The Adventures of Augie March* and *Henderson the Rain King* foreshadowed, toward a more balanced diet of emotions in his conception of Herzog. In a letter to Professor Mermelstein, one of his last, Herzog denounces "the advocacy and praise of suffering." He argues that "It takes us in the wrong direction"; hence, "I will never expound suffering for anyone or call for Hell to make us serious and truthful. I even think man's perception of pain may have grown too refined." With these words Herzog opts for a thoroughgoing humanism. Pain is a part of one's emotive life but so is joy; and one can reach the glorious East of joy by way of more routes than the Western straits of pain. Although he recognizes that his suffering has been "a more extended form of life, a striving for true wakefulness and an antidote to illusion," he is willing now to open his heart to the joyous burden of being "without further exercise in pain [p. 317]."

Bellow handles this awakening symbolically as a resurrection and dramatically as a brush with death. Lazarus and Christ figure as recurring motifs. "I believe in Lazarus," Henderson asserts, "I believe in the awakening of the dead. I am sure that for some, at least, there is a resurrection [ch. 11]." Similarly, Herzog is characterized by Ramona as a man "who knew what it was to rise from the dead" and with whom she "experienced a real Easter [p. 185]." And even that most dissolute of Bellow's fictional creations, Allbee, in *The Victim*, campaigns like a latter-day Blake for regeneration here and now: "It makes sense to me that a man can be born again.—I'll take a rain check on the kingdom of heaven, but if I'm tired of being this way I can become a new man [ch. 19]." The Romantic faith in man's ability to renew himself in this world, to move through "the brutal stage of life" into "the sublime [so exults Bummidge in *The Last Analysis*]" [7] without waiting for the next world, is obviously an important one for Bellow, even supplying him with the peripeteia of this dramatic farce about "the mind's comical struggle for survival in an environment of Ideas [p. vii]."

All the Bellow protagonists confront death either literally or symbolically and triumph over it both psychically and spiritually. The *locus classicus* of this situation is the conclusion of *Seize the Day*. Throughout the story Tommy Wilhelm suffers congestion of the chest (where his heart is located) and suffocation of the lungs from repression of his feelings. In terms of this controlling metaphor his heart pushes "upward with . . . frightful pressure [ch. 7]," seeking release from his efforts to conform to the self-reliant, calculating commercial man that is the ideal of his empirical-minded father, Dr. Adler. The tears ("the splash of heartsickness" [ch. 7]) that he involuntarily weeps at the bier of a stranger eases this constriction. In language echoing the sea imagery of Milton's "Lycidas," which elegizes the death of an individual into a reaffirmation of the immortality of man, Tommy's sobs of love become "the consummation of his heart's ultimate need [ch. 7]." Henderson similarly stares into the dark pit in Africa (where he had deliberately gone "to encounter death"), surviving a lion hunt, a witch doctor's enmity, and a severe bout of malaria, to rise from his sick bed chanting that he is "unkillable" and eager to do battle with the "dead days" of his past [ch. 22]. Augie "in a way . . . died somewhat" after Thea deserted him in Mexico. By then he knew "how impossible it is to live without something infinitely mighty and great." From this momentary willingness to say "Okay, Death, I'm ready [ch. 20]," which he finally resists, he returns to America and life, the symbolic action of his resolution culminating in his marriage to Stella. That this marriage still keeps Augie in bondage to another, in exile in Europe, without children, attests to the early date of the novel. In 1949, nor for that matter in 1956, with the publication of *Seize the Day*, Bellow had not as yet matured his philoso-

phy of life to the balance of opposites that it presents in
Henderson the Rain King and *Herzog*. A similar compromised resurrection characterizes the ending of Bellow's
second novel *The Victim*. After Allbee's absurd attempt at
suicide and, as Leventhal suspects, near murder of him, the
fortunes of both men improve. Allbee reverses his slide
toward Skid Row; by putting a brake on his drinking and
lechery and adjusting his goals to his limitations, he becomes a success in radio advertising and consort of a faded
movie star. Leventhal finds the job that fits his talents,
becomes a father, and softens in temperament. If neither
victim / victimizer experiences actual rebirth, he unquestionably undergoes renewed growth. Symbolic death of the
old self occurs for Herzog when he gets into an auto accident while visiting his daughter and afterward is
"Stretched limp, looking dead," on the grass [p. 282].
From feeling "the heavy, deadly shadow lying on him [p.
286]," he arises rejoicing in life again, in his true nature,
"A loving brute—a subtle, spoiled, loving man" who
"craves use" made of him [p. 308], and returns to his
home in Ludeyville, "Confident, even happy in his excite-
ment, stable," even if seemingly "almost an idiot" in the
simplicity of his "loving powers [p. 326]."

Each has faced the attractions death offers and resisted
its appeal. Each has withstood the temptation "to be
forced by another to feel his persuasion as to how horrible
it is to exist [*Augie March*, ch. 20]." Each has triumphed
with the heart over the corrosive experience of the mind.

For all its impracticality and inefficiency, the heart's
affection is portrayed by Bellow as a sextant of moral
precision. Interestingly, it is Leventhal's violent visceral
reaction of irritation, disgust, anger, and guilt toward Allbee which, according to Allbee himself, caused in some
indefinable psychic way his moral and social rehabilita-
tion. Heart saves Augie from the sin of Simon, who treats

marriage as a business transaction and sells himself to the highest matrimonial bidder—and garners for himself an extra dividend of spiritual malaise. Heart also protects Herzog from the taint of Madeleine, with her "mixed mind of pure diamond and Woolworth glass . . . as sweet as cheap candy, and just as reminiscent of poison as chemical sweet acids [p. 299]"; and from the defilement of Gersbach, "poet in mass communications . . . ringmaster, popularizer," manufacturing "Emotional plasma which can circulate in any system [p. 215]." Directionless, fumbling, disorganized men, Tommy Wilhelm, Augie, Henderson, and Herzog are led by the dream of their hearts to fashion their lives "in a significant pattern [*Herzog*, p. 303]," to "create a world" they "can live in [*Augie March*, ch. 17]," to "leave the body of this death" and raise themselves "into another world [*Henderson*, ch. 19]." If the pattern is at best only dimly discernible, each demonstrates that the individual, while partaking of the social order, may preserve the integrity of his soul without submerging his fate, like Singer's Gimpel the Fool, in his social role. In the crises of their lives, Bellow refutes the prevalent axiom that the intellect is a surer moral guide than the feelings.

The modern mind has turned in upon itself, caught in vertiginous tautologies of materialistic thought, like the speaker in Auden's poem "Petition," dealing in death, not life. As Herzog admits ruefully, "civilized intelligence makes fun of its own ideas [p. 271]"—the last refinement of the mind! The nihilism of such thought furnishes us with "modern forms of Orphism [p. 317]." "What is the philosophy of this generation?" Herzog asks, and answers himself:

Not God is dead, that point was passed long ago. Perhaps it should be stated Death is God. This generation thinks—and this is its thought of thoughts—that nothing faithful, vulnerable, fragile can be durable or have any true power. Death waits for these things as a cement floor waits for a dropping light bulb. The brittle shell of glass loses its tiny vacuum with a burst, and that is that. And this is how we teach metaphysics on each other. "You think history is the history of loving hearts? You fool! Look at these millions of dead. Can you pity them, feel for them? You can nothing! There were too many. We burned them to ashes, we buried them with bulldozers. History is the history of cruelty, not love, as soft men think. We have experimented with every human capacity to see which is strong and admirable and have shown that none is. There is only practicality. If the old God exists he must be a murderer. But the one true god is Death. This is how it is—without cowardly illusions."

. . . Proudhon says, "God is *the* evil." But after we search in the entrails of world revolution for *la foi nouvelle*, what happens? The victory of death, not of rationality, not of rational faith. Our own murdering imagination turns out to be the great power, our human imagination which starts by accusing God of murder. [p. 290]

In the lives of Tommy Wilhelm, Augie, Henderson, and Herzog, Bellow (like his great predecessor Blake) rejects this rationalized death in favor of *"moral realities"* and "the divine image" of man: "Three thousand million human beings . . . each a microcosmos, each infinitely precious, each with a peculiar treasure [*Herzog*, pp. 175–176, 178]." For as Blake insisted in "The Divine Image":

> . . . Mercy has a human heart,
> Pity a human face,
> And Love, the human form divine,
> And Peace, the human dress.
>
> .   .   .   .
> And all must love the human form,
> In heathen, turk, or jew;
> Where Mercy, Love, & Pity dwell
> There God is dwelling too.

This shock of recognition Romantics from Wordsworth to Bellow have affirmed.

The Group and the Individual

Bellow has been a member of the Committee on Social Thought at the University of Chicago; and a problem of Western civilization that fittingly has absorbed his attention is the survival value of individualism in a society increasingly organized according to the rationale of what is best for the gross national product. Aside from the dubious amusement that the futile rages and childlike impracticalities of Joseph, Wilhelm, Leventhal, Augie, Henderson, and Herzog afford the "true disciple[s] of Thomas Hobbes"— the "organizational realist[s]" and "poet[s] in mass communications [*Herzog*, pp. 78, 125, 215]"—Bellow admits that their "bread-and-butter" value to society is negligible. But he refuses to write off their individualism as a biological dead end, social mutation, or archaism. Affectionately and fervently, he sees them as performing the civilized office of keeping alive in man his agony of consciousness, his tragic sense of life, his old-fashioned dread of death, his spiritual awareness of self. Since these characters are learning how to maintain simultaneously their individualism and their membership in the group, they also serve to remind us of man's gift for survival and his hard-won social victory.

F. J. Hoffman in a perceptive essay contends that the Bellow hero is bent on finding some kind of accommodation with society, on changing his separation for conformity, his rebellion for adaptation.[8] "Bellow's hero moves *into* society," Hoffman rather sweepingly asserts, "with a desperate hope that the human dilemma will be solved in community recognition and action."[9] Although he acknowledges the importance for Bellow of the development of the individual, he believes that the goal of the Bellow novel is emphatically the assimilation of the individual into society. Yes, says Marcus Klein, but in assent shifting

Hoffman's emphasis away from total absorption, after alienation in our time comes accommodation—"that simultaneous engagement and disengagement . . . that tricky distance between the sense of one's self in one's freedom and the sense of society out there."[10] Klein has a disconcerting tendency to blur Pygmalion with Galatea, so that one is not always sure whether the artist or his fictional creation is currently engaged in making tentative advances. Nevertheless, I would agree with his diagnosis that equilibrium is the ideal aimed for in the Bellow novel; but, if I read him correctly, wish to demur at his inference, perhaps not wholly intended, that the Bellow protagonist, with the questionable exception of Henderson and his "Nietzschean idea of heroic self-transcendence," continues locked into "the exercise of personality for its own sake."[11]

Bellow's celebration of identity has a purpose. He recognizes that man cuts the umbilical cord tying him to the community at large at the risk of his sanity. As an urban American Jew he knows that man draws his nourishment from the surrounding culture. It is not the movement of the individual toward the group, however, which he considers necessary—and here I think both Hoffman and Klein err in direction of emphasis—but the maintenance of oneself apart from the many, while continuing paradoxically to exist within the whole. For, as Bellow has asserted on more than one occasion, public life tends to drive out private life. The tenor of Bellow's remarks in his article, "Some Notes on Recent American Fiction,"[12] clearly points to the importance that he places, first, on the survival of the individual in an age when the encroachment of the public realm on the private "steadily reduces the power of the individual"; and, second, on the artist's obligation (and need, if his vision is not to become a parody of historical hypotheses and social formulas) to find answers to the question "What is man?"

"I myself am not convinced that there is less 'selfhood' in the modern world," he avows as a testament of faith against those contemporary fictional soothsayers who lament that "The power of public life has become so vast and threatening that private life cannot maintain a pretence of its importance" and who consequently ask "The Self . . . to prepare itself for sacrifice." "Undeniably the human being," he admits, "is not what he commonly thought a century ago"; but, he adds, "The question nevertheless remains. He is something. What is he?" Bellow, here, is calling with the prophetic voice of Blake for writers to cleanse the eyes of vision. His own novels are increasingly courageous attempts to confront this "issue of the single Self and the multitude," unblinded by popular shibboleths, and to define anew for our age the integral Self, which has replaced the "sovereign Self of the Romantics" and "the decent Self of Kipling." Joseph and Leventhal submit to assimilation of a sort; but Henderson travels the same route of social affirmation, all the while hollering contrariwise about each man's right to what Schlossberg in *The Victim* calls the need "to be myself in full [ch. 21]." One also recalls Augie's simultaneous love fete with the human race and his lifelong resistance to being owned by anyone. For him to do less would have been for him to deny all. At the end of *The Victim* Allbee sums up this viewpoint succinctly when he says, "When you turn against yourself, nobody else means anything to you either [ch. 24]." Herzog's agony similarly is that of a man involved in "the total reconsideration of [his] human qualities [p. 203]," bent on the peculiarly modern task of growth in self-consciousness ("changing" Herzog calls it) to insure his continuation as a man. And at the end of his bout with standardized society Herzog considers it an achievement, while having struggled through to what can only be called a victory for the inviolacy of his selfhood, that he is "much better now at [the] ambiguities [p. 304]" of living among people.

Civilization exists, Bellow would have it, only so long as the individual can retain his selfness intact. Anything less leads to death and genocide. Is not this, in part, the parable of the fate of the Arnewi in *Henderson the Rain King?* They leave no margin for questioning the dogma of the communal mind. And death greets their passive conformity. Similarly, King Dahfu of the Wariri dies in submission to the cultural will of his people, while Henderson survives through resistance to it. Not in automatic conformity nor in quixotic individualism but, rather, out of the tension that comes from the pull of the two extremes on man does Bellow conceptualize hopefully the establishment of a "locus of reality and value." [13] Out of this vortex evolves the dramatic and symbolic patterns of his novels.

This tension is developed with maximum effectiveness in *Seize the Day* in the multiple ironies of Tommy Wilhelm's confrontations with Tamkin and Dr. Adler. Both men embody facets of the American ideal. Dr. Adler is forever reminding Tommy of the need to be self-reliant and financially independent. In keeping with his medical background he emphasizes the visible and the material. Tamkin preaches a breezy optimism no less calculating and pragmatic than his counterpart's debased Emersonism. The rich complexities of Bellow's social and psychological insights are indicated by the ambiguities in Tommy's effort to relate to the world of Tamkin and Dr. Adler. Tommy is undergoing the crisis of middle-age. Beset with both marital and economic troubles, complicated by a paralyzing sense of his own inadequacy, he looks to both men's professional capacity as healers to solve his problems. Dr. Adler, Tommy's real father and a healer of "the real ailments" of bodies [ch. 3], gives sound financial advice in cautioning Tommy about

Tamkin but falsely withholds from Tommy his love. Tamkin, a substitute father and a healer of minds and souls, answers Tommy's cry for love but fleeces him in the bargain. Tamkin serves Tommy eventually as both confidence man and savior. Both men—Dr. Adler, an old man trying with massages to arrest time; and Tamkin, an opportunist dealing in stock futures—advise Tommy to take advantage of the "actual, immediate present . . . [to] Grasp the hour, the moment, the instant [ch. 5]"—to seize the day! It is ultimately Tamkin, the bogus psychologist, who accurately diagnoses Tommy as a man of heart and urges him to follow the dictates of his true soul. And it is Tamkin the swindler who, through the embezzlement of Tommy's last few dollars, works to release Tommy's pent-up tears and restore him to his true self. Hence, Dr. Adler's advice to Tommy about Tamkin proves, in a profounder sense than the economic, to be as false as his paternal relationship.

The configurations of Tommy's relationships to Tamkin and Dr. Adler are evenly negative and affirmative. His involvement in their commercial world and his emotive dissociation from it is characterized in the equipoise of the language of his thoughts after breakfasting with his father:

> . . . since there were depths in Wilhelm not unsuspected by himself, he received a suggestion from some remote element in his thoughts that the *business of life,* the real *business*— to carry *his peculiar burden,* to *feel shame and impotence,* to *taste these quelled tears*—the only important *business,* the *highest business* was being done. [ch. 4; my italics]

This equipoise is evident in Tamkin's linking of *M*oney with *M*urder, *M*achinery, *M*ischief; and in Tommy's rejoinder, "What about *M*ercy? *M*ilk-of-human-kindness? [ch. 4]." And it is present in Tamkin's description of the two souls

that inhabit each human bosom: the true soul which fulfills man's need to "go outward" in love of "something or
somebody"; and the pretender soul which satisfies man's
need to perform such socially acceptable acts as giving
"some money to a charity." Tamkin concludes that "The
interest of the pretender soul is the same as the interest of
the social life, the society mechanism [ch. 4]."

Plurality or individuality? One is reminded inevitably of
Augie's initial paraphrase and *subsequent reversal* of Hera-
clitus (too often overlooked by critics) at the start and at
the end of his adventures: "I said . . . that a man's character was his fate. Well, then it is obvious that this fate, or
what he settles for, is also his character [ch. 26]." All
Bellow's novels are concerned to a greater or lesser degree
with this theme, specifically as it touches upon the peculiar Jewish sense of the indivisibility of inner- and outer-di-
rected needs. All Bellow's protagonists (including the
white Anglo-Saxon Protestant Henderson) on one level of
experience are marginal Jews whose dissociation from
Jewish religious values is a measure of their divergence
from a socially approved sensibility.[14] In comparison to
Wilhelm's pathetic gulling, however, Herzog's seriocomic
confrontation with society transcends its explicit Jewish
ethos to reflect historically profound responses to the
place of the individual in the life of a nation.

Moses Herzog is no Hans Castorp. And Ludeyville, Mas-
sachusetts, is certainly no Schatzalp, Switzerland. Yet *Herzog* and *The Magic Mountain* are similarly serious sum-
mings-up of climates of opinion. Both Herzog and Castorp
image in the successive actions of their lives the crises of
their times. For seven years Castorp lives on a Swiss mountain top withdrawn from the world below. In the atmosphere of low vitality of a tuberculosis sanitorium, he
dreams away the days like one under a spell, while the
thunder from below of European ideologies faintly pene-

trates his isolation in the form of the old-fashioned Victorian debates of Naphta and Settembrini. For seven months and more Herzog dashes frenziedly about Europe and America, immersed in imaginary epistolary warfare with social and political thinkers, past and present. Castorp is awakened from his enchantment by the holocaust of World War I, descends from the Schatzalp, and is lost to our sight, booted and helmeted, running with thousands of soldiers across the no-man's-land of Europe in senseless taking and retaking of nameless hills. Herzog retires to his farmhouse in the Berkshires to see his crisis of identity through to its conclusion, appositely preoccupied with the allied problem of how man can retain his sense of human individuality in a mass society where even goodness is associated with "technological transformation [p. 204]." If the symbolic movement of *The Magic Mountain* is inexorably a descent from the heights to the plains below where the individual wish is submerged in the national ambition, then that of *Herzog* as underlined by the controlling metaphor of a mountain [15] is one of ascent, of aspiration to the heights from where past and future become visible and private and public lives can be joined. Neither can evade his fate. Castorp succumbs to his cultural environment and moves from dissociation to self-immolation. Herzog feels equally the pull to easeful conformity and the necessity of existential existence, the twin forces of his age.

Whereas Castorp's schizophrenia is pre-World War I, pre-Marx, and in effect, pre-Freud; Herzog's manic-depression is post-World War II, post-Freudian salvation (when anyone with the price of a couch and the jargon of a psychology textbook can set himself up as a social welfare headshrinker), and post-Marxian revolution (although revolts in Marx's name continue to be plotted, hatched, and aborted). His anguish is that of the intellectual of the post-McCarthy era, occupying the periphery of a power that is manipulated by politicians and consensus men. His is the confusion of the liberal mind, which seeks to help man to the full life but abhors the authoritarian methods of mass persuasion; the mind which needs to believe in the goodness of man's heart but fears the corruptibility of man's mind. By turn "the organizational realist [p. 125]" coldly controlling the *Massenmenschen* to their mutual benefit and the "tragical mammal [p. 258]" wallowing in "potato love [p. 176]" for their individuality destroyed in the name of collectivity, Herzog poses the dilemma of the idealistic reformer.

Like so many of his academic colleagues at midcentury —intellectual, liberal, and messianic—Herzog sees himself as a potential benefactor of mankind—indeed, as possibly man's last best hope. He wants to do what he can "to improve the human condition [p. 107]." At extreme moments of euphoria, he conjectures that if he is right, "the problem of the world's coherence, and all responsibility for it," become his. But inevitably misgivings compromise his almost sublime megalomania. He remembers that the despised Valentine Gersbach "was a regular Goethe. He finished all your sentences, rephrased all your thoughts, explained everything." "Readiness to answer all questions is the infallible sign of stupidity," Herzog sneeringly concludes, "a harmful, Prussian delusion [p. 155]." Yet during the years of his marriage to Madeleine, he was afflicted with intellectual pretensions, full of pride in his capacity to mastermind a new humanism. He saw himself as Nietzsche's "last man"—"the unitary and sufficient Self produced by a proud bourgeois and industrial civilization" [16]—personally responsible "in his icy outpost" of Ludeyville for Western survival, "lying in bed in an aviator's helmet when the stoves were out," fitting "together Bacon and Locke from one side and Methodism and William Blake from the other [p. 127]." He and his confreres are dangerously susceptible to the inviolate idea. They easily succumb to the chief temptation of the intellectual—overweening affection for "an imaginary human situation invented by their own genius and which they believe is the only true and the only human reality [p. 304]." Madeleine curses him as "sick with abstractions [p. 123]." He "took seriously Heinrich Heine's belief that the words of Rousseau had turned into the bloody machine of Robespierre, that Kant and Fichte were deadlier than armies [p. 119]." Hence, as a member of the intelligentsia, an historian of ideas, a kind of second generation Jewish Lovejoy, he is afflicted with an inordinate sense of "personal responsibility for history [p. 128]." He sees himself by means of his books and lectures as an inevitable leader. Not for nothing is he called Moses. The German meaning of his surname—duke—is an unsavory reminder of centuries of *Kriegleiter*. All the Herzogs, he is fond of recalling, are aristocratic in manner. Herzog envisions himself in another context as a patriarch, "family man, father, transmitter of life, intermediary between past and future, instrument of mysterious creation [p. 208]," not just of the Herzog name but of all human society.

Ironically, this grand vision of the individual's historical role is the disease which has recurrently plagued our century with epidemics of dictatorship. For Herzog the ancient Hebraic veneration for ideas has been momentarily grafted onto the modern intellectual taste for totalitarianism. And in one sense Herzog's recovery of mental and emotional balance is in direct relation to his agonizing diagnosis of his megalomania, and agonizing middle-aged reappraisal of his place in society.

First, were he to succeed as an intellectual leader, Herzog comes to realize, he would be responsible for what in the deepest reaches of his personality he most abhors, the installation of his thought as an official opinion to be foisted on all who wish salvation. With great conceptual skill, Bellow contrives the narrative so that the years of Herzog's marriage to Madeleine coincide with the years when he is preparing his "grand synthesis [p. 207]" of Western thought; and the aftermath of her divorce from him, with his soul-searching disillusionment in ideas as panacea and in the intellectual as *Gauleiter*. Madeleine's is a distinctly modern consciousness. If Herzog's disorder is disorganization, hers is "super-clarity [pp. 303–304]." Aware of goals, not averse to use of power tactics to gain her ends, and contemptuous of people as things to be manipulated, she is a master of "mental politics" and "the power to hurt," for "the strength to do evil is sovereignty [p. 126]" Herzog righteously tells himself. As such she is a distinct threat to the moralistic, Old Testament impulse, which basically informs Herzog's temperament. She functions on one level of the story as a measure of his temporary mental aberration. During the years of his second marriage (itself an anomalous memorial to his temporary estrangement from the true course of his life), he works at a treatise, he fondly tells himself, on which depends "The progress of civilization—indeed, the survival of civilization [p. 125]." The knowledge he slowly regains after being discarded by Madeleine like so much used-up scrap is that he had been pursuing power goals akin to hers. He had been one of those "diseased, tragic, or dismal and ludicrous fools who sometimes hoped to achieve some ideal by fiat, by their desire for it. But usually by bullying all mankind into believing it [p. 67]." In seeking to bind Madeleine as the first of eventually all mankind, he had bound himself— to paraphrase a Blakean proverb, which Herzog ironically applies to his and Ramona's relationship [p. 66]. He had wished "to pull the carpet from under all other scholars, show them what was what, stun them, expose their triviality once and for all [p. 119]." The certainty of being right, with its "flow of power," flooded his bowels and flushed his body. He luxuriated in the "victories of anger." With supreme ego, he was intent upon a "definition of human nature [p. 129]" that would be good for all time. In short, he wished to make man over into his own image! He suffered from "the chief ambiguity that afflicts intellectuals, and this is that civilized individuals hate and resent the civilization that makes their lives possible [p. 304]." With the reformer's contempt for what he is bent on bettering, Herzog saw "bourgeois America" as a "crude world of finery and excrement. A proud, lazy civilization that worships its own boorishness [p. 133]." The masses, liberated by production, lead empty private lives. His book would provide a metaphysics for the modern technological milieu, which would obviate this vacuum. And like Blake's Urizen, he viewed his efforts as a "holy cause [p. 128]." To effect this end, he comes to realize in horror, is, however, to exercise the hard-headed, political talents of the "organizational realist [p. 125]," to follow the historical determinism of Hegel, who "was curiously significant but also utterly cockeyed," to "make others live according to his way of thinking—*ex ipsius ingenio* [p. 123]," to efface the individualism that he is intent on bettering. Essentially a prophet in the old dispensation, he had mistakenly confused eighteenth-century French and German political economy with his Old Testament concern for morality, justice, and humanity.

That Herzog's heart is not in such *Realpolitiks*, his Jewish emotionalism makes plain enough. That his mind also finds it alien, his fondness for quoting Blake reveals only too clearly. Despite the temporary deviations of his mind, he can say with his friend Nachman that he keeps his "heart with William Blake [p. 133]," whose lifelong evangelism was to convince each man of his uniqueness and to labor to "Create a System" of thought of his own, so as not to "be enslav'd by another Man's [*Jerusalem*, ch. 1, plate 9]." Blake, Rousseau, Rilke, and Kierkegaard are all favorite authors of Herzog; and all violently resisted wearing the collar of another man's mind. But it is not until his return to Ludeyville from Chicago that Herzog at last clearly recognizes how fully he "had committed a sin of some kind against his own heart, while in pursuit of a grand synthesis [p. 207]." No wonder Herzog had scribbled only disjointed fragments, "his old valise . . . swelled like a scaly crocodile with his uncompleted manuscript [p. 207]," and was hung up in his book on the chapter dealing with Hegel and Rousseau! He has been divided against himself. One part of his mind keeps reminding him that modern rationalism represents "reality opposing the 'law of the heart,' alien necessity gruesomely crushing individuality [p. 123]."

As Blake never wearied of expounding, to codify one's thought so that it can be worshipped, obeyed, and believed, is to introduce death into life. And for much of his ordeal, Herzog is fascinated by the death instinct, by the curious human wish that "it would hurry up," would "come soon [p. 326]." For a time he too, like the contemporary generation he excoriates (which has enshrined Forest Lawn as a substitute for Heaven), unwittingly believes in the philosophy that "the one true god is Death [p. 290]," glad to step into his coffin "as if it were a new sports car [p. 291]." His memory becomes custodian of "all the dead and the mad" and nemesis of "the would-be forgotten [p. 134]." On a tour of Europe to regain his health of mind, he visits cemeteries and the sites of vanished ghettos. His resignation of his professorship and retreat into the Berkshire hills are expressive of the same temporary denial of life. The unkempt grounds and the dusty mouse-infested furniture of the house in Ludeyville, with the house itself "in bad repair [although of sound foundation and frame]" and out of the way, "Miles from a synagogue [p. 307]," provide us with an objective correlative of Herzog during the years of his marriage to Madeleine and its aftermath.

Ludeyville as a reflection of Herzog's false ambitions is also used by Bellow to underline the Jewish theme. Herzog denies that he can be considered quixotic, first because "A quixote was a Christian and Moses E. Herzog was no Christian," and second because he lives in the "post-quixotic, post-Copernican U.S.A. [p. 286]." Yet he admits that he had bought Ludeyville as a "symbol of his Jewish struggle for a solid footing in white Anglo-Saxon Protestant America [p. 309]." It is, like his second marriage, a bid for membership in the country club. He had divorced a traditional good Jewish woman to combine with a Catholic convert, only to find that the marriage had isolated him not only from all of society but from all mankind. A sign of his recovery is his decision to sell the Ludeyville "estate."

The turning point for Herzog comes *dramatically* when he is involved in an automobile accident that endangers his daughter's life and leaves him lying stretched on the grass as if dead and *thematically* when he begins to acknowledge the rightness of "the old-fashioned dread of death." For not to dread death, he tells Luke Asphalter, "makes life a trifle not worth anyone's anguish" and "threatens the heart of civilization [p. 272]"; and conversely, to dread death is to love life. For a time in his desire to be the modern Aquinas he had mistaken systematic theorizing for creative reasoning; he had "devalued the person" in the "multiplied power of numbers [p. 201]" to "the raw material of technological transformation [p. 185]"—to the dehumanized "filthy garments" of Blake's trinity of devils, Bacon, Locke, and Newton. For a time he had tried to convince his innermost soul of the truth of this image of man as commodity—and the trope of man as a business product recurs in his musings and letters. But the true bent of his mind—temporarily stultified by infatuation, pride, and ambition—is best illustrated by his remembrance that as a high school valedictorian, he had told the "Italian mechanics, Bohemian barrel makers, Jewish tailors *The main enterprise of the world, for splendor . . . is the upbuilding of a man. The private life of one man shall be a more illustrious monarchy . . . than any kingdom in history* [p. 160]." During the years of his *Götterdamerung*, he was unable to follow his own youthful advice. He carried his friend Shapiro's "fine monograph" with him "all over Europe in his valise," committed to reviewing it but unable to set down to the task, until in desperation in Venice he ground out something he knew was a "botch [p. 69]." He had not liked Shapiro; the man had made eyes at Madeleine and charity was absent in his heart. His recovery is marked by the generosity with which he belatedly congratulates Professor Mermelstein for scooping him and offers carte blanche use of those parts of his "projected book" which he will "never return to [p. 315]." In this desire to be used he returns to the faith of his forebearers, echoing their sense of the sacred role of the Jew in the world.

The ordeal of Herzog encompasses both his personal life and his intellectual life, the breakup of his marriage and collapse of his academic career and the contraction of his "superman" role in the world's history of thought. His is the crisis of the liberal humanist that Lionel Trilling has written so movingly of in *The Middle of the Journey*. Power demands that he adopt the enemy's weapons and methods —and ultimately, as Blake was so acutely aware, his point of view. The *homo sapiens* in Herzog, however, triumphs by a narrow squeak, reasserting all its humanity and individuality. He still proceeds *ad hominem*. But his assertion of individuality is of humbler stuff than was his previous Urizenic effort to codify *self* into a compendium of human nature. He no longer cares to bind others to his concepts, and thus "oppress them [p. 134]." His involvement in the

history of thought had been in the interests of man but out
of contempt for mankind in the mass. In the process he had
fallen apart, like his friend Hoberly, unwittingly bearing
false "witness to the failure of individual existence" and
thus serving "the Leviathan of organization even more de-
votedly [p. 208]" than its adherents. The upshot is that
Herzog now accepts his nature for what it is: "part-time
visionary, cheerful, tragical mammal [p. 258]," and "spe-
cialist in . . . spiritual self-awareness; or emotionalism; or
ideas; or nonsense [p. 307]." Such a person is incompetent
to cope with the high "level of organization and automa-
tism [p. 268]" of contemporary mass existence. In a revealing comparison with his brother, Willie, a competent,
quiet businessman "of duty and routine," Herzog rhapsodizes:

> Under the old dispensation, as the stumbling, ingenuous,
> burlap Moses, a heart without guile, in need of protection, a
> morbid phenomenon, a modern remnant of other-worldli-
> ness—under that former dispensation I would need protec-
> tion. And it would be gladly offered by him [his brother]—
> by the person who 'knows-the-world-for-what-it-is.' Whereas
> a man like me has shown the arbitrary withdrawal of proud
> subjectivity from the collective and historical progress of
> mankind. [p. 307]

"What kind of synthesis," he asks himself ironically, as he
muses on his recent derangement, "is a Separatist likely to
come up with? [p. 322]."

In one sense—and it is important for understanding Bellow—Herzog's "proud subjectivity" involves him more in-
tegrally in human affairs than the vaunted reason and common sense of the "mass man," who in his pride becomes "a
man of the crowd" and "The soul of the mob," by "Cutting
everybody down to size [p. 86]." It is Herzog who responds with compassion for the people he observes caught

in the impersonal coils of justice. Waiting to see his lawyer Simkin at city court, he wanders into several courtrooms where trials are in process. Each depicts an individual dehumanized and perverted by the abrasive pressures toward conformity of a totalitarian society. Herzog is horrified by the bureaucratic impersonality of the proceedings, involving such horrible deeds done to a fellow being as the brutalization from childhood of a demented, crippled girl. When she herself is grown and a mother, the girl responds toward her own child with the same kind of brutality that she has suffered, finally killing it by wrenching free its clutching, loving hands from around her waist and slamming the child repeatedly against a wall. In his heart, Herzog weeps in protest against the mass organized indifference of "the lawyers, the jury, the mother, her tough friend, the judge," whose calm restraint is "inversely proportionate to the murder [p. 237]." With the passionate indignation of Matthew Arnold decrying the desexing of another victim of society in the laconic newspaper report, "Wragg is in custody," [17] Herzog tries posthumously to imagine some modicum of human aid and dignity for the murdered child. Echoing the cry of Macbeth at the endless despair of life, Bellow tells us that Herzog "was wrung, and wrung again, and wrung again, again [p. 240]."

In this profound emotion for one's fellowman is sounded in ringing peals the triumph of the individual heart. It still bears passionate testament to the existence of "primordial feelings of a certain sort [p. 307]" and to the truth that "man is somehow more than his 'characteristics,' all the emotions, strivings, tastes, and constructions which it pleases him to call 'My Life' . . . more than such a cloud of particles," which are the "mere facticity" of his sojourn on earth [p. 266].

Judged by the standards of public life and national purpose and mass civilization, Augie, Wilhelm, Leventhal, Henderson, and Herzog fall short of the standardized ideal. They are ineffectual, weak, bumbling; but they transcend these faults in our regard because of their intense compassion. Himmelstein, Gersbach, and Shura Herzog are contrariwise all "true disciple[s] of Thomas Hobbes [p. 78]," cynically using man and manipulating the modern social structure to their own advantages. Herzog, with all his emotional confusion, is a living reminder that they—and we—are human, raised above the animal level predicated in *The Leviathan*. He is a "loving brute," who makes "his sacrifice to truth, to order, peace," by allowing his fellow beings to use him [pp. 308, 272]. He is a testimony to the radically regimented world of the Himmelsteins "impregnated with modern ideas," that man *can* shoulder "his great, bone-breaking burden of selfhood and self-development," that he need not sacrifice his "poor, squawking, niggardly individuality [pp. 92–93].

At the extreme he is the sacrificial offering through whom modern collective society may reaffirm its affinities with the more than human. This bitter pill about the burden of selfhood Herzog at first shrinks from swallowing. To Sandor Himmelstein, he shouts shortly after Madeleine has sent him packing, apropos of her wanting a divorce, "I'm not going to be a victim. I hate the victim bit [p. 82]." Yet it is the passion of Christ, Bellow suggests, that Herzog and all individualists like him experience symbolically for the sake of mankind at large. For man, as Bellow's characters show, can in this century achieve and maintain his identity and yet hear "the still sad music of humanity" [18] only at the price of periodic solitariness. This hard-won insight was the lesson of Wordsworth and his generation, who were also the first Western men to respond to the challenge that modern technological utopianism forces upon the individual. In the solitary communings of Herzog, who addresses the world, living and dead, Bellow has come a long way from the defeatest cry of Joseph, at the end of *Dangling Man*. Hence, there is increasing importance for the Bellow story of a protagonist who persists, in Tony Tanner's words, in "solitary self-communings." [19]

Herzog's years with Madeleine are in their symbolic action a kind of death to the world of his true self; but he stubbornly resists this modern trend of death-in-life. *"He could not allow himself to die yet,"* he tells himself after suddenly recalling that his mother had "died so young [p. 27]"; and at the end of the book, in a message to his dead mother thanking her for the life she has given him, he adds that he is "still on the same side of eternity as ever," which is "just as well," for he has "certain things still to do [p. 326]." With his divorce he begins the trauma of rebirth into the essential Moses Herzog.

This rebirth is conveyed, aside from Herzog's own growing acceptance of himself as he is, in part, by his dawning love for Ramona, by his rejection of Asphalter's death exercise, by his inability to kill Madeleine and Gersbach, and by his cessation of letter writing (a carry-over from the days when he was intent upon renovation of the world, instructing the quick and the dead, the great and the near great, past and present). During his dinner date with Ramona, he washes himself in her bathroom, and recalls the "old Jewish ritual of nail water, and the word in the Haggadah, *Rachatz!* 'Thou shalt wash.' " He further recalls that "It was obligatory also to wash when you returned from the cemetery [p. 181]"—surely a reminiscence calculated to indicate Herzog's own return from the dead, that is, his rebirth. Afterward he listens to Ramona characterize him as one who "had experienced the worst sorts of morbidity and come through by a miracle." "Here was a man . . . who knew what it was to rise from the dead. . . . with him she experienced a real Easter. She knew what Resurrection was [p. 185]"—words that pointedly call attention to

themselves in the strangeness of their use by a Jew. It is
fitting that her palinode should be followed by their eating
together and then by their making love—both aspects of
the "Dionysiac revival [p. 186]"—and that the novel
should end with Herzog back at Ludeyville, basking in the
"sparkling summer weather" of the Berkshires [pp.
309–310], at last with "no messages for anyone. Nothing.
Not a single word [p. 341]," quietly awaiting Ramona for a
dinner of his own making.

In the persons of Augie March, Tommy Wilhelm, Henderson, and Herzog, especially, Bellow, like his great predecessor Blake, asserts the primal " 'law of the heart' in Western
traditions [p. 119]" as a counterbalance to the modern law
of the dehumanized mind. So Herzog wryly reminds Shapiro: "We are survivors, in this age," which, "trained in the
cunning of reason," "lies closer to the vision of Comte—the
results of rationally organized labor [p. 75]." Obsessed
with universal concerns rather than with practical relativi-
ties, with the "tribal" claims of "ancestor worship and
totemism [*Herzog*, p. 78]" rather than with the suburban
ideals of group anonymity and assimilation, they are Bellow's loving tribute not only to his own Jewish heritage
(which in America is passing into the mainstream of national life) but also to the core of feeling that Rousseau
celebrates (*"Je sens mon coeur et je connais les hommes"*)
and Herzog humbly quotes [pp. 340, 129], which separates
man from the animals. By implied contrast Bellow is also
diagnosing the ill of our century: the displacement of the
individual heart with all its inefficient subjectivity in favor
of the "beautiful supermachinery" of "organized power,"
"tremendous controls," "mechanization," and "multiplied
power of numbers [*Herzog*, p. 201]." In these terms *Herzog* is a worthy successor to *The Magic Mountain;* and
Bellow is a writer who will appeal strongly to intellectuals,
yet who will give them little comfort.

Character and Narrative

Assemble the following ingredients: *Huckleberry Finn* and the picaresque tradition, *Wilhelm Meister* and the "Bildungsroman," Byron's *Don Juan* and self-castigating social satire, and *Sartor Resartus* and vatic pomposity. Take two brothers of contrasting personalities, one all will and rationality, the other all heart and sentiment. Involve them from adolescence in circumstances (depression years of the 1930's, Jewish family background, desertion by father) and with a rogue's gallery of people. Stir thoroughly so that everything is contiguous—and formative of each brother's character. Let the oldest pursue wealth coldly and deliberately at the expense of his soul. Let the younger drift seemingly from job to job as he seeks his true self, maturing his soul and finding a happy life. For leavening agent, add a series of amorous adventures, acting upon the young man to bring him knowledge of life, its pain and anguish, and its joy and satisfaction. Combine with universal philosophy, irony, and pyrotechnic language at great length. Like life itself let it have no conclusion—other than death —and end with the two brothers still living.

The book resulting from such a mixture, of course, is *The Adventures of Augie March*. With the exception, perhaps, of Leslie Fiedler, Saul Bellow has the most cultivated mind of practicing Jewish-American novelists. His books display acquaintance with an impressive amount of Western thought, and, what is more to the point, a broad knowledge of European and American literary traditions, and a great capacity for assimilation of these traditions. *The Adventures of Augie March* is not his only novel to use older literary models effectively. *Henderson the Rain King* relies for more than a touch of its effect on our knowledge of its great predecessors *Gulliver's Travels* and *Candide*. And is not Bellow in the semiepistolary *Herzog* a psychologically (as well as literarily) matured Richardson?

Equally impressive is Bellow's skill in translating these models into contemporary idiom. Augie is recognizably a lineal descendant of Huck Finn. Yet what in his characterization or his adventures can be identified as imitative of the Missouri boy's odyssey on the Mississippi? The world of Hannibal in 1830 has effectively been transplanted to the Chicago of 1930. And the Irish-American castoff of a ragamuffin ne'er-do-well, has been completely metamorphosed into a Jewish-American "orphan" of a run-away jack-of-all-trades. Whereas Huck is embroiled in his age's major question of slavery, with its dilemma-posing crisis of public morality and law versus private loyalty and love, Augie is beset with the problems of his time's economic failure, with its social pressure on young men to pursue lives dedicated to financial success or social and economic reform, even at the cost of their personal integrity. In his inability to conform, Augie provides us with a valid image of the social rebel in the Depression years (just as Huck does for the West prior to the Civil War): urban, lower-middle class, Jewish, intellectual, idealistic. Similarly, Henderson is at once a gulled Gulliver wandering with astonished, yet shrewd, eye among the Arnewi and Wariri, and a naively hopeful Candide sitting at the feet of the native philosophers Willatale and Dahfu—all reincarnated in the modern figure of a jaded cynic qua conscience-tormented existentialist.

This eclecticism also gives texture to Bellow's style, which is equally adept at piling up descriptive details reminiscent of the Chicago school of realists, and at exploiting motif and symbol with the best of the symbolists. In his handling of form, particularly the inseparable problems of point of view, plot, and theme, Bellow clearly shows his mastery of the novel. In his preface to the New York

Edition of *The Ambassadors*, Henry James rejected "the first person, in a long piece," as "a form foredoomed to looseness." Four of Bellow's six novels sin against this dogma: *Dangling Man, The Adventures of Augie March, Henderson the Rain King,* and *Herzog.* One cannot technically call *Herzog* an "autobiographical" novel; yet the first person figures so extensively in the letters of Herzog that for all practical purposes it belongs in this category. Of these four novels, *The Adventures of Augie March* and *Henderson the Rain King* illustrate, like the indefiniteness of *David Copperfield*, the tenuousness of an uncontrolled central observation and the blunting of discriminations in the relationships of the characters, against which James inveighed. That this is not without calculation Bellow's deliberate choice of the picaresque mode would indicate. Norman Mailer, perceptively reading his contemporaries with a novelist's eye, notes this peculiarity of Bellow's narrative as a "major weakness." Bellow "creates individuals and not relations between them, at least not yet," Mailer writes. "Augie March travels alone, the hero of *Seize the Day* is alone, Henderson forms passionate friendships but they tend to get fixed and the most annoying aspect of the novel is the constant repetition of the same sentiments." [20]

One's weakness, as Coleridge was fond of noting, is frequently the contrary expression of one's strength. This is almost certainly so with Bellow, who tends to identify life with the private self—in Henderson's words, with the spirit waked from sleep—and whose novels tend through their structure to reflect this philosophy. The moral picaresque becomes a perfect vehicle for Augie's endless succession of broken, abandoned, and deserted human attachments, periodically and haphazardly renewed, which represents not so much aimless drifting as it does (like his brother Simon's "mismanaged effort to life. To live and not die," [ch. 26]) his struggle to keep himself free of all those friends and family who would own him like a thing and make him over into their image of what he should be. Paradoxically, he has to go into the wilderness and like the prophets of old live on worms and locusts before he learns to know his real self sufficiently to entrust it to the faceless rigidities of society. The same made-to-order vehicle also supports the angry lunges of Henderson into and out of marriage, from the city to the country, to Europe, and finally into the fastness of Africa, in flight from the "Society" which always "beats" him [ch. 5].

It is in the other two novels, *Dangling Man* and *Herzog*, however, that Bellow brilliantly exploits the first person, turning a possible structural shortcoming into a virtue. Essentially a cerebral novelist more than a teller of tales, he is concerned with the mind's confused response to ideas and the heart's blind grappling with joy and pain in the never ending *rapprochement* of the one and the many. Hence the inherent inertia of plot, but compensatory strength in exploration of thought and feeling, of the first person narrative fits his artistic proclivities perfectly. The persistent *donné* in the Bellow novel is the emotional and spiritual crisis of the hero, and despite his essayesque inclinations, Bellow shows much skill in solving the literary problem intrinsic to his practicing the novelist's art, his need to find a narrative form that mirrors the inner life of the protagonist. In *Dangling Man* and *Herzog* he depends less on traditional forms, fashioning instead structures uniquely responsive to the demands of the theme. Little happens in *Dangling Man*, as Joseph waits month after month for a faceless bureaucracy to draft him into the army after having notified him of his imminent call-up; but this cessation of normal activities, as Joseph shrinks from contact with friends and relatives and debates with himself the moral propriety of volunteering himself, finds the perfect vehicle in the day-to-day journal he keeps, so expres-

sive of stopped action, of life that has temporarily
switched off *doing* and turned on *musing*. These journal
entries duplicate in their self-conscious air the narcissism
and antisocial predilection of Joseph. With equal brilliance
the letters of Herzog are adapted to his pedagogic habits,
gregarious nature, and temporary confessional needs. Dom-
inating the first half of the novel, they solve the problem of
Herzog's dual *aperçus* inherent in the simultaneity of multiple time schemes in the novel. The narrative spans the
four or five days of Herzog's stay at Ludeyville, during
which interval the previous years of Herzog's life are given
in the form of letters and brooding reminiscences. These
last days mark his recovery from the crisis of his second
marriage. Thus the flashbacks contain a dual point of
view: Herzog reacting with anguished immediacy at the
time to his experience, and Herzog commenting ironically
in the present on his past follies. This distancing of Herzog
lends credence to his depiction of Madeleine, Gersbach, and
the rest. The letters, further, stand as a brilliant tactic for
giving a semblance of division of point of view between
Herzog's subjective epistolary thoughts and his "objective" reminiscent reports of past events. Such a structural
strategy also permits full play of Bellow's interest in the
inner life of his character, while keeping the narrative
demands of the novel to a minimum. It emphasizes the
now, the dogma of *Seize the Day*, with its optimistic under-
song of the heart's response to impulse and immediacy. At
the same time form and point of view allow Bellow to
explore the relationship of the person to society, while
fully implying his faith in the importance of the individual.
In their isolated communion with the world through journal and letter, two men bare themselves to our view as they
agonizingly come to terms with themselves about the extent of their involvement in the group.

Given such lack of emphasis on narrative and such tension of endlessly shifting relationships between individual and state, few of Bellow's novels understandably have inevitable endings. An exception is *Dangling Man*, in which Joseph's being drafted into the army brings a painful phase of his life to a close. Despite the huddled and hurried conclusion of *The Adventures of Augie March*, as if Bellow had become bored with the life and times of his hero, which might seem to argue otherwise, Bellow is quite adept at contriving concluding episodes, which reverberate with symbolic overtones that satisfy emotionally and aesthetically. *Seize the Day*, with its generally recognized moving conclusion, *Henderson the Rain King*, and *Herzog* most fully illustrate this point.

If Bellow has not heeded the Master's admonitions in every instance, still he has learned, however indirectly under James's example—as have most novelists in this century—that the novel is a work of art with form and unity realizable through means other than the what-happens-next story line—through balance and antithesis of structural elements, imagery, motif, and symbol.

In *The Adventures of Augie March*, for example, Bellow counteracts the loose episodes of the picaresque tale not only with a marriage of it to the purposefulness of the *Bildungsroman*, but also with a concatenation of parallels and antitheses of characters and situations. These can be grouped into the givers and the takers, both ironically containing within themselves Janus-like the contrary qualities. There are those "tutors-in-life" who wish to "give" something to Augie, to provide him with advantages, and in the process to own him; and those who ask Augie for help, and in doing so give him the chance to express feeling for his fellow man and hence exercise and develop his capacity for love. It is the latter class of people who really educate Augie. Despite this tightening of the novel's form, Bellow seems to have succumbed to the pitfall of the naturalist in the conclusion. Dreiser apparently gave exorbitant space to Frank Cowperwood's jail term in *The Financier* because he could not resist documenting prison life. Similarly, Bellow wished to utilize his knowledge of the merchant marine during World War II. The disastrous consequences for the two novels are similar: the aesthetic incongruity of an overlong section of the book, coming crucially toward the end, which has slight, or, in the case of *The Adventures of Augie March*, redundant thematic function.

Bellow's concern for the trapped condition of modern life appears, as I have already mentioned, in the recurrent image in all his novels of bondage. As Henderson says, we are all slaves of the times [ch. 12]. This enslavement takes a variety of forms. In *The Adventures of Augie March* it is linked with Augie's desire to escape his social and economic background; and, as one might expect, it appears usually in conjunction with those who would make him over in their image. In a sense, Augie is in a struggle for survival; and Bellow underscores this motif with the recurrent images of war, Roman Praetorian Guards, and Roman generals. In *Henderson the Rain King*, the bondage image follows Blake in identifying our own body and mind as prison and turnkey.

To offset the tyranny of mind Bellow advocates love, heart, and flesh, which he underscores in the ancient antithesis of man and animal. Hence, the repeated identification of Henderson with pig, lion, and bear, as he strives to free his spirit from the sleep that is death of the heart. In *Herzog* the tyranny of the mind is the special one of modern society, in which the positivist "benefactor" programs the life of every citizen as if it were part of the day-to-day routine of a business, with the Himmelsteins "touting the Void as if it were so much saleable real estate [p. 93]." The issue, here, as Herzog (and Bellow) see it is ultimately one of the persistence of the "poor, squawking, niggardly" indi-

vidual vis-à-vis the historical necessity of the dreary dehumanized group. Passionately, urgently, Bellow would have
us realize that order does not issue necessarily out of conformity, that human well-being does not depend upon totalitarian methods, that virtue does not come in ready-made
packages.

NOTES—CHAPTER 5

1. J. V. Levenson, "Bellow's Dangling Men," *Critique*, III (1960),
3–14.
2. Ihab Hassan, "Saul Bellow: Five Faces of a Hero," *Critique*,
III (1960), 28–36.
3. All citations are to the following editions: Saul Bellow, *Dangling Man* (New York: Vanguard Press, 1944); *The Victim* (New
York: Vanguard Press, 1947); *The Adventures of Augie March* (New
York: Viking Press, 1953); *Seize the Day* (New York: Viking Press,
1956); *Henderson the Rain King* (New York: Viking Press, 1959);
and *Herzog* (New York: Viking Press, 1964).
4. Saul Bellow, "The Writer and the Audience," *Perspectives USA*,
IX (1954), 102. Cf. the fifth Memorable Fancy in Blake's *The Marriage of Heaven and Hell*, where the Devil says that "Jesus was all
virtue, and acted from impulse, not from rules."
5. Saul Bellow, "The Writer and the Audience," *Perspectives USA*,
IX (1954), 102.
6. Saul Bellow, "Distractions of a Fiction Writer," *The Living
Novel*, ed. Granville Hicks (New York: Macmillan, 1957), pp. 1–20.
For a further consideration of this theme, see James Dean Young,
"Bellow's View of the Heart," *Critique*, VII (1965), 5–17.
7. Saul Bellow, *The Last Analysis* (New York: Viking Press,
1965), p. 118.
8. Frederick J. Hoffman, "The Fool of Experience: Saul Bellow's
Fiction," *Contemporary American Novelists*, ed. Harry T. Moore
(Carbondale, Ill.: Southern Illinois University Press, 1964), pp. 80–
94.
The debate among critics over the relationship in Bellow's stories
of the individual to society enlists new partisans almost daily.
David D. Galloway, "The Absurd Man as Picaro," *The Absurd Hero
in American Fiction* (Austin, Texas: University of Texas Press,
1966), pp. 82–139, sees the Bellow hero as engaged in an unending
quest for an identifiable role in society, forever "faced by the crossroads where 'one path leads to the society, the other away from the
community [p. 110].'" Keith Michael Opdahl, *The Novels of Saul
Bellow* (University Park, Penna.: Pennsylvania State University,
1967), defines this tension as a conflict basically between two opposing kinds of characters: "a man of love who seeks joy within

the limits of his nature and a hard-boiled man of will who would impose his desires upon the world [p. 5]." He argues that the goal of the Bellow hero is "religious transcendence," an immolation of the immature self as a means of achieving loving union with a community. "Bellow insists that his hero stop holding on to himself, but he creates a situation in which the victory of love is a throwing away of the self. He creates protagonists who desperately need community, but portrays a community in which the price of admission is destruction [p. 6]."

For other recent treatments of this theme, see Patrick Morrow, "Threat and Accommodation: The Novels of Saul Bellow," *The Midwest Quarterly*, VIII (1967), 389–411; and Howard M. Harper, Jr., "Saul Bellow—The Heart's Ultimate Need," *Desperate Faith* (Chapel Hill, N.C.: University of North Carolina Press, 1967), pp. 7–64.

And so the dialogue continues, sounding its perilous way.

9. Frederick J. Hoffman, "The Fool of Experience: Saul Bellow's Fiction," *Contemporary American Novelists*, ed. Harry T. Moore (Carbondale, Ill.: Southern Illinois University Press, 1964), p. 80.

10. Marcus Klein, *After Alienation: American Novels in Mid-Century* (Cleveland: World Publishing Company, 1964), p. 30.

11. *Ibid.*, pp. 65, 61.

12. Saul Bellow, "Some Notes on Recent American Fiction," *Encounter*, XXI (1963), 22–29.

13. Marcus Klein, *After Alienation* (Cleveland: World Publishing Company, 1964), p. 57.

14. Cf. Maurice Samuel, "My Friend, the Late Moses Herzog," *Midstream*, XII (1966), 3–25.

15. Cf. Patrick Morrow, "Threat and Accommodation: The Novels of Saul Bellow," *The Midwest Quarterly*, VIII (1967), 409.

16. Saul Bellow, "Some Notes on Recent American Fiction," *Encounter*, XXI (1963), 25.

17. Matthew Arnold, "The Function of Criticism at the Present Time."

18. William Wordsworth, "Tintern Abbey," 1. 91.

19. Tony Tanner, *Saul Bellow* (Edinburgh: Oliver and Boyd, 1965), p. 104.

20. Norman Mailer, *Cannibals and Christians* (New York: The Dial Press, 1966), p. 127.

6/ Leslie A. Fiedler and the Hieroglyphs of Life

America: Ares and Eros

THE STORIES of Salinger and Fiedler are modern commentaries on the old-fashioned notion of romantic love. Salinger envisions love as an indiscriminate embrace of all being. Such an ideal is nonsexual and leads inevitably to denial of the individual. This ironic reversal is succinctly epitomized, although probably unintentionally, by one of the Four Great Vows on which the Glass children (so we learn in *Zooey*) are nurtured: ". . . however inexhaustible the passions are, I vow to extinguish them [p. 104]"—to which noble effort Seymour began to direct his intellectual and spiritual talents (we learn in *Hapworth 16, 1924*) as early as the age of seven. Leslie Fiedler's preoccupation with the sexual infantilism of the American male is too well known to need exposition. Less understood is the profound sense of social and psychological disorder which underlies his conflation of love and death. In *King Lear* disorder within the individual and the family leads to disorder within the state; in Fiedler's novels the disorder within society betrays the primitive sexual energy of the essential man into neurotic dissonance. When he attempts to honor his human birthright of creativity, man finds himself frustrated into fulfilling his cultural heritage for self-destruction. Hence, an irony similar to that found in Salinger's "Upanishads" informs Fiedler's mythographic tracts about the continuum of love and death that cramps the psyche of the American.

With considerable bravura the author of *Love and Death in the American Novel* intertangles the Yin and Yang of existence in his two novels *The Second Stone* and *Back to China*, and the three novelettes collected under the title *The Last Jew in America*.[1] Ares and Eros mingle, we are told [ch. 6], when Clem Stone and the pregnant Hilda Stone (no relation) adulterously meet in embraces that are "half an assault"; their "living tongue[s] played back and forth between their skulls," their kisses "like the touching of skeletons" that annulled momentarily the promise of life in the "boneless bulge in her belly [ch. 1]." Similarly, Baro Finkelstone fornicates with Shizu, always seeing last of all tacked over the bedroom door two stills from the movie *Hiroshima, Mon Amour* of the twisted rubble and burned people of the city behind "her flushed bobbing head" ("Shizu straddling him as she really preferred") "fading as he faded from consciousness in the final explosion of love [ch. 2]."

In this conjugality of love and death, Fiedler sees the hieroglyphic life of the American at strife with the constructs (customs and prejudices) of his culture, which are, ironically, on one level of meaning the expressions of his own deepest feelings. "The white, largely European settlers of America have had," Fiedler contends, "from the earliest times, to work our their personal fates and national destiny in the presence of two alien races."[2] Out of his love-hate relationship with Negro and Indian, the American has fashioned a society that is a parody of his ambivalent rage for racial marriage-murder of self. The ultimate irony is that man's Shavian-like will to love refuses to be a faithful bed partner to the immolative wishes of the society bitch created and civilized from a rib of his own being. Fiedler's two novels are high-spirited explorations of this theme of betrayal.

Rome: Metamorphoses of Stone

The Second Stone considers the racial fixation of the American, with its overtones of self-betrayal, specifically in terms of Jew and Gentile, although conflicts among the Caucasian and Negro delegates to Mark Stone's First International Conference on Love provide a peripheral duet of love-hate. Against a backdrop of Rome, the "cemetery" of Western civilization, Jewish Mark Stone talks endlessly and dispassionately about "Marriage, Adultery, and *Amor Purus*" at the three-day Conference [ch. 1], while his one hundred percent American wife Hilda, thirty-five years old and three-months pregnant—an "aging little girl [ch. 2]" American woman still virginal in mind and spirit [ch. 4], who does not want to be a mother—submits with her body to his Gentile boyhood friend Clem Stone. Hilda's betrayal of her husband reflects not only her rejection of his intellectual position on love but also her intransigent reluctance to acknowledge the union of Jew and Wasp with her marriage and with the fetus in her womb. In hers and Clem's ambivalence toward Mark, Fiedler fictionally represents his belief that "Americans at the moment seem unwilling to surrender a distinction it pains them to maintain." [3]

In Mark Stone's concept of *Amor Purus* is summarized the basic dramatic, rhetorical, and thematic conflicts of the novel. *Amor Purus,* he declares in his opening address to the Conference, is "not *pure* love in the ordinary sense at all; for what the ordinary sense would interpret 'pure' to mean is fleshless. And without flesh, there is no love, no human love, that is to say." The true definition of *Amor Purus*—and here Mark's sensual subtlety equals his metaphysical fastidiousness—is the kiss: ". . . the contact of naked bodies but without final consummation." This Talmudic vision of the kiss as a union of two spirits, he points out with pedantic cheerfulness, is "Andrea Capellanus' *Amor Purus*, but it is also bundling, necking, not unlike the odd sexual experimentation of the Shakers. Not an American invention perhaps (for in the earliest Christian Church, the relations of priests to what were called then the 'Beloved Ones' were surely somewhat similar), but the cultural possession in our time of America, a part of that much traduced American Dream, which is the very opposite of materialist." After indulging in this dazzling display of historical synthesis, he ends in a conflation of the sacred and the profane that elevates the sexual habits of the American adolescent into the *ne plus ultra* of love: ". . . a contact of the flesh fleshly whose end is not reproduction, but which is not, on the other hand, a mere parody of the act of reproduction; a meeting of soul and soul which is not a blasphemous parody of mystical communion: an American *tertium quid* acted out by kids in the rear seats of hot rods [ch. 4]."

Here is the ultimate revolt against the cult of genitalia of our times, as Fiedler in language echoing Mark Stone's speech has argued in his essay "The Alteration of Consciousness."[4] Whether the *reductio ad absurdum* of Mailer's unlimited orgasm or the *coitus reservatus* of Capellanus' *Amor Purus*, the denial of life masquerading as love comes to the same dead end. The implications for the racial problem of love without coition, the contact of bodies "without procreation" and "without the expenditure of seed [*WE*, p. 161]," are equally clear. By means of such an ideal, Mark Stone preaches, man will realize the semblance of assimilation with his fellow beings, while furtively main-

taining the distinctions between races which, as Fiedler
caustically remarks in his essay "Indian or Injun," both
white and colored men find "more and more psychically
important to maintain, as it becomes more and more difficult [and painful] to do so [*WE*, p. 115]."

Fiedler underscores this witty analysis of the psychic
substratum of American culture, with its idolatrous worship of sterility in the name of genitalia, by staging his
"Love Story" against a kaleidoscope of love-death refractions. The cynical sponsor of the Conference on Love is the
sinister-comic Magruder, a millionaire manufacturer of
contraceptives. The Conference is scheduled for May 1, the
date of the Communist International Festival of Labor.
Both events are attended, in part, by the same delegates.
Inevitably, metaphysical ideals are compromised by racial
prejudices and international politics. The delegates—fag-
gots, masturbaters, eunuchs, black zealots, and white op-
portunists—drop their "show of passion for . . . universal
love" and split into partisans of hate and spite. Soon the
destructive tactics of power politics are disrupting the
exalted orations on love. Eventually a screaming May Day
mob stones Mark, the apostle of the Love Conference.
Clem is a novelist hung up on a war novel. His wife, a
writer on motherhood and child raising, has had her Fal-
lopian tubes tied off in Sweden and goes in for symbolic
adultery at parties. Deserted by her (she has returned to
America and her mercantilistic Jewish parents), Clem ardently leads Hilda through the ruins of Rome, from cooling
fountain to dank catacomb, until charnel vault and cathe-
dral chapel meld at last in his mind into one vast "womb-
tomb-jewel" of blinding mosaic motherhood. This motif
climaxes in Clem's recognition that a *Pietà* becomes a Crucifixion when turned ninety degrees. "The artist-son hangs
from a rough-hewn female tree, a tree of stone," he muses,
and "his mother is the cross on which he dies [ch. 6]."

Thus Fiedler pinpoints the psychogenesis of the American's ambivalent longing for the extinction of the melting pot, by merging life with death, love with sterility, and European experience with American innocence.

The urge toward racial purity, which recurrently surfaces as an expression of the obverse side of the American ideal, is no less a fiction, Fiedler observes, than the dream of indiscrimination. Blonde Hilda may let herself be led to Clem's bed, moved as much by his white Anglo-Saxon Protestantism, as she is repulsed by the everlasting invitation of her husband to partake of his symposium on the "meeting of mind and mind in love [ch. 4]." But adultery for the girl-woman and boy-man, who are running from their obligations to others, proves no more satisfactory than Mark Stone's "love feast" of talk [ch. 4]. Each, in his embalmment of the spirit, realizes the social standards of sterilization. Furthermore, the marriage of Americanism and Jewishness, which Fiedler gleefully analyzes in the essay "Jewish-Americans, Go Home!" as the nuptials of a mythical Gentile and a mythical Jew,[5] is a fact of the American milieu of the past twenty years, as the two Stone marriages are meant to symbolize. The intractable sameness of Mark, the apostle of unitive verbal love, and of Clem, the devil's advocate of divisive physical love, is dramatized by Mark's *Amor Purus* speech, which is filtered through Clem's thoughts as he dozes in the audience, until we are uncertain what of the reported speech is part of Mark's actual opening address to the Conference and what is part of Clem's dream. The identity of their last name also underscores their psychic oneness, as does the punning of their first names on the twin halves of *Mark* (Sam *Clemens*) Twain's personality.

Ultimately then the two Stone households are betrayed back into love and togetherness by the life drive whose paradoxical impulse, as Clem recognizes, is (ironically like the American psychic crisis) both creative and destructive, painful and soothing—the love that is self-crucifying and that "lives through crucifixion, lays out in tears the dead destroyer of the self and of the world [ch. 6]." Selma Stone out of erotic yearning begs Clem to come home. Responsive to the productive-immolative urge of conception imbibed from Hilda and from their church-womb-tomb crawling, he burns his manuscript on the war dead and turns toward America, daughter, sterilized wife, and job with his Jewish father-in-law. Mark and Hilda Stone break through their wall of intellectuality and come together emotionally, their I-it relationship shattered by her new role of adulteress and his of cuckold, both crying recklessly at the Conference banquet, Mark beating Hilda on the head and shoulders with a rolled-up copy of *Thou* and stuttering "I-I-I-I," less like the beginning of a sentence than like the wail of "Ai! Ai! Ai! Ai!" of his ancestors [ch. 8].

The pyrotechnics of dialogue and exposition which advance these ambiguities cause us to gasp at the inventiveness and accumulation of surprises. In the end, however, this first novel leaves one disappointed. Like the effect on us of a display of fireworks, in which the bright sparks fade into after images momentarily before blacking out, Fiedler's story always seems to be on the verge of saying something profound about the interrelation of human love and social habit—but the words and form never quite fix the fleeting insights into a permanent impression. Fiedler is too clever, too volatile, for his own good. Take the matter of the novel's prototype. *The Second Stone* parodies *The Marble Faun*—but only gratuitously. Hawthorne's murky, but passionate, exploration of the seamlessness of good and evil through the catacombs of Rome becomes in Fiedler's hands a Yiddish romp through adulterous bedrooms. Presumably Clem as the "Second Stone" shares Donatello's growth in understanding of himself as a poor bare-forked American through his sexual initiation into the mysteries of love and death. Otherwise the climactic meditation of Clem before the Rondinini *Pietà* of Michelangelo—as well as his puns on stone fountains—becomes superfluous. Clem learns through his epiphany that the female principle is hieroglyphic. As a stone survives its form as statue, so a mother survives her son: ". . . a stone forever virgin, though possessed before the son is at the breast or born or sown in the womb." And so man's fear of the violability of blood proves to be imaginary. The ovular gift to man of life in the twin forms of sonhood and fatherhood, on the other hand, is "pain and comforting [ch. 6]"—the legacy of Adam which, Faulkner was fond of telling us, every woman is born with the knowledge of. This cryptic profundity, we are to assume, gives Clem the psychic strength necessary to accept the coming of age in America with all its racial ambiguities. But why blur the issue with Mark Stone who surely as the "First" Stone also partakes of Donatello's fate? Or, for that matter, why blur the issue with all the other stones that splash water, get cast at the cuckold Stone by the adulterer Stone, and in general clog the story? And why the perverse reversal of roles of the light-dark women? Blonde Hilda Stone—an aging American girl-woman—somewhat somnambulistically plays dark Miriam's part of catalyst for the primal instincts of the human heart, while brunette Selma Stone portrays the emancipated Jewish-American mother—full of Beat jargon and the latest views on life—whom light Hilda would surely have become, given the opportunity of another time and place. Antic punster and literary show-off is more visible here than visionary artist.

Fiedler is clearly trying to define the blank facade of contemporary American civilization. He seems to identify the intellectualized effort of our machine society to homogenize life into fixed pop-art shapes as a pretense of our inner life that the national goal of assimilation is being realized, while we merrily continue the old division of Jew and Gentile, Negro and Anglo-Saxon. But this Balkanization of people, he sardonically insists, is forever doomed to betrayal by the aniconic world, by the hieroglyph of motherhood. Too often, however, he substitutes paradoxical action and verbal wit ("soul is a four-letter word," "no more a-mor" [chs. 1, 5]) for the more difficult artistry of plot and profundity of thought. In *The Second Stone*, the dialogue and international theme remain narrative tricks learned at second hand from Hawthorne and Henry James. In *Back to China*, set for the most part on the home ground of Montana, Fiedler moves a great way toward solving the problem of an idiom which honestly renders his distinctly midcentury attitudes and reactions.

China: Philoprogenitive in Perpetuity

The narrative of *Back to China* in its multiple betrayals with a racial origin is a more comprehensive fictional portrayal than *The Second Stone* of Fiedler's mythographic fixation that the national problem, sexual and political, of America's race relations is a projection of the deeper reaches of the individual American's psychic life, of his insistence upon Anglo-Saxon exclusiveness with its sense of loss of paradise, and of his guilty wish for suicidal melting-pot union with the other races. Shizu, Baro Finkelstone's Japanese mistress, betrays her American Indian husband, lies to Baro that she is pregnant, and plays a bewildering game of deception about her origins. Her betrayal, however, is not one-sided. Her husband George married her, a member of an enemy nation and race, out of hatred for a country which has betrayed his race. Indeed white, yellow, and red races *trompent* one another on all levels of human experience. Jew and Gentile play an endless confidence game with each other. One generation deceives the next. The player king is Baro: self-betrayed, betrayer of his wife, of Hiroshige, and of George. Not only does he cuckold George but he compromises his and George's "common flight from consciousness and belonging" with a "stupid dream of a Fellowship" for George [ch. 5].

Baro Finkelstone, the hero of *Back to China*, is a middle-aged idealist of the obsolescent thirties stamp. While serving with the Marines in China at the end of the war he had compulsively submitted to sterilization, performed by a Japanese doctor, as an atonement for the bombing of Hiroshima. America in its use of a radioactive bomb, he contended, had "killed the future." The effect of radiation on the unborn had resulted in destruction of "what is not yet in being, possibility itself [ch. 3]." As an American who had chanted "Bomb Japan" during the Sino-Japanese War, he felt compelled to assume his part in the guilt of Hiroshima by sharing the death of its future. Now twenty years later he is still trying to resolve his ambivalence toward life and death that this radical endorsement implied.

Fiedler skillfully pictures Baro's act of conscience as not only a flight from adult consciousness that is inexorably betrayed by the contrary push toward life but also as a flight from the American social ideal of the racial equality of man. Sterilized, he could enjoy sexual union with his oriental girl friends without sharing the responsibility for blurring the white race with the colored ones. Previous to his sterilization he had run from the orgy his Japanese friend Hiroshige staged for him and fifty American soldiers. He had also run from a more refined girl whom Hiroshige supplied him under the mistaken notion that he was fastidious in matters of sex. Instead he had explored the nirvana of opium. Not until after his vasectomy had he been desirous of pulling an oriental woman into bed with him. In key with the time's obsession with death, Baro thus aligned himself with nonexistence. In answer to the Japanese doctor's warning that a vasectomy is irreversible, he had cried in scorn, "Only death is irreversible, and there can be no death where there has been no life first [ch. 4]." So, in the land of an ancient civilization, aided by one of its modernized citizens, Baro had tried to deny his complicity with the future, by arresting his maturity, thus removing himself from the life stream and fixing himself in time and in childhood innocence. Ultimately China becomes for him a collection of memories of prepuberty girls obscenely associated with sex.

Back home after the war, a professor in a Montana university, he continues to be obsessed in the deeper reaches of his mind with the extinction of the nonwhite races. His being a Jew substantiates Fiedler's belief that "Jewishness is currently taken as a patent of . . . Americanism [*WE*, p. 89]," here ironically reversed to the Jew willy-nilly becoming the beneficiary of the American neuroses. At a peyote-eating service of the Native American Church, for example, as the Indians pray to God Baro tries to chant back to them "some holy words of his own, some prayer in Hebrew," but all he can remember are the first two words of the *Kaddish*, the prayer for the dead [ch. 3]. And he is not entirely innocent of subconscious complicity in the death of George, his Indian student, mentor into the mysteries of opiates, and seemingly at times father figure.

The irony, however, is that circumstances betray him, circumstances that appear uncannily with only the slightest shift in point of view like the demi-urge of the life force. He can evade neither the procreative stream of time nor the assimilative push of the American *Zeitgeist*. No longer able to create life, he spends the next twenty years pursuing the young—Indian, oriental, and occidental alike—as if in the sexual possession of each girl he would reestablish his participation in "the ordinary shared incarnation of youth [ch. 5]" and the aborted dream of America. His experimentation with the younger generation's arsenal of drugs—"peyote, and Marijuana and LSD. . . . Transitone and Dozidol and Lassitan and Harunobuphile . . . nutmeg and morning-glory seeds [ch. 1]"—also reflects his extraordinary urge to create the semblance of virility through hallucinatory intensification of his life.

Time has betrayed his efforts to arrest it in another way as well. Despite his aping of their subcultural jargon and practices, he is out of touch with the new generation. He still functions within a syndrome of values of the thirties and forties, when "Stop the rape of China" and "Bomb Japan" were the slogans—hence, his redemptive membership in the sixties in the "Ban the Bomb" movement. Yet one of his hip students asks him, "Who digs Hiroshima any more? . . . Nobody. *Nobody digs Hiroshima.* That's the message." Baro *cares* about people, ideas, peace. The new generation "couldn't care less." Arrested in time he still finds the smooth little-girl faces and figures of Japanese girls exciting. The new generation goes for the erotic mysteries of the Negro. "Get a tight little spade chick for yourself," his hip student advises, "that's something different, something my generation understands [ch. 4]."

The bitterest irony of all involves his Gentile wife, who has never been told that he was sterilized. Denied motherhood, she has turned frigid, guiltily taken to drink, and become so obsessed with her presumed failure as a woman that, after twenty years, she drunkenly seduces one of Baro's students and conceives. Then she makes love to Baro later that same night for the first time in ages. Remembering only the love-making with Baro she is happily convinced that he is the father of her unborn child and that at last she has not failed him. "Oh, Baro," she exclaims, kissing his temple, the rim of his ear.

> "I've been so upset, so afraid I would stop being a woman without ever having been a mother, without bearing your

child. I've felt so guilty always, so guilty for letting you down. I know it's what stood between us always, getting worse and worse until I just couldn't, you know what I mean, couldn't *let* you any more. What was the point if it was all for nothing, a mockery? I could see the way you looked at me, Baro, when you thought I wasn't watching, the way you despised me for being barren, though you pretended not to want children. Oh, Baro, you never fooled me for a minute with all that business about Hiroshima and the third world war, when all the time your heart was aching to become a father." [ch. 6]

The cosmic irony of the betrayal of his ideals by his wife's urge to conceive, which has led her unwittingly to cuckold him, awes Baro. The most drastic effort he could devise to remove himself from complicity in the continuity and assimilation of the species has not been enough. *"Hiroshige, George,"* he shouts silently to the listening dead—a Japanese and an American Indian, whose status as foster father and as foster son to him marks the degree of his assent to the ideal of brotherhood before he became, not unwillingly, an accessory to their deaths. *"I will be the father of a son,"* he adds, *"who will be the father of sons. George, Hiroshige, we will not any of us utterly die. And yet I am sterile* [ch. 6]." The hieroglyph of motherhood is here more clearly than in *The Second Stone* ascendant over the contrary seductive drag of oblivion.

Betrayed by his culture, which indoctrinated him with the national ideals of racial brotherhood and economic equity in the thirties and then with the national virtues of death and of war in the forties, Baro reacts guiltily. He endorses another surety of his culture—belief that the sexual innocence of childhood corresponds to the primal innocence of *Homo Sapiens*, only to find himself betrayed again. In submitting to sterilization, Baro committed a crime against both history and human nature, as well as against his own faith in the racial ideal of One World; and for twenty years his true self protests this outrage by chasing after the follies of an adolescent generation. Fiedler uses the flashback imaginatively to combine these themes of national destiny and individual will to life. Basically two places and two moments figure in the novel: China 1945, the end of the war when Baro was sterilized; and Montana 1965, the present (of one day's duration) when he learns of his wife's pregnancy. Structurally the story alternates between these Yins and Yangs of national and human aspiration, weaving a series of ironic configurations in time and space that unite into a coherent statement about the inevitability of self-betrayal in human affairs. In China in 1945 Baro, in ambivalent response to national murder, rejects human existence and flees from love. In Montana in 1965 he finds himself instinctively avid for life, pursuing its seductive incarnation in the strong young body of every girl he sees. Fiedler cleverly uses typography to suggest the cramped restricted existence of Baro (intensified contrariwise by his going in for the hallucinatory expansiveness of drugs) since his vasectomy. The Montana scenes in the present are squeezed on the page in narrower blocks of print than the China scenes in the past.

This inventiveness characterizes both Fiedler's virtues and his faults as a writer. The most damning criticism that can be leveled against him is a prolificacy that he still finds irresistible, and which still substitutes for the solid virtues of hard thought and solid plotting. He cannot resist offering, like so many red herring, a bewildering variety of reasons for Baro's vasectomy. Besides his white man's ambivalent feelings of love-hate for the nonwhite races and his desire to atone for Hiroshima, Baro is also portrayed as suffering from arrested development, in search of a mother rather than a wife, and longing to be punished by a hated father. Such facile Freudian clues to what motivates him gratuitously underscore the symbolic action of the narrative that sterile Baro embodies the infantile American dream of primal innocence as well as the correlative myth of racial purity.

The Wild West: Jew, Spade, Wasp

The seeming harshness of the above criticism should not blind us to the fact that Fiedler's control of his subject improves with each book. In his latest effort, the three long stories "The Last Jew in America," "The Last WASP in the World," and "The First Spade in the West," the symbolic action again insists, with increasing fictional conviction, on the mythic submergence in America of the Jew and Negro into the deepest psychic pools of the American mind.

"Deep in the mind of America," Fiedler has written, "there exist side by side a dream and a nightmare . . . of the American frontier, of the West (where the second race is the Indian), or of the South (where the second race is the Negro). In either case, it is the legend of a lost Eden, or, in more secular terms, of a decline from a Golden Age to an Age of Iron [*WE*, p. 113]." Fiedler is at his best picturing this mid-century American "supermarket" culture as it overlays the lingering, blurred carbon of the mythic Far West—now a tinny imitation of a Hollywood copy of the real pulsating fact. The college town of Lewis and Clark which figures in these three stories is a convincingly rendered western city with its tawdry downtown and sudden spaces. Fiedler realizes the peculiar dislocation of the American, "refused . . . any identity except the general one contained in a name," his Americanism which to the rest of the world "is an abusive epithet [*WE*, p. 102]," by planting against the familiar western background the alien figures of Jew, Negro, and Indian who do not belong, yet whose assimilation of American manners etches the dislocation that much more in relief. Fiedler had already experimented in the Montana setting of *Back to China* with a sardonic portrait of civilization as a betrayal of the chthonic life. An instance is his description of a service of the Native American Church that Baro Finkelstone attends in the hope of getting back to the pure religious experience from which he had felt himself excluded. The maize (marked "LITTLE GIANT WHOLE KERNEL"), fruit, and tobacco used in the worship come in tins and "sacred sacks of Bull Durham." The Indians speak a patter combined in equal measures of the hip talk of college fraternity brothers and the brassy slang of sideshow pitchmen. Which makes Baro feel "the whole silly pretense at something primitive and authentic . . . [to be] an *ersatz* of tradition, dreamed in the shadow of TV antennas and rusting disabled cars and tricked out with merchandise snatched from the shelves of some reservation general store [ch. 3]."

"The First Spade in the West" superbly captures the ambiguous blessings of assimilation. Ned York, the town's one Negro businessman (he owns and operates a bar), guards his hard-won reputation for respectability as nervously as any white member of the Junior Chamber of Commerce. With assiduous middle-class cultivation of his image, he expects to be elected by the Kiwanis Club as the Man of the Year, a sign of acceptance by the white community that he figures will impress his son and daughter.

The surrealism of life in the civilized west, the lack of identity coupled with the make-believe of civic and cultural roots that finds its facsimile in the false fronts on the Main Street buildings, is etched in Currier and Ives tints in the description of the funeral of one of Lewis and Clark's leading (that is, richest) citizens. Elmira Gallagher is a childless, widowed harridan who dies on her wedding night, after an all-night drinking bout followed by a sexual binge with the worried and reluctant Ned York, while her middle-aged homosexual gigolo bridegroom lies in sodden drunkenness on the living-room floor. An ex-vaudeville trooper who had found herself stranded in Lewis and Clark years before and had just stayed on and on, she is buried in a garish display of America-First frontier sentimentality from the stage of the decrepit theater in which she once had performed:

> In the first row alone, there was the mayor, three State legislators, the editor of the paper, the presidents of both banks, the dean of the School of Business Administration from up at the college, five clergymen; and the county chairman of the Republican Party, who read a long telegram from the senior United States Senator, ending, ". . . and be assured that I am with you in spirit in this hour of our common loss, firm in the conviction that the pioneering impulse which burned in the hearts of Lewis and Clark and was revived in Mike and Elmira Gallagher still survives in the uncorrupted and incorruptible West." . . . And all the heads in the audience bowed . . . so that Ned could look down at them, row after row; the crew-cut skulls of the jocks from the High School, the bald or graying domes of old Indian fighters and second-hand car dealers and lumber merchants and professors of God knows what, plus the carefully waved heads of the ladies who had walked around in curlers all the day before the funeral to be ready for the occasion. [p. 189]

Here is point of view with comic racial dimensions: the Guard of Honor standing at the four corners of the coffin, made up of "a beatnik from the East, a little sheeny with a shoe-clerk's moustache, a big fat queer who'd struck it rich, and a spade," all "dressed like cowpokes," looking with sly grins at each other down on crew-cut, bald, and permanent-waved heads—proto-American stereotypes tricked out for the profane occasion and fixed like wax-works in devotional attitudes of silent (that is, non-) prayer for the dead [p. 191]. The understated burlesque of Wild West, Main Street, teenagers, and small-town society makes its point with effectiveness. In its arrested modes of conduct this tableau of deluded mid-century America is a

convincing dramatic correlative, with its devastating identification of love with death, sterility with immaculateness,
form with life, to the stone *Pietà* in *The Second Stone*. Like
the "Sioux or Ute or whatever the hell" they are (thus
George alludes to his tribal relatives, scathingly admitting
his loss of racial and cultural identity [ch. 3]) in *Back to
China* who celebrate their love of God with the canned corn
and peaches of a supermarket civilization, the American,
Fiedler seems to say, has fashioned his loves and hates into
the profane masks of a wooden-indian and dime-store my-
thology.

A caustic vision of society's cannibalism, its suicidal
impulse, its radical threat to the psychic energy of the
individual is broached in the fiction of Fiedler. He hints
bleakly that the life of society is an externalization of the
unconscious mind, and society's predilection for self-destruction an expression of the radical contradictions in the
individual. Although his most recent stories reveal a deep-
ening of pessimism, his despair so far has not developed
into full-throated profound outcry. It has invariably stumbled up against his antic wit. Fiedler's bumptious personality will not let him peer very far into the abyss before his
ironic contemporary mood diverts him into cool laughter.
Ultimately he prefers to dismiss what Blake called the
dismal iron circle of history in favor of the cosmic joke
that man's will to procreate inevitably and comically nulli-
fies his propensity to err in the direction of death. In this
respect Fiedler in his exuberant celebration of man's hieroglyphic life is an attractive novelist.

NOTES—CHAPTER 6

1. Leslie Fiedler, *The Second Stone: A Love Story* (New York:
Stein and Day, 1963); *Back to China* (New York: Stein and Day,
1965); and *The Last Jew in America* (New York: Stein and Day,
1966). All quotations are taken from these editions.

2. Leslie Fiedler, "Indian or Injun," *Waiting for the End* (New York: Stein and Day, 1964), p. 114; henceforth referred to as *WE*.

3. *Ibid.*, p. 115. Fiedler is alluding specifically to the relationship of white and colored.

4. Leslie Fiedler, "The Alteration of Consciousness," *Waiting for the End* (New York: Stein and Day, 1964), pp. 155–169.

5. Leslie Fiedler, "Jewish-Americans, Go Home!" *Waiting for the End* (New York: Stein and Day, 1964), pp. 89–103.

7/ Edward Lewis Wallant and Bruce Jay Friedman: the Glory and the Agony of Life

The Polarities of Love

IN *The Pawnbroker*, after Jesus Ortiz has fatally taken the bullet meant for Sol Nazerman, Sol sits hunched against the "abrasive roar" of milling people, "his body becoming worn down under the flood of it, washed down to the one polished stone of grief, of *grief*."

> All his anesthetic numbness left him. He became terrified of the touch of air on the raw wounds. What was this great, agonizing sensitivity and what was it for? Good God, what was all this? *Love?* Could this be *love?* He began to laugh hysterically, and the voices in the store stopped. [ch. 28]

In *Stern*, on the morning that he is to go to a rest home for treatment of an ulcer brought on by anxiety over his failure to avenge a neighbor's insult to his wife, Stern awakes feeling "Down deep at the center of him . . . a small capsule of glee that he was going to the home on this day; if dark and terrible things happened then to his family, he could not be held responsible. How could he prevent them

if he was away in a home?" Later that day, as he is driven
by his wife to the home,

> Stern watched his wife's knees, apart as they worked the
> pedals; he imagined her dropping him off at the home, then
> going immediately to a service station and allowing the at-
> tendant to make love to her while her feet kept working the
> pedals so that she could always say that she had driven all
> the way home without stopping. She pulled into the driveway
> of the Grove Rest Home in the late afternoon and Stern,
> saying goodbye, squeezed her flesh and kissed her through
> her dress, as though by getting in these last touches he could
> somehow ward off the gas station attendant. [pp. 110, 112]

Both Wallant and Friedman concern themselves with the
theme of love; but, as is illustrated by the two selections
just quoted, they are polarities apart in their treatment of
the subject. Wallant's handling of his material is intense
and often oppressive, with the tragic never wholly absent;
Friedman's is irreverent and often indecorous, with the
ludicrous ever present. Wallant has in his manner a touch
of the poet, Friedman of the stand-up comic. Yet these
mannerisms mask quite contrary responses to life. For
Wallant, love leads man to joyous awareness of his being
human; for Friedman, it traps man in isolating cul-de-sacs
of fright. Although both are indefatigable creators of bizarre characters, Wallant's approach to man is essentially
religious, Friedman's psychological. Wallant tenderly cru-
cifies his people so that he can resurrect them, Friedman
ribaldly dresses his so he can expose their parts.

Edward Lewis Wallant

Each of Wallant's novels [1] presents basically the same
protagonist. He is spiritually and emotionally paralytic, a
man anesthetized against the presence of others. Each narrative depicts his painful emergence into life through "the

impenetrable glass that held the heat of people away" (to quote Wallant in an early story [2] foreshadowing the central situation of the novels). In this progression from simple sensation to the full attainment of feeling, each protagonist carries about him some of the uncanny aura of Wordsworth's solitaries as he perilously traverses the ambiguous reaches of his selfhood. Angelo DeMarco in *The Children at the Gate* and Norman Moonbloom in *The Tenants of Moonbloom* are introduced to us as beings as yet unviolated by emotion; Yussel Berman in *The Human Season* and Sol Nazerman in *The Pawnbroker*, as beings desperately insulated from the nightmare of feeling. Unmarked angel (Angelo DeMarco), frozen organism in false maturation (Nor[th]man Moonbloom), vulnerable bare man (Berman), naysayer of men (Nazerman), each is determined to remain, like Angelo, "unassailable within the cool vessel he had made of himself, able to patch the minor cracks of lonely moments, to deflect the encroachment of a girl's laughter or of people's murmured conversations on porches or doorsteps in the summer night [ch. 1]." "Don't think, don't feel. Get through things—it is the only sense," Sol Nazerman advises Tessie who is in agony over the slow death of her father. "Imagine yourself a cow in a fenced place with a million other cows. Don't suffer, don't fear. Soon enough will come the ax. Meanwhile, eat and rest. Don't pay attention, don't cry! [ch. 23]." Alone and unfeeling each pursues this policy in his daily contact with the maimed, the lost, the abandoned—with bleeding, suffering mankind. Angelo visits the wards of a hospital twice daily, methodically taking ice cream orders for a drug store. Moonbloom makes weekly rental collections in four tenement dwellings, dreamily writing fake receipts at each stop. Berman repairs the worn plumbing of ancient buildings, impersonally removing the accumulated muck of time. Nazerman stands all day behind the wire window of his Harlem pawn shop, uttering repetitious aphorisms to his customers.

Love! sexual, spiritual, communal, defines Wallant's answer to the grinding despair of a Sol Nazerman and a Yussel Berman. Hence, Wallant portrays their absence of feeling as identical with dehumanized malformation, imprisonment of the spirit, and death. Sol Nazerman's body is a symbol of his negation of life as much as it is a saturnine tribute to man's inventive cruelty and dark ambivalent urge equally toward creation and destruction. A survivor of Nazi torture chambers, he had been sadistically operated on, bones removed and grafted elsewhere, until every part of him was "wired and patched ingeniously," his body become "a great accumulation of strange severances, of poorly connected cogs and gears and ratchets, off balance, the imbalance overcompensated for, and so balanced again," and his soul full of "dark and littered corners [ch. 18]." To a woman who offers him her love, he responds "in a dry, aching voice": "do not think of becoming intimate with me. . . . You would be guilty of necrophilia—it is obscene to love the dead [ch. 22]." Similarly, Berman lives "a sort of living death, himself something that hovered in a private limbo," during the "solitary weeks" following his wife's death [ch. 8]. He returns from work each night with "the feeling of being physically engaged in some worn piece of machinery. There was a sense of automation, of knowing exactly what each movement would be, one after another, like a movie he had sat through innumerable times. There was no pleasure in it, only a sort of bleak ease, for it demanded nothing from him [ch. 12]." Stonily he refuses the aged and the afflicted who answer his advertisement of a furnished room for rent; and pitilessly he ejects a roomer, after a few days, because he cannot "stand to live with someone as miserable as me [ch. 9]."

Retention of the child's outlook into manhood is equally repugnant to Wallant. He coolly (in the case of Moonbloom comically) condemns this naïveté as emotional retardation. Contrary to Salinger's sentimental vision of childhood innocence as the only virtuous, viable response to the world, Wallant equates childhood with the daylong "sleep-walking" of Angelo DeMarco and Norman Moonbloom. Sammy, the Jewish hospital orderly who takes Angelo under his wing, always addresses him as *Bubi;* and the conjunction of this word of endearment for a boy with the sound of *boob* surely reflects Wallant's complex point of view. And Moonbloom, we are told repeatedly, lives a muffled existence within the placenta-like covering of his skin, which is likened to an eggshell and to the blanket his grandmother wrapped him in as a child. "Like me, you are essentially humorless and unalive," Moonbloom is told by one of his tenants [ch. 4]. Wallant underscores Moonbloom's desuetude by describing that "sleepwalker's" non-reaction to one of his tenants: "He saw her pale full neck as she rested her head on the back of the couch-bed, her white-sweatered breasts, heavy in their rise and fall. Slowly, passively, he turned over and over, used to his own pulsing silence. From where he was, she was just weight and warmth [ch. 4]." We are introduced to him as he sits in a rented cubicle of a realtor's office, telephone to his ear, reducing his brother's conversation to "rannana rannana," while "One of the many O's" from the sign on the window "made a daguerreotype of his blinded face." When he stands up the *O* makes a "target of his chest," that is, his heart [ch. 1]. With superb shorthand, Wallant is telling us that Moonbloom is unfractured by experience, still a cipher, a nullity.

Each of Wallant's protagonists travels the route from "nonexistence" to "being" through a feverish illness in which he confronts his past (least developed in the case of

Angelo's illness in *The Children at the Gate*) and is forced
to acknowledge what Jonathan Baumbach has called "the
fact of having been alive."[3] Indications of their liberated
senses are the acute impressions on Moonbloom's eyes
when he recovers from his fever, the release of Berman's frozen emotions in "simple, childlike weeping [ch.
16]," and the laughter in exultation over the deaths of their
own self-containments of Angelo and Nazerman after the
deaths of Sammy and Jesus Ortiz. Each then confirms his
human guise through his involvement with the people
around him. Moonbloom with his own hands repairs the
apartments of his tenants. Angelo assumes the discipleship
of life granted him by Sammy's self-sacrifice, gives Sammy's insurance money to his mother, and begins his human
pilgrimage in the world. Nazerman finds himself unable to
deal objectively, calculatingly, with his customers and begins to purchase their articles for more money than they
are worth. And Berman renews his awareness of people in a
daylong ramble through the city, until returning home in
the evening he witnesses a street fight, reluctantly agrees to
testify at police court, and observes wonderingly that he as
well as all the other bystanders are daily *"witnesses . . . To
themselves* [ch. 17]." Both he and Nazerman subsequently
reaffirm their past relationships to others.

As Wallant presents it, acceptance of more than the
sensation of existence is a painful process for each of
these men. One can easily characterize their shrinking from
life as modern instances of the fear of assuming existential
responsibility for one's actions. Nazerman dreads the event
of the squeaking machinery of his body and mind coming
undone and his being "forced to live in the chaos [ch. 18]"
of uncircumscribed acts, daily testaments to his existence.
Yet in Angelo and Moonbloom, Wallant presents men less
in flight from life than as yet unawakened to it. Wallant
will not allow himself—or man—either the easy solution of

angry despair that was Nathanael West's or of dissociation that is the pop artist's. To exist is to be smudged. We cannot avoid the dirt of life, no matter how hermetically we might be sealed off from it. This surely is the significance of the drunkard's vomit splashing on Moonbloom's trousers as he walks somnambulistically through the city [ch. 4]. In spite of Nazerman's determination to get through his daily rounds without involvement in other people's affairs, he is unable to eliminate the need for thought and feeling. Circumstances force him into poignant self-questioning. In a delirium of nervous exhaustion brought on by the approaching anniversary of his wife's sexual humiliation and death in a Nazi camp, he protests his gangster employer's involvement in white slavery, even standing up to the gangster's threat of death. Afterward he ponders, "So it isn't death that I am afraid of," and asks, "Then what is it that makes me tremble and ache? Why does my breast distend and threaten to burst? [ch. 26]." What afflicts Nazerman are the growing pains within himself of the Tolstoian ideal (as defined in *My Confession*) of grieving, loving identification with all mankind. If we would be human and whole, Wallant insists, we have no alternative to this redemptive anguish.

The exhilaration that overwhelms them, and which is occasionally communicable to others, more than compensates for the pain that Wallant's solitaries find they have substituted for the earlier vague sense of their having missed something in their lives. In the conclusion of *The Tenants of Moonbloom*, Norman, Gaylord (the Negro superintendent of the building), and Bodien (the plumber) in uproarious laughter remove the hideous bulge in the bathroom wall that has been tyrannizing Basellecci. Drunk not only on Basellecci's liquor but also on Moonbloom's exaltation, which he has been imbibing in equal draughts, Gaylord acting as a vise grips "the pipe with both hands from behind the plumber, so that it appeared he was embracing him" and roars:

> "That Norman Moonbloom got a idea he can *do* something to the world. He thinks he's a giant superman. He's so crazy he makes me crazy too, makes me think I'm building the pyramids in old Pharaoh country, or maybe the friggen Yewnited Nations. You hooked us, Norman, you got us mainlinin' the same fix you been taking. Hah, Basellecci, Bodien, ain't we all drunk on the same stuff he been drinking? You lousy rat, Moonbloom, this man here is dying, Bodien here is a disbarred plumber without no future who won't have another plumbing job after you go. And me, me, I'm just a poor shine with nothing to look forward to except sweeping up other people's shit till I'm too weak and old to do even that. So how come, how come I'm happy as a friggen lark? You got me drunk, Moonbloom; you got me so drunk I'll *never* sober up." [ch. 26]

A few hours later Norman sits in his office, waiting for his brother to come and fire him for spending too much money on the upkeep of the apartments. He notices that the last letter of his name painted on the window, which had been slowly flaking off, "had now been totally scraped away. Somehow it freed the word, opened it up so that the *o's* bubbled out endlessly, carried the crooning sound of the name out to an infinite note of ache and joy. It thrilled him with his own endlessness, and, almost laughing, he followed its course. Moonbloooo-ooo [ch. 26]." In the muck and stench of death, in contact with the soiled, the weary, the sick, and only there, where further contact with dirt can only cleanse, grows and blossoms into light the rapture of existence. So Wallant says about Moonbloom caked with the "wet vomit of brown thick liquid [ch. 26]" from Basellecci's bathroom wall as he cleans up the dirt of his last repair job, and implies about Berman as he struggles in basements and attics amidst bathroom oozings and rat droppings at his plumbing trade, and about Angelo as he brings ice cream and cold drinks to the hospital sick lying amidst "the odors of ether and feces and sweat [ch. 2]," and about Nazerman as he trades old dreams for new with the flotsam and wreckage of humanity that files into his shop. "Dreams and flesh, imaginings and real smells and feelings. Love too," Berman muses as he looks around him at people on the street. "And look at them all, full of those dreams, the dreams mixed with the smell of them, the smell and sound and sight of the whole staggering summer night [ch. 17]." Each, in the agonizing discovery of his ineluctable humanity, performs for us symbolically the same divine service.

Wallant's language in depicting this perilous exploration of the terrain of one's identity is designedly sacramental without being formally religious. Shortly before he discloses ("betrayed" is the word Wallant uses) to the Sisters running the hospital that Sammy has been lovingly giving opiates to his patients to ease their pain, Angelo accepts cookies and grape juice from Sammy during their usual late evening talk. Sitting significantly in a hospital wheelchair, Angelo eats and drinks, his body and brain dazed by the communion with Sammy, feeling "as though something had been removed from him and something else put in its place [ch. 11]." Nazerman, the Everyman of this century, is pointedly identified with Christ, "the figure of a heavy man, awkwardly transfixed on a cross, a man with blue cryptic numbers on his arm [ch. 25]." In this union of man with Christ, in whose essential humanity all beings participate, Wallant reiterates his fundamentally spiritual view of human growth. Contemporary man's life, as he portrays it, is in effect a mystic participation in crucifixion and resurrection. And Moonbloom, carrying the rubbish of the bathroom wall downstairs to the basement, raves drunkenly, "There's a Trinity—Love, Courage, and Delusion, I mean

*Ill*usion"—words whose momentary confusion of prefixes and whose echo of (but divergence from) Faith, Hope, and Charity underscore Wallant's reverent but unsentimental conception of life. Love dilates each one's being into ecstatic union with the world. A "small, dusty man," Moonbloom felt himself "huge, united with all" his tenants [ch. 26].

Wallant wrote, in a sense, always the same story. The protagonists of his three published short stories [4] exhibit similar suspended metabolisms. They differ from the heroes of the novels only in their not experiencing a resurrection of sensibility. In this respect the title and action of "When Ben Awakened" are ironic.

Wallant needed, however, more space than the short story gave him in which to develop the drama of the dead resurrected, the sleeping awakened, the unborn born. He very early turned to the novel, whose large canvas allowed him a conceptual frame in which isolated protagonist is opposed to teeming humanity. This antithesis of the one and the many brilliantly poses the human situation and the grounds inherent in it for a reconciliation of the contraries. The microcosm of tenement dwellers, hospital patients, and pawn customers becomes the norm toward which Angelo and Norman, Berman and Nazerman, each works his hazardous way. Through the economy of this paradigm Wallant explores anew the crux of the American experience. It is not accidental that Moonbloom's tenements house a cross section of mankind—Jew, Chinese, Spaniard, Italian, German, Negro, Anglo-Saxon; nor that each apartment is a physical correlative to the essential confinement of its inhabitants, who move within the isolation of their own emotional worlds, only occasionally touched by the pain of another.

Wallant offers no panacea for this human dilemma. He portrays man's nature as inextricably linked to the fact of being an animal (pervasive bestial imagery underscores this assumption). He sees the mire in which man breathes and moves as the necessary condition of his spiritual illumination. Like the Keats of "Ode on Melancholy" Wallant accepts the continuum of sorrow and joy (Moonbloom never laughs without also feeling pain); all his characters labor under some kind of emotional stress that is the glorious price they pay for being human. Hence, the Wallant protagonist moves from the isolation of occasional physical contact with others to the proximity of emotional reaction to them; but he does not change their fate nor unite his with theirs, other than that in his emotional reaction to them he now shares in their common fate of being human. Moonbloom's disinfection of Karloff's room does not prevent that centenarian's death. His repair of Basellecci's wall does not cure that person of his cancer. Katz still attempts suicide; Paxton still departs for happier places; the Lublins continue to live with the horror of their uncle, the Jacobys with the anxiety of uncertain lovers. In figuring the cost of repairing the apartments, Norman sees himself as "a mariner, adrift in a night without stars" and longing for a sextant to chart "his personal latitude and longitude [ch. 16]." But the voyage of discovery into himself discloses to Norman simply that his manhood links him unalterably to other men, a knowledge that offers at once a precise and a vague sextant for human affairs.

Besides a spatial arrangement of the insulated one and the afflicted many, Wallant organizes his stories temporally, juxtaposing the numbed present to a vital past. It is as if his hero must become aware of time, of the slow ticking of destruction within his own body, before he can acknowledge his life. Moonbloom dreams during his illness of scenes in his childhood and subsequently, when well, even revisits his hometown; Sammy tells outrageous tales of his past, which disturb the mute equanimity of Angelo; and both *The Pawnbroker* and *The Human Season* alternate scenes in the present with ones from the past. This confrontation of the circumstances of the past becomes confirmatory of life in the present.

For Wallant, suffering has lost the traditional sacramental meaning that it has for the pious Chasid Moshe Gabriel in Isaac Bashevis Singer's novel *The Family Moskat*. In this novel, Gabriel tells his daughter Lottie, who insists that she will not have children because mankind suffers so much, that "All good comes only through suffering [pt. VIII, ch. 5]." Yet Wallant will not, like Lottie, deny life simply because pain is a fundamental, senseless condition of life. Instead, he insists upon his hero's acceptance of this harsh truth as the sign of his attainment of maturity. "It's so lonely," Sammy warns Angelo in *The Children at the Gate* (of life?), "not to suffer [ch. 11]." And the thought occurs to Norman Moonbloom after making love for the first time at thirty-three that "joy resembled mourning [ch. 16]."

Like the Romantic poem of exploration, as opposed to the Neoclassical poem of representation, each novel probes the effect on a cauterized sensibility of the despairing cries for help of suffering mankind. Each novel concludes with a beautiful return to a scene similar to that which opened it, with this difference: the isolated sensibility has progressed from angry or indifferent immunity from life to fervent acceptance of it. At the beginning of *The Pawnbroker*, Nazerman trudges stony-eyed up from the river toward his shop, stolidly unresponsive to morning greetings or to the beautiful summer day. In the conclusion, as he leaves the pawnshop and walks toward the river, his eyes are filled with tears for Jesus Ortiz' death. Thus, blinded by mourning, he at last makes contact with people, bumping into them, feeling them and "their peculiar odors of sweat and breath, of dirt and hair, the smell of the great mortal decay that was living because it was dying." He clears his eyes and sees "the ineffable marvel of their eyes and skins [ch. 28]." In this moving conclusion, reminiscent of the ending of Bellow's *Seize the Day*, Nazerman cries with all men for the dead, but also for himself and the living. Caught now in the flow of humanity he makes his way to the subway "to take the long, underground journey to Tessie's house, to help her mourn [ch. 28]" the death of her father, which is also for him to resume his life. And so essentially begin and end *The Human Season*, *The Children at the Gate*, and *The Tenants of Moonbloom*.

These are *Bildungsroman* of a special sort. Wallant deals with the coming of age, not in years, not in conventional education and acceptance of society's manners and rules, but in sensibility. It is the terrors of growth and change in the human heart (as the organic metaphor in the title of *The Human Season* suggests) that are all-important to him. Man is born to die, and lives to love, partaking equally of anguish and happiness. In Nathanael West's *The Dream Life of Balso Snell*, Balso quotes an epigram of C. M. Doughty that is applicable to Wallant's view of man: "The semites are like to a man sitting in a cloaca to the eyes, and whose brows touch heaven [ch. 1]." Less in *The Human Season*, but with fervor in the three novels that followed it, Wallant presents the maturation of the spirit in acceptance of this fact, as the key to survival in this world. Wallant's was a religious temperament, which dealt with this secular and terrible century in lyrical terms. With an unmediated imagination that miraculously retained its exaltation, his was a tragic vision, which expressed an unequivocal reverence for life. With almost terrifying tenderness he was able to sit tearfully mired in the mud of human experience and watch with loving joy the stars above. Through his premature death in 1962, America lost a moving and promising novelist.

Bruce Jay Friedman

The irony of the titles *Stern* and *A Mother's Kisses* [5] underscores the paradox at the center of Friedman's hilarious look at life. With a name that mocks him, Stern walks in a fog of fantasied ambushes. Meg and her seventeen-year-old son Joseph waltz in manacled circles at the end of an umbilical tether, giving and receiving wide gurgling kisses that feel to Joseph "as though a large, freshly exposed, open-meloned internal organ had washed against his face [p. 181]." In both books outrageous banter and exaggerated actions hint at the mysterious yearning that goads us into word and deed. With gaiety of manner and drollery of language that hides not too convincingly his despair of heart and skepticism of mind, Friedman defines for us the unspoken horror of family antagonisms and the pretzel-like entanglements of human relationships.

In this world of laughter qua betrayal love is the chief culprit, a pretty cupid discovered to be a dirty-mouthed urchin, whose unfulfilled promises strew the wake of his pollinating progress from human to human. So Joseph and Stern and the other lost, misguided figures in Friedman's books learn to their constant bewilderment. At summer camp, the sexual wonders of a girl's body are approached by Joseph "as though she were a wonderful store; he had four minutes to take anything he wanted before the owner came back from dinner [p. 54]." But the girl is a pathetic mental case who disconcertingly reminds him "of a girl in his neighborhood who was always going off summers to have things done to her head, later to appear on the street tightly wedged between her parents, smiling sweetly." Consequently, her reactions are frequently irrelevant. Her passion belittles as often as it flatters Joseph. When she kisses him her body shudders with the tremor of "a strange, malarial-type reaction that might have come on with equal force had he been a mosquito." At an inopportune moment of necking, she cranes her neck and lets loose with a "Nawwrrr" that sounds like "a sudden plumbing defect in a far-off house at midnight [pp. 44, 46]." The "defective-plumbing sound" dampens his ardor. He leaves off further glorious exploration, "feeling somehow that the store owner had returned, trapping him among the high-priced German binoculars [p. 55]." Joseph's other amorous hopes end in equally truncated disillusionment or frustrated flirtation. He gets up nerve to dance with "a girl whose sweeps and bobbing dips" were the talk of the canteen dance floor and whose "Lindy-hop-hardened" behind he had always wanted to touch [p. 184]. But he knows only three breaks and has to lead her off the dance floor in disgrace after the third repeat of them. With an overcoated gang of boys he bathes a girl, taking his turn at scrubbing her back and sentimentally half falling in love with her in the process, until "a little relieved to find her lethargic of speech, killing her off slightly as a romantic possibility [p. 187]."

For Joseph, only familial kisses remain constant, ambiguously comforting, always available—but somehow never wholly satisfactory. Here love primps with lascivious leer and enticing wink, garlanded with incestuous taboos, that leave him faint with guilt. From his bed in the dinette he lies awake for hours so that he can glimpse his sister undressing in the foyer after coming home from a date. (She sleeps in the living room of the three-room apartment in a bed that turns into a bookcase with three shelves of Balzac during the day.) He keeps a breath-taking tabulation of all the times he has seen her nude or "coiled and moist in her slip." He has a recurring dream in which

she settled comfortably in his bed and allowed him to explore her body, her face sweet, patient, neutral. He loved the dream, wishing he could arrange to have it run on schedule.

Sometimes, late at night, in lieu of an undressing, she would come and stand alongside his bed, eating some cookies, stooping to touch his hair. He had a hanging, half-awake shred of a memory involving cold, wet, milky, low and lassoing half-mad kisses in the darkness. [p. 143]

The same sexual fantasies oppress him in his relationship with his mother. Besides also catching an occasional glimpse of her undressing, he remembers a time when, "Massive-breasted in a white brassiere," she "had done a great deal of voluptuous midday lying around in the living room, asking him to get her things [p. 139]," and remembers other times when he had crawled into her warm, odorous bed, never sure whether he really wanted to be there under the covers with her [p. 223]. Meg contributes to his bewilderment by talking of sex in front of him with libidinous innuendoes and by kissing him on the ear in the same manner as the French girl at summer camp had while they danced. When Meg accompanies him to college to see that he finds a place to live, she wangles them a room in a crowded hotel by passing themselves off as lovers who have "this one night together" because tomorrow she has to get back to her old man so he will not suspect anything [p. 207]. And like a jealous lover Joseph fends off marauding males that Meg is forever attracting; in turn she sends the police in search of him when he stays out on a date too late. "I'll be your social life [p. 269]," she raucously informs him. All this maternal sexuality, of a vaguely disturbing variety, leaves Joseph frustrated, rebellious, uncharitable. If he spontaneously kisses her and puts his head on her shoulder, "taking a good smell of her sweater," he feels nice in the enclosure, but then he detects "a mysterious cry starting up from the bottom of him" and he withdraws [p. 86]. He takes Meg to the movies, where all around them couples are necking. "Would you hold your mother's hand?" she asks him. "I would," he answers, "but what's the point? [p. 230]."

As Friedman defines it, love acts less as release into full emotional life than as psychological confinement without parole. Not joyous union but bitter-sweet separation is the keynote of the human love portrayed in Friedman's novels. The ending of *A Mother's Kisses* poignantly dramatizes this irony. For weeks Meg has been scheming not too subtly to wean Joseph away from college and back home, while he has been trying halfheartedly to convince her that she should return alone. He finally wins out. As he sees her to her train seat, suddenly Joseph wants her to "Stay another few days." But he kisses her hair in bidding her goodbye and returns to the platform. Then, involuntarily, he begins to leap on and then off the first step of the passenger car,

> repeating this action several times in what might have been a new leg exercise for soldiers in transfer. He had to stop when the train began to move, and then he trotted alongside it until he came to the end of the platform. Stopping there, he began to holler things after his mother, first softly, then at the top of his lungs, anything he wanted to: "What was the rush?" and "You're not great at all."
> "I never enjoyed one second with you," he shouted, and kept on, fairly much in the same manner, until the shriek of the engine no longer covered his words. [pp. 285–286]

Even more than *A Mother's Kisses* the symbolic action of *Stern* brilliantly dramatizes Friedman's acrid view that love's bitterly ironic gifts to man are estrangement and anxiety. Driven by sexual desire to marry his wife, he submits knowing "he was bound to her for a hundred years." His marital experience "together with her" in their new home is "as though a small, cold jail cell of steel had dropped out of the sky, encircling" him, "surrounding his movement [p. 42]." The house is purchased by Stern with a loving desire to move his family out of the ghetto and into the country, even though this means for him an endless pilgrimage daily into the city. Nothing, however, works out right. The act removes him from the protective friendships of his old urban Jewish neighborhood to a Gentile community. There his little boy, without playmates, stands day-long "sucking a blanket on a barren lawn [p. 110]." His wife is insulted, knocked down, and called a kike. Obsessed with the need to avenge her, Stern's love for his family curdles into erotic anxiety and finally into an ulcer—a mush-rooming "pain flower [pp. 74, 135]" in his gut. He appeals to friends for comfort, but they are insulated from outside cries of help by the deafening roar of their own pain. His Negro artist friend Battleby reacts incredulously, as if to say, "you don't understand. The conversation is about me. I talk about things that have happened to me, and I don't get into other things." When Stern insists on airing his hurt and involving his friend as a member of another minority group, Battleby finally offers him the lesson that Wallant's characters are so painfully unlearning: ". . . you have got to abstract yourself so that you present a faceless picture to society [pp. 96–97]." Only when Stern deserts his family for five weeks in a rest home is the great sexual "flower" of his ulcer replaced by "a thin, crawling brocade of tender-ness that seemed to lay wet on the front of his body [p. 134]."

When it is not producing cancerous growths, love is shown as less a communion of two souls than a thing of sexual mechanics, endlessly disappointing. Before depart-ing for the rest home, Stern makes love to his wife "as though to nail her down, to stake a claim in her during his absence, to mark her, change her in some way."

> She watched him like a great-eyed fourth-grade girl, but then her eyes closed, her skin became cold, and she clung to him with a nervous, clattering whimper, doing a private, rising-up kind of thing. He went at her with a frenzy, as though by the sheer force of his connection he could do something to her that would keep her quiet and safe and chaste for two weeks,

but when he fell to the side he saw with panic that she was unchanged, unmarked, her skin still cold and unrelieved. [pp. 110–111]

The surrealism of the sexual experience is wonderfully depicted in an incident that occurs to Stern while he is in the rest home. With two other young inmates, one recovering from "bad blood [p. 123]" and the other from a leg amputation, he keeps a tryst with a Puerto Rican girl friend of theirs. She leads them to her room "down a long corridor with lined-up rows of hair-drying machines [p. 150]." While the two youths play at sitting under the hair-dryers, Stern and the girl, who speaks like a Gilbert and Sullivan heroine, make love in her room. "Sweet riddance," she says of the boys. "Now, my knighted author, will you be with me on the highest of all levels? . . . explore forbidden avenues with deponent thine. . . . Then thrill my secret fibers. . . . We are pages in a book of sonnets." Stern in his frenzy fails, however, and "after a few seconds she rose and said, a little irritatedly, 'Oh you thrilled me all right. You really thrilled me.' " In the incongruity between the girl's operatic vaporings and her unabashed lust (contraceptive ready at hand), the sordid setting, and Stern's failure, Friedman devastatingly burlesques romantic notions of love and sex. In a *Walpurgisnacht* aftermath, Stern and the two "tattered, broken boys" opt for the solidarity of friendship over the dissociations of sex; they transform the Puerto Rican girl into a jack-in-the-box, making her straddle a broomstick on which she is jiggled up and down, while she tries to tell Stern of a book she plans to write "on the sweetness and bile" of her life [pp. 152–156].

The faceless masses—automatized, crippled, gross, and bizarre—people Friedman's two novels, providing us with a yardstick of the 1960's, not unlike the urban horrors depicted in the crowded canvasses of Hogarth and Rowlandson and the novels of Dickens. The daily routine of Joseph's father limns with a few skillful strokes the subterranean life of the many. On his way to work he proudly informs Joseph that he always stops at the same corner to buy his morning paper. In the subway car, he adds, "I usually stand at this end and hold on to a strap." Returning home at night, he remarks with self-satisfaction, "Now is when I read my paper [pp. 14–15]." With such a routine existence people easily lose their personality and become things, as Dickens has shown powerfully in *Great Expectations*—and as Friedman with some of the same power shows in *Stern* and *A Mother's Kisses*. They may work mindlessly for years, like Stern's father at cutting shoulder pads, or like Joseph's father at couch-making; then suddenly they lie on their backs on a plank, as did Joseph's father, for two years bathrobed and unshaven. Or, like Stern's closest neighbor in the country, an ancient man with a thin chest, they sit vegetating all day in the sun on a folding chair until they become a dehumanized part of the landscape. They have "a garbage problem," like his neighbor's wife, who is "always carrying a bagful out to a wire basket in front of her house to burn it [p. 31]." They have orgasms solitarily and at assembly-line regularity, like the French girl who dances with Joseph at summer camp, uttering "a series of hopeless little noises, as though valuables of hers were being dropped from a speeding train." But the breathless release which the French girl is so ecstatic over is meaningless, because, as she laments, "The only trouble is I'm off again [p. 32]." They count out the days of their old age "wearing truss-like old-man belts and gadgets [p. 39]" and interrupt the love-making of their roomers, "elasticized old-man gadgets dangling [p. 41]." Such had been one of Stern's experiences with his future wife during their college days. They enter rest homes, half-men suffering from degrees of decapitation, tired blood, and softening of the bones, to be draped over banisters "like a blanket [p. 121]" or propped against walls, down which they forever slowly slide. Appropriately ruling over this Bartholomew Fair at the rest home Stern attends is a powerful Negro orderly on steel crutches, who walks complicatedly in a clatter of "clamps and gears turning, leg sections rasping and grinding [p. 116]," forever shifting, arranging, tugging, and yanking at elaborate mechanisms.

A Mother's Kisses defines the frustrated love of Joseph and Meg specifically in terms of the Oedipal complex, while *Stern* defines the cowardly love of its hero in terms of anti-Semitism. Actually, Friedman casts a wider net than these limited themes require. He scrutinizes some of our treasured sexual assumptions, and with the art of the caricaturist focuses the blurred outlines of what for us has lamentably become humdrum. Take, for example, Joseph's adolescent tendency to conceive of romance in terms of cinema clichés. The French girl at summer camp is automatically metamorphosed by his daydreams into the celluloid world of a Hollywood movie, her voice the sounds "coming from a small French music box, in the guest room of a château in Nancy [p. 31]." But Friedman does not let us—or Joseph—forget the nether side of love. Joseph next meets the Viennese girl whose kisses sound like plumbing defects. She is a frightening reminder that the anatomical accidents of oral and anal orifices, of the mystery of creation and the excrescence of death, are profoundly linked. The despairing inferences of Friedman's portrait of human love is reminiscent of the skeptical idealism and blasted hopes of Byron. Shorn of its platonic and romantic trappings, love reduces to a physical appetite, at times bewildering in its emotional confusion of sexual desire with maternal security and at times frightening in its voracious meld with the other psychic hungers of cruelty, hatred, envy, dread. If human love is betrayed in *Don Juan* by the pretensions of society, it is isolated and alienated in *Stern* and *A Mother's Kisses* by the psychological sports in man. Born with a faulty emotional apparatus that is blindly optimistic, man's neuralgia-prone efforts at love perennially re-enact his banishment from paradise.

The Polarities of Love: Ut Poesis

The worlds of Wallant and Friedman are complementary. Together they comprise a large vision of the glory and the agony that is the human experience of love. Both see man torn by the fury of his existence. Wallant, however, expresses tragic faith in the redemptive processes of love. Not to feel emotive kinship with humankind is to be divorced from time and self-awareness, buried (or unborn) in the truncated angularities of one's own body, while to love with uncalculating immolation of self is to know the extra dimension of being that transforms individuals into communicants of shared pain and joy. Friedman acknowledges only the farce of man's defective pursuit of love, a hopeless chase after the other half of his divided identity as much as after the externalized image of his desire, which leaves him breathless and frightened with a catch he no longer wants.

In structure and language their novels exhibit the coherence of these unified views of life. Wallant's skepticism, his humanistic *Je ne sais pas*, comprehends a meaningfulness in the events of human lives; and the carefully conceived strategy of his novels is meant to validate this faith. Blake wrote in *The Marriage of Heaven and Hell* that "Eternity is in love with the productions of time" but that "Without Contraries is no progression." Through the hallucinations of his past life that intrude their vital facts upon his blank present, and through the synchronized interaction of his soul sensitized by illness with the emotional reality of those around him who pray and sweat, dream and fornicate, laugh and weep, the Wallant protagonist progresses with Blakean inexorability toward rebirth as a sentient being. The miracle of this resurrection is movingly documented in prose that weeps for the Babylonian captivity of us all, while singing of the spiritual joy at the heart of existence. Listen to the conclusion of *The Children at the Gate*, which describes Angelo's departure from home and entrance into life at last:

> He began to walk toward the bus station.
> Suddenly he seemed to hear the dim burble of children's laughter coming from the pavilion, behind the main building where he couldn't see it, and in that distant, cascading sound, carried like a chip on a torrent, he thought he heard the word *boychik*. And a blade twitched into his heart, beginning that slow, massive bleeding he would never be able to stop, no matter what else he might accomplish. He was surprised and puzzled as he walked with that mortal wound in him, for it occurred to him that, although the wound would be the death of him, it would be the life of him too. [ch. 17]

The Friedman novel has no apparent strategy of plot. Its action does not progress, it swirls and eddies. At the end as in the beginning, Stern fears the kike man. Not Joseph's getting into college, but his continuing emotional entanglement with his mother is the theme of *A Mother's Kisses*, and this remains unresolved to the conclusion. This downplay of narrative design reflects Friedman's belief, despite his commitment to psychological materialism, that a profound irrationality obtains in human affairs, that the line between fantasy and reality, thought and action, impression and object, is forever wavering and blurring. Events ultimately are motiveless. That they happen, not why, inevitably then becomes central. Hence Friedman concentrates on the rich texture of surface details, with its emphasis on the tactics of incident and caricature. He is a Jewish Dickens tipped into impudent acceptance of the illogical. And the merry gifts of his prose stretch our sensibilities to the same awareness. Here is a rendering of Joseph's first day of college:

A young woman with spreading hips and great sopping rims around the armpit areas of her blouse came in then and headed for the front of the room. She turned out to be the teacher and Joseph, who had taken an aisle seat in the back row, was ashamed he had inhaled as she passed by. When the room was filled, she said, "I'm Miss Greco. To sum up all we know about Elizabethan customs and everyday practices, our New York fellow in the back. All stand at your seats while answering in class."

"Am I supposed to know that already?" Joseph asked, getting to his feet. "Are we supposed to come in here with that under our belts? They were superstitious."

"Jesus," said the dwarflike boy in the front row, slapping his great head in disgust and stamping his feet.

"Bravissimo," said the teacher, and Joseph was relieved to hear her go on as though his one-liner had given the class a leg up on the whole Elizabethan picture. She called then upon a muscular fellow in the rear who used the word "dichotomy" several times in his answer and kept kissing his wrist to make points now and then about Elizabethan sensitivity. At the end of his talk, the teacher kissed her own wrists to let him know he had gotten across to her. A middle-aged man who had taken down every word spoken thus far and seemed to have filled up several notebooks asked, "Are we all supposed to kiss our wrists while answering?" He turned out to be a Navy Commander on extended leave from submarine duty to take the course in pastoral literature. The classroom had been occupied one hour previously by home economics students; Joseph noticed that the desks converted into sinks and miniature electric ranges. There were some brownie crumbs left over on his seat from the last group and he found himself nibbling on them nervously in the hope he would not be called on again. There were four girls sitting in his row; midway through the lecture, he looked over to see a heavily ribbed, familiar-looking sweater heading his way, being passed along from girl to girl. "Hold it, class," said the teacher. Joseph turned to see his mother near the door. "I'm terribly sorry," she said. "I wouldn't have interrupted for the world. But he ran outside without anything on and you could die from the weather."

"All set?" asked the teacher, and when the sweater arrived at Joseph's desk, he held it aloft, saying, "I've got it now."

"He'll kill me for this," said Joseph's mother, turning to leave, "but what can I do? I'm one of those crazy mothers." [pp. 224–225]

Here are the polarities of sanity for our time. To step beyond them is to court sainthood—or madness.

NOTES—CHAPTER 7

1. Edward Lewis Wallant, *The Human Season* (New York: Harcourt, Brace and World, Inc., 1960); *The Pawnbroker* (New York: Harcourt, Brace and World, Inc., 1961); *The Tenants of Moonbloom* (New York: Harcourt, Brace and World, Inc., 1963); and *The Children at the Gate* (New York: Harcourt, Brace and World, Inc., 1964). All quotations are taken from these editions.

2. Edward Lewis Wallant, "The Man Who Made a Nice Appearance," *New Voices 3: American Writing Today*, ed. Charles I. Glicksberg (New York: Hendricks House, 1958), p. 351.

3. Jonathan Baumbach, *The Landscape of Nightmare* (New York: New York University Press, 1965), p. 148.

4. Edward Lewis Wallant, "I Held Back My Hand," *New Voices 2: American Writing Today*, ed. Don M. Wolfe (New York: Hendricks House, 1955), pp. 192–201; "The Man Who Made a Nice Appearance," *New Voices 3: American Writing Today*, ed. Charles I. Glicksberg (New York: Hendricks House, 1958), pp. 336–353; and "When Ben Awakened," *American Scene: New Voices*, ed. Don M. Wolfe (New York: Lyle Stuart, Inc., 1963), pp. 94–100. This last story obviously derives from an early draft of what eventually became *The Children at the Gate*.

5. Bruce Jay Friedman, *Stern* (New York: Simon and Schuster, 1962) and *A Mother's Kisses* (New York: Simon and Schuster, 1964). All quotations are taken from these editions.

8/ J. D. Salinger and the Crisis of Consciousness

Prolegomena to FRANNY, ET AL.

Franny and *Zooey* were analyzed not long ago by Daniel Seitzman [1] for their overtly Freudian description of the heroine's psycho-spiritual crisis. One cannot do justice in summary to the range of evidence and good sense of Seitzman's argument; in brief, his conclusion is that Franny's sexual problem, her love-hate reaction to Lane and to other men, is reflective of her religious straits. In emulating the pilgrim in *The Way of a Pilgrim* by repeating the Jesus Prayer, Franny is pursuing a spiritual ideal identified with her saintly brother Seymour and his teachings. But Seymour the older brother has also been a father figure and continues after his death as an Oedipal image for her. To love another man is for her then to deny her love for Seymour; and to deny Seymour emotionally is to deny him intellectually and spiritually as well. Thus, although she is attracted erotically to Lane, her feelings are rendered ambivalent by her effort to realize Seymour's religious goals.

Why did Salinger choose to formulate Franny's spiritual ordeal in psycho-Freudian terms? The artistic problem that he faced with *Franny* was how to portray religious crisis (essentially an inner experience) in dramatic form other than in the impossible medieval one of confrontation with devil and angel. Graham Greene solves the problem in part by placing his heroes in violent, primitive settings where the supernatural does not appear out of place. Greene's least successful story has a modern urban background—which is Salinger's literary milieu! To complicate the problem for himself, Salinger the professional storyteller, the one-time writer of slick magazine tales, knows that a boy-girl situation (boy bent on sexual conquest, girl on resistance to his advances) is a plot convention expected by the reader. He also knows that to give the boy-girl situation without romantic complications will confuse the reader and arouse the Pavlovian response without satisfying it with the expected condiments. So Salinger portrays Franny, not mooning wordlessly over the Jesus Prayer in her room (which is where she should have been and where approximately we find her in *Zooey*), but on a weekend football date with an old beau. Furthermore Salinger, who cannot help being a man of his time and thinking with the assumptions of his time, inevitably uses a psychological (née Freudian) vocabulary to define Franny's and Lane's spat, even though the preoccupation of Franny and the action of *Zooey* indicate that her travail is religious, not sexual. And Salinger's incredibly deft technique makes of the restaurant confrontation between Franny and Lane a psycho-sexual joust that reverberates with clues, unwittingly revealed by the combatants, of subconscious motives, desires, and antagonisms, until it is no wonder that readers have conjectured irrelevantly about Franny's possible pregnancy! The same ambiguity of effect warps "A Perfect Day for Bananafish," prompting readers to attribute Seymour's suicide to his marital or sexual inadequacies rather than to his spiritual maladjustment. And why not? By including the dramatically contrapuntal scene of Muriel in the hotel bedroom, polishing her finger nails and chattering inanely on the long distance telephone to her mother, while Seymour broods suicidally on the beach, Salinger asks—insists—that we account for Seymour's death in the conventional terms of the formula story.

As if the strategic confrontation of life in the type of story Salinger has written here does not pose enough inherent problems, the dualism of *Franny* (not unlike the purposeful and purposeless powers informing Isaac Bashevis Singer's fictional world) involves Salinger in thematic contradiction. The religious aims of Franny and Seymour presuppose a voluntary effort and a goal attainable by that effort. Otherwise the morality of their action becomes an irrelevant by-product, which Kant's pietistic Lutheran temperament as much as his eighteenth-century rationalist mind was quick to recognize when he was defining the limitations of the practical reason. Yet the psychological underpinning of the story with its scientific determinism contradicts this voluntarism. Not only is the pilgrim's way unavailable to all men, but external circumstances affect the distance he may travel down the road. *Ecce* Seymour's suicide and Franny's nervous collapse!

Is Salinger then dramatizing in the moral action of "A Perfect Day for Bananafish" and *Franny* a simple dualism—and nothing more? The answer is more pluralistic than the question would indicate. One can discern multiple directions that the Glass saga might be taking. (1) Salinger believes sincerely in the Zen ideal and is trying fictionally to explore the ways in which the true spiritual life can be realized in a modern materialistic society. (2) He has taken us in with a devastating irony that sneers at the ideal of the spiritual life—which leaves still unanswered the question of what he is saying positively. (3) He is trying to render fictionally an image of modern sainthood, but, because the realization of sainthood in actuality is rare, his artistic integrity leads him instead to portray human failures to achieve the Zen ideal. What comes from his pen, influenced by the conventions of the *New Yorker* short story, are psychological studies of the disorders attendant upon the individual effort in a materialistic culture to pursue the pilgrim's way.

The third possibility not only more clearly fits the symbolic action of "A Perfect Day for Bananafish," *Franny*, and *Zooey*, but also offers reasons for the turn that the most recent Glass stories have taken. It is reasonable to assume that Salinger's commitment to Zen is sincere and has grown in fervor. The endings of *Zooey* and *Seymour: An Introduction*, which portray both Franny and Buddy gaining the quietude of spiritual insight, if not full *satori*, would suggest that Salinger is serious and hopeful about his and the unique Glass children's ability to follow Zen teachings —even though his artistic honesty continues to pose details of psychological trauma and failure. Assuming that the religious direction taken by *Zooey*, *Raise High the Roof Beam, Carpenters*, *Seymour: An Introduction*, and *Hapworth 16, 1924* is indicative of Salinger's intentions, one is not entirely unfounded in suspecting that the psycho-sexual tactics in *Franny* represent an unavoidable misdirection of the story's strategy, or at best an unnecessary complication or overlay of theme. Hence, Salinger's determination to move away from the well-made story with its built-in expectations and toward the loosened "sincerity" and intimacy of his subsequent stories, and hence his increasingly narrow restriction of the drama of his stories to the intimate confines of the Glass household and his growing identification with key members of the family. But here a new problem assails Salinger. In *Franny*, the youngest of the Glass children suffers a crisis of consciousness. In *Sey-*

mour: An Introduction and *Hapworth 16, 1924*, particularly, the creator qua narrator of the stories seems to be suffering the crisis.

Epilogue to SEYMOUR: AN INTRODUCTION, ET AL.

Salinger's imagination has begun to impose upon the reader. Like the initialed mystery of his name and the childish nicknames of the Glass children, his prose nowadays darkens more than illuminates, obscures more than enlightens. Despite the steady maturation of an incredibly skillful technique, Salinger finds himself writing words that multiply fractionally, so that more and more adds up to less and less. The paradox is that he seeks greater depths of communication. Unfinished dialogue, telephone conversations, letters, diaries, and bathroom mirror messages are brilliantly manipulated within the linear limitations of the print-bound media to approximate what Marshall McLuhan calls the immediacy and disjunction of the new electronic media and what Salinger would define as the comprehensiveness and simultaneity of the Zen visionary experience.[2] Contrariwise, this strategy of Salinger's language inadvertently also images a breakdown of communication in our century (in spite of the paper blizzard, or, if McLuhan is right, because of it); for the unfinished, disjointed, and cut-up dialogues of his characters reflect the retreat of mechanized mass man into indirect articulation. Salinger's exploration of the spiritual ways in which man's sensibility can reach out to touch another's has become, paradoxically, a rendering of the incommunicability intrinsic to the modern scene.[3]

Most intriguing in this reversal of situations is that in *The Catcher in the Rye* and the stories chronicling the Glass family, Salinger has become less and less a recorder of the phenomenon and increasingly a mute testament to its truth. His receptivity to this distinctly modern problem mirrors a crisis of consciousness in J. D. *Buddy*franny-zooeyseymour-Salinger, whose exacerbated sensibility seems to be reflecting ever multiple refractions of reality, with infinity apparently the end in mind. Since Buddy is, of all the Glasses, the most complete spokesman for Salinger (the blurring of the two identities has reached the point where Buddy has laid claim to Salinger's one novel and four of his short stories), *Seymour: An Introduction*, which is Buddy's most ambitious creative effort to date that we have been shown, is probably the best work to examine for clues to the imaginative impasse which appears to be presently troubling Salinger.

Stanley Edgar Hyman comments in a review of Salinger [4] that the Glass series have progressed in little more than one decade from one of the finest short stories of our time, "A Perfect Day for Bananafish," to one of the most appalling ever written, *Seymour: An Introduction*. He applauds Salinger's steady drift away from the well-made story of the *New Yorker* into the ever widening pool of experience, but, he carps, a maturing writer breaks through limiting forms into fuller and deeper forms, such as those of *Moby Dick* or *Ulysses*, not into anarchy and incoherence. *Seymour: An Introduction*, the most representative of this new open form that Salinger now espouses, in its delineation of a protagonist beset by a crisis of consciousness, is not, however, without its defenders. John O. Lyons [5] contends that Salinger has resuscitated the effective literary stance of the early nineteenth-century Romantics, whose experience presupposed (1) the mysterious interrelation of things, with the identification of art and reality, and (2) the writer as the subject of his art, with form in endless process, not a completed product, of creation. Joseph L. Blotner [6] (in the same issue of *Wisconsin Studies in Contemporary Literature*) would consign Salinger to an even earlier literary epoch, asserting that Buddy's "interminable, reminiscent colloquy with the reader" represents a fictional study in "something like hysteria" and that if Salinger continues this mode of the anti-short story far enough he will be writing "something very like Aubrey's *Brief Lives* or the *Conversations* of William Drummond of Hawthorndon [pp. 104–105]." Henry Anatole Grunwald in the introduction to his edition of Salinger criticism [7] argues along somewhat the same lines that Salinger is concerned not so much with a characterization of Seymour as with pulling off an indirect revelation of Buddy's personality. And Ihab Hassan [8] contends that Salinger is engaged in the risky experiment of constructing stories which will convey through form a sacramental view of life and through language the Zen ideal (espoused by Seymour and his disciple Buddy) of the silence of things.

Rather than attempt still another rhetorical exegesis of the astonishing direction that Salinger's muse has taken, I wish to approach this question of Buddy's wordiness as posing for Salinger a problem in point of view that is, in origin at least, more psycho-religious than literary. Indeed, the point needs to be emphasized. We cannot in any final critical judgment separate the religious and artistic intentions in Salinger's work.[9]

Buddy as portrayed in *Seymour: An Introduction* is a man wracked by contradictions. He presents the anomaly of a Zen enthusiast in retreat from sensation and of a creative mind in unmediated contact with the world. He is "a species of literary shut-in," living alone in a "cringing, little house" (surely a trope for his sensibility), "set deep in the woods and on the more inaccessible side of a mountain," where he sees "very few people during the working week or year." [10] Despite this refinement of surroundings for contemplation, his portrait of Seymour remains unformulated and incomplete, because he cannot discriminate among his memories. "It would help enormously," he cries forlornly, "if some kind soul were to send me a telegram stating precisely which Seymour he'd prefer me to describe." When Buddy tries to characterize Seymour he gets "a vivid-type picture" of Seymour "simultaneously at the ages of approximately eight, eighteen, and twenty-eight, with a full head of hair and getting very bald, wearing a summer camper's red-striped shorts and wearing a creased suntan shirt with buck-sergeant stripes, sitting in padmasana and sitting in the balcony at the R. K. O. 86th street [pp. 198–199]."

In short, the whole stream of experience impinges on his sensibility. Like Seymour's face ("the last absolutely unguarded adult face in the Greater New York Area" [p. 202]), Buddy's sensibility has no built-in defenses. It reacts to *all* stimuli, swelling into "a thesaurus of undetached prefatory remarks [p. 125]." When he narrates an incident about Seymour, irrelevant, minor, and insignificant details jostle each other in noisy clamor to gain his harried attention. A reminiscence of Seymour's answer to an innocuous question put by their father Les balloons with expanding surface: instantly Buddy recalls "Seymour, sitting in an old corduroy armchair across the room, a cigarette going, wearing a blue shirt, gray slacks, moccasins with the counters broken down, a shaving cut on the side of his face that I could see [p. 173]." Hence, Buddy comes close to a breakdown in communication when he gives up trying "for Selectiveness with a description" ("I can't sort out," he laments, "can't clerk with this man" [p. 189]) and, engulfed in particulars, begins to give us Seymour, hair by hair, and ears by eyes by nose by skin to get at the face. Seymour has become "much too large to fit on ordinary typewriter paper [p. 176]," he confesses, ostensibly paying tribute to his brother's larger-than-life saintliness but also betraying his own unmediating sensibility. Buddy is the victim of what Coleridge and Wordsworth a century and a half ago recognized epistemologically as a despotism of the senses, which destroys one's self-identity and hence one's imaginative control of experience.

Understandably, Buddy's effort to reduce his memories to aesthetic form leaves him exhausted and even physically ill. A "little pentimento" about Seymour's instruction in how to shoot marbles starts him "sweating literally from head to foot [p. 237]." The description of Seymour's nose, he tells himself, will "only hurt a minute [p. 206]." The subject of Seymour's ears causes his hands to sweat and his bowels to churn. "The Integrated Man is simply not at home" he laments [p. 204]. And after recalling the show-business environment of his childhood, he suffers an attack of hepatitis. But, again, the anomaly: joy not frustration puts him on the sick list. "Professionally speaking," he confesses at the outset, "I'm an ecstatically happy man." Still, he admits, "an ecstatically happy writing person is often a totally draining type to have around [p. 115]." Moreover, he is prone to self-immolation. The "true artist-seer" is "dazzled to death by . . . the blinding shapes and colors of his own sacred human conscience [p. 123]." If a pun on *consciousness* is not intended here, certainly the persistent pressure of Buddy's "confession" in the story makes it eminently applicable. For the artist-seer, the man of unmediated imagination, sensation becomes less the genesis of creativity than the destroyer of healthy artistic control. Aesthetic joy is identifiable, as Buddy in a hesitant side step admits, with liverishness. Openness of the senses, aliveness of the spirit, is akin to inflammation of the organs [p. 176]. No wonder Buddy believes that Seymour, an *echter Dichter*, carried "the Muse of Absolute Joy" on his back like the monkey of addiction [p. 172] and that Beethoven increased and improved in creativity "after he ceased being encumbered with a sense of hearing [p. 129]."

The joy Buddy has in mind here is concomitant with the

Zen ideal of *satori,* "to be in a state of pure consciousness" (so he defines it, quoting Dr. Suzuki, in a letter to Zooey),[11] of the flow of things in the universe. In such a comprehension of the natural way of things, self-effacement paradoxically is not involved, because self does not exist. In fact, the realization *is* that there is no self. Hence, one is reinstated in the natural flow without the artificial barrier of a sense of otherness. The experience is clearly akin to the "spots of time" in Wordsworth's life when the external world ceased to exist for him apart from the image of that world in his mind.

Why then Buddy's illness? Both Seymour and Buddy are writers as well as Zen neophytes; and literature and Zen— despite the cosmic paradox of such great Chinese Taoist poets as Chuang Tzu—seek irreconcilable goals. Seymour, the holy guru as bananafish,[12] gorged himself on sensation in an effort to achieve nirvana. Buddy wishes to emulate Seymour in the same religious gesture at indiscriminate love of all things. Yet he also nervously wishes to practice the highly discriminating art of writing, which we learn from Seymour is also Buddy's religion [p. 186]. The two gestures, contrary to Seymour's tendency to confuse them, are incompatible, the one a private apprehension of being, the other a public rendering of objects. Wordsworth, whose greatness as a poet lies, in part, in his ability to communicate his experience aesthetically, kept the two separate in his mind. If, for him, at moments of identification with nature, as he tells us in *The Prelude,*

> the light of sense
> Goes out, but with a flash that has revealed
> The invisible world [VI, 600–602],

like an enormous short-circuiting of perception brought on by an overload of the senses with the world of objects, still his poetic rendering of the experience *selectively* invokes the visible world. Buddy's problem is his failure in straining for communicable form to keep these contradictory impulses separate.

One may start from another angle, Buddy's likeness to Seymour, and one will arrive at the same broken sentence and blank sheet of paper. To Buddy, a junior tagging after his brilliant two-years-older brother, Seymour (who represented "all *real* things" to the other Glass children [p. 123]) was an ideal to be jealously, despairingly emulated. Seymour was the tireless person who made Buddy the "Second-Fastest Boy Runner in the World [p. 246]," who played daemon-inspired games of ping-pong and football and inimitable stoop ball superior to any kid in the neighborhood, and who was *"never* wrong [p. 248]." The similarity of the two brothers, as contrasted to the four younger Glass children, is physical as well. Their noses and lack of chins were "close to being identical [p. 206]." Buddy unwittingly reveals his subconscious desires when, in alluding to his story about Seymour's suicide ("A Perfect Day for Bananafish"), he admits to having described "the young man, the 'Seymour,' who did the walking and talking . . . not to mention the shooting," not after Seymour but "oddly" after "someone with a striking resemblance to—alley oop, I'm afraid—myself [p. 131]." In a backhanded fashion in one of his parenthetical disclosures, Buddy later acknowledges that his efforts at a description of Seymour involve his own ego, his "perpetual lust to share top billing" with his older brother [p. 248]. Hence, the act of recreating Seymour becomes for Buddy an endless, terrifying exploration into himself.

In this respect Buddy is a true Romantic, and *Seymour: An Introduction* as Romantic a work as Byron's *Don Juan* or Wordsworth's *The Prelude*. "I *yearn* to talk, to be queried, to be interrogated, about this particular dead man [p. 166]," he exclaims; but he cannot enjoy being his "brother's brother for nothing [p. 248]." The price he must pay is personal discovery. Each scrap of fact about Seymour has attached to it a revelation about Buddy. It is this note of the *intime* that the baffled Buddy is "really not up to [p. 174]." At the beginning of his attempt to write about Seymour he distinguishes between professional speech and private speech. The one is a joyous exercise, the other a sweaty penance. His trouble is that the story of Seymour blurs the two activities. Hence, he is unable to get on with the tale and envies the reader's "golden silence [p. 158]." He stalls with ballooning details about Seymour. The "drama of reason" Coleridge once called the luxuriant spread of parenthetical expressions in his prose, that presents "the thought growing, instead of a mere Hortus siccus"; [13] and Buddy echoes him in tagging his "early [and late]-blooming parentheses . . . the bowlegged—buckle-legged—omens of my state of mind and body at this writing [p. 114]." Understandably his "psychedelic" attempts at re-creation of his and Seymour's past selves end in sweaty silence—or, the same thing, in hepatitis, Buddy's inventive variation on bananafish gorging. Like Seymour, he can give out with "cries of pain" and "cries for help" at intervals, only to "decline to say in perfectly intelligible language where it hurt" at length [p. 121].

But what of Salinger? In the fictional charade of the Glass family Seymour functions as surrogate of Buddy, and Buddy as alter ego of Salinger. That much is evident. Less apparent are the implications to date and for Salinger's future in this literary ploy of a tale about a pseudonymous alter ego's surrogate, which pretends at once to distance the author from and to merge him with the flow of experience.

Seymour: An Introduction represents, in its portrait of Buddy, a skillful dramatization of a creative mind at the crossroads; a mind in agony over the spiritual problem of how to travel simultaneously the bisecting roads of the actual and the ideal that meet somewhere between this and the next world and between oneself and another man's being. That is certainly an ethical theme which this and the other Glass stories explore, but there are also important considerations about creativity implied in the rendering of the theme. (If this assumption confuses the author with his fictional creation, then the author himself must be indicted along with me as an accessory.) The writing of *Seymour: An Introduction,* with its attempt to create a modern saint, images an unbearably paralyzed ambience of the creative spirit. It retails *sub rosa* a terrifying confession of the havoc wrought in the Romantic mind when it grapples in isolation with inchoate raw experience. One is reminded of the din, the painful bellowing and energetic despair, of the efforts of Los, Blake's personification of the imagination, to give form to matter. One cannot easily forget that the fires of Los's energy eventually burn out and Los lies inert, frozen, in the "nerveless silence" of "a cold solitude and dark void," [14] foreshadowing Blake's own verbal silence the last twenty years of his life.

The signs in Salinger's work are similarly there to be read. Buddy-Salinger admires Seymour's poems for their impersonality. The more autobiographical they "appear to be, or *are,* the less revealing the content is of any known details of his actual daily life in this Western world [p. 155]." They fulfill the ideal of Zen, revealing emotion and personality without "spilling a single really autobiographical bean [p. 172]." That is to say, when Seymour is least "personal," least involved with "self" (since ego according to Zen is purely illusion), he is most truthful. It is not entirely coincidental that all the Glasses have more than a touch of the actor in them, which is another way of achieving this ideal. But Buddy, significantly, is less the poet-mystic than Seymour and less the actor than Franny or Zooey. Like Salinger he is a storyteller. *Seymour: An Introduction* is his sprawling prose effort to emulate his brother's achievement. Interestingly, however, he produces the exact reverse of Seymour's double haiku. Prodigally, he distributes autobiographical beans about on the page, ignoring the niceties of literary expression in his frenzy to realize the *koan*like wholeness of Seymour. In short, a persona has not helped Salinger to achieve the distance necessary for imposing imaginative form on experience. He identifies as closely with Buddy as Buddy with Seymour, and Seymour is committed to the Taoist goal of indiscriminate embrace of the world. Few men's nervous systems have the appetite for such a program, and few artists the synthesizing powers for such a task. Buddy-Salinger seems to comprehend this; yet, like the old vaudeville team of Gallagher and Glass, he finds himself unable or unwilling to update his routine. As early as *The Catcher in the Rye*, Buddy-Salinger's most impersonal and still most successful book (even though and perhaps in part because least ambitious), Holden Caulfield is made to reject the careful selectiveness of Hemingway's manner as phony [ch. 18]. A thorough Romantic, Buddy-Salinger will embrace all experience—*or none.*

The ambivalence of that aim appears everywhere in his stories. "Don't ever tell anybody anything," Holden warns the reader. "If you do, you start missing everybody [ch. 26]." His ideal of a future is to pretend to be a deaf-mute married to a real deaf-mute. "Then I'd be through with having conversations for the rest of my life," he thinks, adding details to his fantasy that unmistakably parallel Buddy's real-life situation: "Everybody'd think I was just a poor deaf-mute bastard and they'd leave me alone . . . and I'd build me a little cabin somewhere . . . and live there for the rest of my life [ch. 25]." Yet, although he does not tell his "whole goddam autobiography," he does spill *all* "about this madman stuff [ch. 1]." In *Raise High the Roof Beam, Carpenters,* Seymour summarizes in his diary a conversation he had with the analyst of his fiancée's mother: "I told him . . . [apropos of the Gettysburg Address] that 51,112 men were casualties at Gettysburg, and that if someone *had* to speak at the anniversary of the event, he should simply have come forward and shaken his fist at this audience and then walked off—that is, if the speaker was an absolutely honest man." In further discussion with the analyst about his being a perfectionist, Seymour defends indiscriminate experience, "on the ground that it leads to health and a kind of very real, enviable happiness," even though he recognizes that "for a discriminating man to achieve this . . . he would have to dispossess himself of poetry, go *beyond* poetry. That is, he couldn't possibly learn or drive himself to *like* bad poetry in the abstract, let alone equate it with good poetry. He would have to drop poetry altogether [p. 86]." Here the indiscriminate embrace of all experience leads inevitably to the Taoist's silence. One of the still unanswered mysteries about Seymour is why his loving absorption of all life became nihilistic for him, ending in his suicide. As a poet could he have mistakenly confused verbal silence with personal nihilism? Whatever the illogic of his act, it inadvertently substantiates Cadmium Greene's rhetorical question (in Earl Rovit's novel *The Player King*) about whether "the pathetic yen for Zen" is not one of the "sickly suicides" of our time—"the deceptively buoyant bubble of air in the veins." [15] In the climax of "A Perfect Day for Bananafish," Buddy-Salinger does not shrink from the integrity of the artistic act. To unite with all life indiscriminately is to deny any immediate object of one's love. As Seymour's mother-in-law is reported to have said in *Raise High the Roof Beam, Carpenters,* Seymour has "never learned to relate to anybody [p. 68]." The net effect of Franny's step from "squalor" toward love at the end of *Zooey* is similar. When Zooey hangs up the telephone after telling her about Seymour's parable of the Fat Lady who is Christ, for whom he used to shine his shoes before going on the radio, "Franny took in her breath slightly but continued to hold the phone to her ear. A dial tone, of course, followed the formal break in the connection. She appeared to find it extraordinarily beautiful to listen to, rather as if it were the best possible substitute for the primordial silence itself [pp. 200–201]."

The heroic effort, to date, of Salinger to portray the Glass children's flirtation with religious enlightenment— willy-nilly, Buddhist, or Christian (why not Judaic?)—by way of telling *all* about them constantly threatens to end in the same stellar nothingness or in its complement, the cancerous formlessness of the recent stories. His meld with Buddy has not altered but rather intensified this problem. For Buddy to achieve *satori* is for Salinger to court a nullification potentially disastrous for writing; whereas for Buddy to fall short of enlightenment is for Salinger to develop a psychological theme other than a paean to the attainment of the full spiritual life in America. Salinger is an instance of the artist, whose effort to unite the personal and the impersonal, the involved and the detached, into equilibrium seems destined, so far, to failure. Unlike Isaac Bashevis Singer, he has shown a decreasing ability to remain dissociated from the fictional world he creates, and an artistically distressing (even though humanly laudable) predilection to better the world rather than simply to know and to represent it.

Nothing in Salinger's latest story, *Hapworth 16, 1924*,[16] published six years after *Seymour: An Introduction*, refutes these conclusions. Buddy has lapsed into silence. As a substitute, however, he has finally screwed up his courage sufficiently to let us look at one of Seymour's writings: in

the words of Seymour, a "very long, boring letter" written
"at blissful random [p. 62]," more inchoate in structure
and cute in tone than any of the stories which preceded it.
Salinger has dispensed with the alter ego of Buddy—who at
least pretended to some of the ordering instincts of a writer
of fiction but who is here reduced to the ineffectual role of
copyist—and succumbed to the self-indulgence of the
seven-year-old Seymour's account, in a letter to the folks
back home, of his and Buddy's adventures at a summer
camp in Maine.

The by-now familiar obsession of Seymour—even at
seven—is only too evident. "It is not in your son Buddy's
nature or mine or your son Walter's to be in the least
shocked or disgusted by any sweet, earthly side of humankind," he tells his mother and father. "Indeed, *all* [that key
word again] forms of human folly and bestiality touch a
very sympathetic chord within our breasts! [p. 36]." Even,
he assures them, the beautiful, "despised, touching pim-
ples," blemishes, and cysts on human bodies [p. 39]. Not
even sibling rivalry upsets Seymour's euphoria. He is full
of schoolgirl praise of that "droll and thrilling companion
[p. 42]," that "dear, comical [p. 50]," and "maddening,
indomitable [p. 56]" younger brother of his, the "most
resourceful creation of God [p. 39]." He quotes Blake's
Proverb of Hell, "Damn braces, bless relaxes," and proudly
assures Les and Bess that he and five-year-old Buddy are
"damning braces all over the place [p. 62]"—most visibly
in the unfettered renderings of this letter! He even declines
anesthesia for eleven stitches in his leg because he will not
give up his state of consciousness for flimsy reasons. And
his passion for sanctifying all experiences prompts him to
by-pass Caruso in favor of Mr. Bubbles, of Buck and Bubbles, "merely singing softly to himself in his dressing
room" in Cleveland [p. 100]. The same indiscriminate appetite has him reading all the books on God or merely

religious works from A to Z, all books in the public library on the structure of the human heart and on the formation of the callus, and all the back comic strips of Moon Mullins. Some idea of the rambling sprawl of the story is suggested by the list of books Seymour asks to be sent to him. It occupies one-fourth of the letter—with gratuitous interspersed remarks, again "at random [p. 92]," about Charlotte Bronte's carnal attractions and other such "insights" of a seven-year-old genius into the authors he is reading!

Buddy-Salinger's resort to the letter of a seven-year-old is a resourceful tactic for giving credence and inevitability, if not aesthetic responsibility, to such insouciant dips into the pool of experience. But the trick does not hide the growing desperation of this reliance on the mouths of little babes. The child as saint grows somewhat stale in repetition—and quite suspicious when, as in this case, he is merely a ventriloquistic device for the voice and thoughts of the author.

Stanley Edgar Hyman's estimate—following publication of *Seymour: An Introduction*—of the cul-de-sac Salinger has gotten himself into still holds true. "His highway has turned into a dirt road, then into wagon ruts, finally into a squirrel track and climbed a tree." [17] From his tree top only the great empty sky unfolds in primordial quiet. It would seem that the ambiguity of the Glass name as metaphor has its insidious consequences. A limitless viewpoint can be as harmful as one narrowed to opacity. It is not accidental that Buddyfrannyzooeyseymour are Glasses, bent on not just the myope's refracted *aperçus* of the bay but on the mystic's wide-eyed vision of the world, a luminous purchase on eternity.

Given Salinger's proclivity for a dramatic frame in his Glass stories, the way down from his tree and back onto the highway may be found with the prosaic eyes of one of the non-Zen Glasses, whose point of view has not yet been explored. Surely Gallagher and Glass offer Salinger's religious mystique few of the temptations to identify with them as have their progeny. If their outlook is not the route to spiritual salvation, it may prove the turn to aesthetic redemption, for they too are artists of a sort, with a practical idea of what does not "go" with audiences. On the other hand, it may well be that his obsessive creation of the Glasses was a wrong move for Salinger and he will never be able to achieve with them, in the words of Ihab Hassan, "the forms of dramatic permanence." [18]

NOTES—CHAPTER 8

1. Daniel Seitzman, "Salinger's 'Franny': Homoerotic Imagery," *American Imago*, XXII (1965), 57–76.

2. I wish to acknowledge particularly the aid of a former graduate student, Anthony Quagliano, whose knowledge of Buddhism and sympathetic understanding of what Salinger is attempting happily reversed the usual roles of teacher-student and saved me from egregious error in my remarks on Salinger.

3. Cf. Charles H. Kegle, "Incommunicability in Salinger's *Catcher in the Rye*," *Western Humanities Review*, XI (1957), 188–190.

4. Stanley Edgar Hyman, "J. D. Salinger's House of Glass," *Standards* (New York: Horizon Press, 1966), pp. 121–127.

5. John O. Lyons, "The Romantic Style of Salinger's *Seymour: An Introduction*," *Wisconsin Studies in Contemporary Literature*, IV (1963), 62–69.

6. Joseph L. Blotner, "Salinger Now: An Appraisal," *Wisconsin Studies in Contemporary Literature*, IV (1963), 100–108.

7. Henry Anatole Grunwald (ed.), *Salinger: A Critical and Personal Portrait* (New York: Harper and Row, 1962), p. xxiii.

8. Ihab Hassan, "Almost the Voice of Silence: The Later Novelettes of J. D. Salinger," *Wisconsin Studies in Contemporary Literature*, IV (1963), 5–20.

9. Warren French's determination to concentrate on structural analysis and to avoid "external considerations" like "borrowings from Zen Buddhism" diminishes the value of his study *J. D. Salinger* (New York: Twayne Publishers, Inc., 1963), p. [8]. Surely Arthur Mizener is more central to a valid critical estimate of Salinger when he writes that "Salinger's constant allusions to the Bhagavad-Gita, Sri Ramakrishna, Chuang-Tzu, and the rest are only efforts to find alternative ways of expressing what his stories are about," "The Love Song of J. D. Salinger," *Harpers Magazine*,

CCXVIII (1959), 83–89. Recent Salinger criticism has gravitated toward Mizener's position; cf. e.g., John Russell, "Salinger's Feat," *Modern Fiction Studies*, XII (1966), 299–311; and Bernice and Sanford Goldstein, "Zen and Salinger," *Modern Fiction Studies*, XII (1966), 313–324.

10. J. D. Salinger, *Raise High the Roof Beam, Carpenters* and *Seymour: An Introduction* (Boston: Little, Brown and Company, 1963), p. 135. All quotations are from this edition.

11. In the story *Zooey*. All quotations are from *Franny* and *Zooey* (Boston: Little, Brown and Company, 1961), p. 65.

12. But cf. Alfred Kazin, "J. D. Salinger: 'Everybody's Favorite,'" *The Atlantic Monthly*, CCVIII (1961), 27–31.

13. Letter to Thomas Poole, 28 January 1810.

14. William Blake, *The Book of Urizen*, V, 4.

15. Earl Rovit, *The Player King* (New York: Harcourt, Brace and World, Inc., 1965), p. 185.

16. J. D. Salinger, "Hapworth 16, 1924," *The New Yorker*, XLI, pt. 3, June 19, 1965, pp. 32–113.

17. Stanley Edgar Hyman, "J. D. Salinger's House of Glass," *Standards* (New York: Horizon Press, 1966), p. 127.

18. Ihab Hassan, "J. D. Salinger: Rare Quixotic Gesture," *Radical Innocence: Studies in the Contemporary American Novel* (Princeton, N.J.: Princeton University Press, 1961), p. 289.

Index